THE ART OF
THEATRICAL
SOUND DESIGN

THE ART OF THEATRICAL SOUND DESIGN

A Practical Guide

VICTORIA DEIORIO

methuen | drama

LONDON • NEW YORK • OXFORD • NEW DELHI • SYDNEY

METHUEN DRAMA
Bloomsbury Publishing Plc
50 Bedford Square, London, WC1B 3DP, UK
1385 Broadway, New York, NY 10018, USA

BLOOMSBURY, METHUEN DRAMA and the Methuen
Drama logo are trademarks of Bloomsbury Publishing Plc

First published in Great Britain 2019

Cover design by Hugh Cowling

A catalogue record for this book is available from the British Library.

A catalog record for this book is available from the Library of Congress.

ISBN: HB: 978-1-4742-5779-4
        PB: 978-1-4742-5780-0
        ePDF: 978-1-4742-5784-8
        eBook: 978-1-4742-5781-7

Series: Backstage

Typeset by Integra Software Services Pvt. Ltd.
Printed and bound in Great Britain

To find out more about our authors and books visit www.bloomsbury.com
and sign up for our newsletters.

CONTENTS

LIST OF FIGURES

INTRODUCTION

The artistry of sound design requires one to objectify a sense that is innate to our being and pervasive in our society. With the proliferation of personal listening devices, we have the ability to fill every moment of the twenty-first century with music and sound; and conversely, if we want to relieve ourselves of this, we use technological tools to cancel out the noise we don't want to hear. By choosing our personal soundtrack, or eliminating the sound around us, we are choosing to isolate ourselves, and our hearing, within a bigger system. We all design our environments to suit our aural wants and needs.

Going to the theater speaks to coming together as a group of people to witness and experience sound en masse. We collectively choose to experience selective sound as a group instead of the norm of a solitary listening experience. Hearing sound in this setting sets the moment of theatre apart from day-to-day life, and is highly entertaining.

When I speak of the artistry of sound design in theatre, it goes beyond the daily existence of noise filtering, surround-sound spectating, streaming radio stations, personalized cellphone rings, and bass-thumping car radios tuned to a satellite. It is about understanding how sound and music affect a human being in a group setting, and what it means to be the artist who thinks in depth about the specificity of relationship between sound and people, and then recreates it with intention.

Within a theatrical setting, the range of dynamics is vast. A sound designer can attain the perception of pin-drop silence as well as shake the foundation of the architecture, and everything in between. What makes an effective sound design is intention. It's about determining the "why" behind every choice you make in order to create an emotional journey for an audience.

This book is a guide to begin your path of study into the art of making sound for a theatrical production. You will come to understand how what one hears can play into our emotional state and how the physics of sound plays upon our physical bodies. And more importantly, how sound designers use that knowledge to artistically support the visual expression of theatre art.

So how do we become objective to something to which we don't give a second thought? Sound can seem intangible and hard to describe. Defining and understanding sound is aided by the application of knowledge to instinctual human behavior. In order to analyze what you do well instinctually, you have to stop, slow down, and break it apart to see what is occurring. This helps you to understand how you are interpreting and facilitating your goal.

Once you slow down and objectively view how you perceive sound, you can then apply additional acquired knowledge. With practice, the new information will become assimilated and ingrained into your way of thinking, and thereby deepen your awareness of your instinct. Once you have applied knowledge, you can then act with intention.

Right now, stop reading, close your eyes, and just listen.

What do you hear? How much do you hear? What were you tuning out? What is contained within the soundscape you are listening to? What is louder and what is softer? What is more to the left or to the right?

You can be asked at any time in your career to imitate environments, so begin by tuning your ears by paying attention to your surroundings as you go through each day. It is the practice of intently listening that will aid in making you a detailed and specific sound designer.

Later in the book we will discuss whether it's appropriate to create a realistic environment for theatrical purposes, because before you took the time to analyze all the sounds you were listening to, you were subconsciously selectively hearing. And if you are creating a sonic journey for an audience, part of your job is guiding their selective hearing to support the storytelling of the piece.

You must also start tuning in to your emotional and physical reaction to sound and music. What instrument makes you react a certain way? Does your heart rate speed up or slow down, and why? Does this piece of music remind you of something specific? Why are you filled with emotion? Just as you begin to hear the sound around you to determine the specificity, you will learn how to put it back together again with emotional and physical intention. This intention can, in turn, apply an artistic purpose to your design work.

As human beings used imagination to develop tools to enable us to do greater work, sound designers have audio toolboxes that help them to achieve reactions to human artistic expression through sound and music. In the past, humans created need-based tools for survival. In our modern world, tools are not designed for need as much as they are defined for specific usage towards a particular outcome.

A knowledge base of a digital audio workstation (DAW) program such as Pro Tools, Logic, Reason, GarageBand, or Audacity is necessary for the exercises in this book. This book is not at any point about the teaching of these programs. It is to provide information that deepens the understanding of how sound affects a human being and how sound designers can use this information to create more emotionally effective and supportive designs.

Another component to sound design in theatre relates to who you are as an artist, because every person will bring something different to a theatrical collaboration. As an artist, you choose what work you want to create and with whom you wish to work. You determine how you communicate and collaborate to achieve a common goal, and you develop your overall aesthetic.

As an artist, you uniquely look at a production through your own lens, and your ears will want to support a particular production in a specific way. Your choices and how you support the whole are what make you unique as a theatre artist in this field. The path you seek artistically will show itself with what work you choose to create and with whom you collaborate. Trust the path will be there if you make life choices you find compelling to you.

Who am I?

My background began with dance. I trained as a dancer from age 5, joined a regional ballet company in central New York at age 10, and was on scholarship at Joffrey Ballet at age 14. I received a BFA in Musical Theatre from Syracuse University. I studied classical acting at RADA and LAMDA before moving to Chicago to become a regional classical actor and director.

In Chicago, the lure of singing and playing in a rock and roll band diverted my attention away from acting and directing, and I found myself surrounded by music once again. I was a member of a cover band and also fronted my own band, which released two CDs of original music.

A theatre company that I helped establish asked if I could write music and sound design for the play *Holy Days* by Sally Nemeth. My response was, "Sure, I can do that," and my sound design career began. From that first show forward, I continually worked as a sound designer. My name was handed from one person to the next and a career that I had never pursued emerged in my life.

It was beneficial that the first regional theater at which I worked was the Goodman Theatre in Chicago, and my career accelerated after that. I started with the local League of Resident Theatres and larger Chicago theaters, and I worked across the country from there. I continued composing and designing and seeing the path of my art following me in my wake.

At the time, I was the only woman in sound design in Chicago. I was garnering awards and accolades; but it was difficult to be a woman pioneer in a field that is dominated by men. I am incredibly grateful to my male sound designer colleagues during this time because I never once felt any sexism from them as a woman sound designer.

In the years that passed, I found a deeper love of directing and, with each show I designed, I learned a great deal from the directors with whom I was working. I have been lucky that I have been able to continue to direct, and the shows I have chosen have had critical success. I attribute that to my years in diverse areas of the theatrical production.

I accepted the position to form a new sound design department for The Theatre School at DePaul University and built a brand new Bachelor of Fine Arts program for the school.

While developing the program, I began scouring for books to help me teach the art of theatrical sound design and couldn't find any that detailed what I do when I design. There were a lot of books about the technology of how to set up a system, or the really specific details of the electrical flow of how sound works, or perhaps even how to break down a script. I found a closer union to cinema sound design where textbooks were concerned.

And I realized that what I had been doing, how I created my art, was not being taught through books. I had to slow down my process, watch every move I made, question every decision, and figure out why I chose to do what I did for my composition and design work. I did this for every show for three years, as I slowly kept adding more and more detail to my courses.

I was asked to join in on a conversation regarding sound design and composition in theatre after the Tony Awards for sound were taken away in 2014. These conversations led to the forming of the Theatrical Sound Designers and Composers Association (TSDCA). I became very active in this organization, helped incorporate its status, and serve as Co-Chair on the Executive Board.

It has been a winding path to get to where I am, and now I am writing the book that I wish I had when I started teaching.

Why Life Choices Matter

When you choose your life based on what you want to do in the moment, you create a journey of experiences that informs every aspect of who you are. Everything in your life experience thus far will inform who you are as an artist. Because of your unique path in life, you will bring something to the theatre that is expressly yours.

As an example, here is how my choices inform me.

Dancer

I feel music and sound in every fiber of my being. I locate frequencies physically and EQ a room by how it feels on my body. I take my past training of knowing how to move to music and apply it in reverse to the theatrical process. When I see movement on stage, I instinctively can feel how the music or sound should accompany that movement. It is my ballet training in mirror reflection.

Actor

I understand what actors needs to help them through their emotional journey, be it subtle or bold influences. And I also know what could possibly get in the way of them doing their best work. I understand the timing of how things work backstage as well as on stage.

Composer

Being a composer has the added benefit of the ability to create something the audience has never heard before that perfectly supports the story they are experiencing. Understanding history and how to mimic a genre or time period's music and sound is an asset to that support.

Director

Directing aids in my collaborative process. A director inspires others to create incredible art that peaks just as the audience gets involved. Having the experience of multiple roles in theatre gives me the unique ability to understand where everyone is in their process and how to collaborate with them to find what is needed to create the collective vision. Compassionate understanding of stressful processes and how differently they work for all involved is beneficial to how you communicate and collaborate with fellow artists.

TSDCA Board Member

Having the perspective of the industry as a whole helps to maintain a standard of practice in my work that is of the highest expectation.

Educator

I learn by teaching others. Their curiosity implores me to learn as much as I can and there are often times when my students will teach me something I did not know.

If there is one thing I can impart by sharing my past and present with you, it would be to entreat you to become a lifelong learner and have humility about not knowing. If you treat every experience with the respect that you will learn from it, you will stave off disappointment and your knowledge will grow exponentially.

How This Book Can Help You

In this book I address the artistry of sound design and how to emotionally affect a human being. In the environment of theatre, sound designers refashion the interaction of what is heard within the environment to reach goals that support an emotional journey through storytelling. We propagate sound in space directly, and perceptively, with dynamic context and aural perspective. As a sound designer you question how you hear, and then take what you hear and realize it in a specific incarnation for an audience. I break down this process into three parts.

Part One—Theoretic Foundation

I explore how human beings experience vibrations in our world—how we perceive these vibrations and create meanings for them—and then focus on the emotional response that is evoked because of this flow of energy and association. Also, I examine spatial awareness of aural architecture, and control of sound, to serve a specific intention. This focus is the basis of how sound designers purposefully create a sonic perception for an audience. This will give you inspiration as to how to recreate sound intentionally for your audience.

Part Two—Contextual Application and Exercises

I then present exercises to define aural technique and give the learner structure by which they can affect an audience to create an emotional journey. These exercises contain examples of how the technique could be used in the actualization of a sound design. In the latter part of this section I delve into a brief recount of the history of music and how it has been recorded in order to apply the aural tools. As artists, sound designers must have an understanding of the other artists' work they will be using or emulating, and the culture that evoked that art.

Part Three—The Collaborative Process

This section details the artistic process of the sound designer in theatre and how an artist collaborates, creates cohesion, and communicates in order to come to a common goal. It is in working with other artists that the sound designer's artistry can flourish.

I do not reference musical theatre reinforcement design, although a great deal of the information contained within, regarding how to affect a human being dynamically, is useful in that discipline as well.

The focus of this book is on supporting text and movement using composition and soundscape, knowing how to create an emotional journey for an audience physiologically and psychologically, and how to work well with others to achieve an effective aural vision.

The further you delve into the world of sound, the more it feels like magic. This book will illuminate how the human body interprets sonic elements, which gives you a deeper understanding of the human body and how it perceives the world around it. You will have an appreciation of how the delivery of sound to a group of people can be magical in its support of an emotional journey. You will understand the details beyond the technical aspect of sound transmission. And it will make you a well-rounded artist that is able to apply psychology, physiology, sociology, anthropology, and all aspects of sound phenomenology to your design.

Because this book focuses on how the artist perceives sound and then constructs it for intentional effect, it can at times feel as though it is going off on a tangent away from theatrical sound design. *This is intentional.* My purpose is to give you a deeper understanding of sound so that you can make your own choices about how to use the information in this book for your specific artistry.

At any time, if you find yourself thinking, "Why is this in this book?" stop, and think about how you may be able to use the information in a theatrical setting. Not everything will speak to all readers, but it is my hope that it will expand your consideration of how sound acts in our world. And as an artist, you use any and all tools to your advantage. The more depth of thought you have in what you are creating, the richer the experience will be for those who experience your work.

I have chosen to not footnote for ease of reading. If you wish to delve further, I suggest looking at the highly detailed books, articles, and scientific theorems listed in the bibliography.

Many thanks to my parents for their unending support; my colleagues who have taught me through collaboration; and especially David Budries, Chair of the Sound Design department at Yale, for his guidance and support in assisting me towards clarity.

PART ONE

THEORETIC FOUNDATION

This section of the book will help define the evolutionary and the associational response in human beings to sound and music. We innately hear a specific way because of the evolution of our species. And our experiences create an understanding through association of meaning and feeling with what we hear. When we combine evolution and association to sound and music, we have a larger grasp of the phenomenology of sound. In the following, the breakdown of exactly what happens when we hear, how we perceive it, and the association of emotion and meaning will be explained.

1

SOUND AND HUMAN PERCEPTION

Humans as Artists

Art can be defined as the expression or application of human creative skill and imagination, producing works to be appreciated primarily for their beauty and/or emotional power. Yet, much of the Western world has come to expand the use of the word to focus on commodity, ownership, history, or specialization, e.g. the art of shaving, the art of homemaking, the art of pizza. And although there can be beauty in the making of pizza or the closeness of a shave, the appreciation of emotional power and observational beauty is the focus to which we as sound designers must draw our attention. The power of the word "artist" should be reclaimed to not have a vague or even at times negative connotation.

Art contributes greatly to the understanding of our existence. As theatre artists we collaborate and problem-solve in the realm of imagination. And we dedicate ourselves to the practice of creating live performances that engage an audience. This form of art is as old as human beings' tradition of retelling a story to pass down history. It is an attractive form of evoking an emotional response and creating meaning for others.

Let's look at what attracts us to dramatic performance in the first place and how we determine what it means for a human being to produce art for theatre.

- Human beings are naturally inclined to ritual and repetition; and for the most part, our storytelling has a beginning, middle, and an end. We crave the set-up, the unfolding of conflict, and the resolution or lack of resolution in the conclusion. There is fullness to a three-part structure: the rise to climax and the denouement that falls after.

- Our stories are reflections of interaction, either showing the past to illuminate the present, predicting a future of possible outcome, or exploring current topics or themes affecting us all right now. We appreciate seeing our lives mirrored on stage before us because it helps to highlight specific microcosms to others who may never have experienced certain issues, conflicts, and resolutions. It's a way to bring understanding and raise social consciousness.

- We wish to feel catharsis or find relief when we release the emotions experienced in theatre. And in the end, hopefully we learn or experience something either comfortingly familiar or excitingly new and unusual to us.

This circles back to how we all love a good story. We support storytelling best if there is emotional power in its association to our lives. And the art of storytelling is the basis of live theatre.

As theatre artists, we wish to evoke response to what we produce. Theatre gives us the platform of a live environment to affect how an audience thinks and feels not only in that specific moment, but also for years to come if it's emotionally powerful. Theatre can be highly addicting as an influential tool of communicating a point of view through metaphor.

If you think back to the first theatrical performance that moved you emotionally, you can remember it with precise detail. It is imprinted upon your memory because of its effect and its power to make you think and feel. As the audience member, you can let yourself go within a story and lose yourself in it by empathizing (feeling the expression presented) and/or sympathizing (responding to the expression presented).

As an artist, the feeling of creating any art is a feeling of losing oneself within something else, and it is typically as enjoyable for the creator as for the observer. A life in theatre is a highly disciplined career, in which we are compelled and often contracted to work long hours to produce our collective art. Recognizing the responsibility of that dedication to what we do, and how we do it, defines us as theatre artists. We produce this work because we enjoy creating an art form that brings entertainment, beauty, and meaning to others.

This dedication shows itself through the intense study of our artistry. When we make the decision to commit to a life in the arts, which is often described as a calling, we make a silent contract with ourselves to know everything about our discipline so that we can use all the tools available to us in order to create. So as we delve further into the study of sound, you will see that it involves so much more than creating structured noise. It is based in specific types of aesthetic responses: evolutionary response and associational response.

In order to be artistic within this field, and affect others' emotional response, you must understand how the body captures vibrations, sends them to the brain, perceives them as sound, and generates a meaning for them. Once you look into the psychological, sociological, anthropological, and physiological properties of sound and the human reaction to it, then you can use these tools in theatrical sound design.

Aesthetic Response

Within the ritual of storytelling there are distinct avenues to approach aesthetic response in theatre. You can create work that immerses your audience so that they are emotional participants in the art. Or, you can create a response to your work that is more of an objective appreciation of the beauty that is happening around them. These internal and external responses to art do not need to live solely on their own and they can be part of the same production, at times living simultaneously.

In *A Christmas Carol* there is a benefit to scaring an audience as if they are immersed in the ghost story. You want them to feel as if Jacob Marley is appearing as a spirit in order to create the illusion for them. But there are times when the story shows the past, present, and future to Scrooge where the audience is observant of the illusion, and therefore they are either empathetic and thereby feeling Scrooge's emotions, or sympathetic in their response to his reaction.

With storytelling, the emotional content can be what makes the most intimate moment beautiful. However, it is important to note that what we perceive as beautiful has a wide range of interpretation. Our success as artists is obtained when we present a collective intention to the audience, and they understand the impression we wish to make with the reaction we wish to evoke.

What I am referring to is the aesthetic response, which is a natural psychobiological function in human beings. In our world there are universal themes that inform the creation of all cultures of the human species, so therefore you can draw conclusions based in the commonality of human aesthetic response that unconsciously appeals to all humans.

Birds will indicate outdoors in the daytime and crickets will indicate rural nighttime; sleigh bells bring the listener directly to winter and possibly Christmas. A church organ has a spiritual effect on some, while others garner the same response from the sound of a Tibetan bowl.

The recognition or response to symbolic content, whether spiritual or secular, is evidence that humans perceive and respond emotionally as one to the world of which they are a part. There are a range of unexplainable feelings that are generated by hearing a melody line soar gracefully, seeing a person in movement with precision, walking into the center of the architecture of a cathedral, or reading words of a poem that transport us to another place and time.

In the twenty-first century, through years of psychological research, we can explain the emotional response to the aesthetic as something that is a mental phenomenon. We are at a place and time where we can discuss this mind–body merger and analyze it in an articulate manner. We can now use words such as kinesthetic (relating to movement of the body) and synesthetic (perception of sense other than the one stimulated). As sound designers we can use these and many other words, and their definitions, to determine how we are going to apply sound to affect an audience.

Art, before psychological terminology, was created solely with the aesthetic reaction in mind. An artist generated their work based on how it made them feel or how it made others feel. They didn't stop to think about how the collective consciousness would influence how sensory perception prescribed the emotional response. This is modern language for what they did instinctually. In the time in which we now live, with this psychological language, we can break down the how and why of art's capacity to produce powerful emotions.

Mind–Body Connection

We have the capability to learn about the size of our boundless universe as well as the minuteness of quantum physics, and with that knowledge we still live within our own proportion of human scale, relevance, and application. For example, we do not have the physical capability to sense infrared or ultraviolet light, but we have learned that they are part of the spectrum of energy in which we live. Human beings use what we sense as our only reality; however, there is much more around us than what we sense.

In the visual spectrum, we have expanded our understanding of the world around us through the use of both the microscope and the telescope. The detail of a world, previously unseen, is rich with life we never dreamed of before the use of these tools. This extension of vision unfolded a deeper understanding to human existence.

Because electronic communication evolved, the realms that were once silent now are full of sound and noise. Listening with electronic amplification can now allow us to hear how whales communicate. Before the technology to do so, we never knew there was sound in the ocean. We have advanced yet further to hear distant stars exploding or the sound of a comet hurtling through space.

The world isn't necessarily noisier, nor do we have the human capability to hear longer distances; it is simply that sound and noise is more pervasive in our daily existence due to technological advances. It's as if our experience of listening has changed, and with that transformation so has our acceptance of where we stand relative to the world around us.

We are bound by our own sensorially perceived confinement, but our sensory limitations can be exceeded by intellectual ability through the use of abstraction. I am not using the term abstraction here as a breakage of determined rules, but in the sense of the quality of dealing with ideas rather than events. Abstract ideas help us comprehend more fully and allow us to dream up anything we want to create as artists. We have learned to train our senses to perceive subtle differences in sight, sound, touch, taste, and smell; and this, along with abstraction of the intellect, is what shapes our reaction to our world.

What we think and feel, and what we know, is internal and personally based on our individual bodily senses and experiences. We determine and measure our beliefs based on our feelings and reactions to the stimuli we encounter daily. And the parts of us that are the essence of who we are—the soul, spirit, and mind—are a collection of experiences and our emotional reactions to them. This is the key to evoking an associational response.

The reason to acknowledge this perspective as important to an artist is that in order to reflect upon the world around us, we must understand our relationship to it. We can look at it in a metaphysical way and reflect upon the bigger picture, or we can look to the specifics of mechanics of how things work. We want to get to the heart of what creates emotional response so that we can duplicate this consistently.

The simple truth is all of our processes are biomechanical. The smallest change in our environment can create an emotional reaction that cortically triggers the need to respond or act. For example, we selectively hear constantly, but if an alarm goes off, it prompts an emotional response that triggers us to act immediately. We can say the alarm scared us emotionally, but it was a cortical response of a human body reacting to a high-amplitude vibration that was unexpected.

It's important to break down these processes so that when we wish to duplicate a reaction we understand what is the catalyst. When we observe the world around us, we think that we are seeing, hearing, touching, smelling, and tasting everything that is in our environment. This is not exactly true. Our bodies are made to remap the energy of the world around us into a usable signal called sensation. Perception is the integration of these sensations.

For example, the psychophysical remapping of a wavelength of light equals color, and the psychophysical remapping of the amplitude of a wavelength of light equals brightness. The distortion of mechanical structure is remapped into touch. Taste and smell are chemical reactions that remap into flavor and scent. And sound is a psychophysical remapping of vibrations.

Most importantly when contemplating psychophysics, remember that it is of a personal nature because of how you personally perceive the energy of the world and apply it to your own experience. Each of us is an individual with unique interpretations of the processes we perceive around us. And although it may be possible that we as individuals see a different color as green, we can all agree collectively that the interpretation of that wavelength of light is the color green.

Sound design is intangible because it is felt as well as heard, and describing sound is difficult. Language obscures nonlinguistic processes and expression. Reactions to images, patterns, and music are part of the human experience and when the brain explains this with language it becomes an interpretation or theory that can clarify what was felt. However, each person perceives, feels, and describes their interpretation in their own unique way.

Although there are many vocabulary words to describe aesthetic response, words create too narrow a view for the concept of consciousness. The aesthetic perception, or art, lives together with consciousness. The human brain stores all of the emotional, non-verbal, and perceptual memories that we experience whether verbalized or not. Our symbolism of dream, myth, and art are a product of our sensory responses and the meanings we have allocated to them.

C. G. Jung, the Swiss psychologist and psychotherapist who founded analytical psychology, has a theory that the collective unconscious, which contains archetypes of what is universally felt to be sacred, predisposes us all to react in the same manner to certain circumstances.

The most challenging part of a sound designer's work is to create an emotional response that is perceived and interpreted both uniquely and universally. It should be unique to the artist creating it, as well as unique to the production in which it is contained. And yet it should be universally understood by an audience to produce a similar collective response, even if the individuals within that audience interpret the meaning slightly differently due to their own separate experience and perception.

Biology, Physics, and Psychology

When we recreate life or dream up a new version of our existence, as we do in theatre, we rely on the emotional response of an audience to further our intention of why we wanted to create it in the first place. Therefore, we must understand how what we do affects a human body sensorially. And in order to understand human reaction to sound we have to go back to the beginning of life on the planet and how hearing came to be.

The first eukaryotic life forms (a term that is characterized by organisms with well-defined cells) sensed vibration. Vibration sensitivity is one of the very first sensory systems, beginning with the externalization of proteins that created small mobile hairs we now call cilia. This helped the earliest life forms to move around, and transformed them from passive to active organisms. The hairs moved in a way that created a sensory system that could detect changes in the movement of the fluid in which they lived.

At first this was helpful because it indicated the presence of predators or prey. Eventually an organism could detect its environment at a distance because of the vibration it felt through the surrounding fluid; essentially it was interpreting the vibration through the sense of touch on the cilia. To go from this obviously simple system to the complexity of the human ear is quite an evolutionary jump that took billions of years, but we cannot deny the link.

If we look at the human ear (Figure 1.1), it is an organ equipped to perceive alternating differences in atmospheric pressure. The inner ear contains the

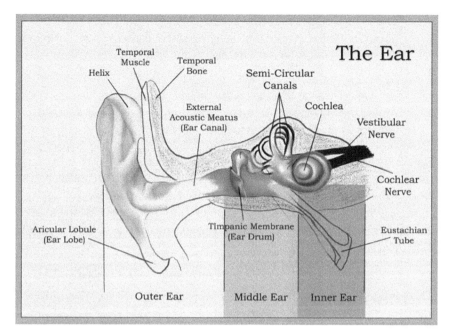

Figure 1.1 The human ear.

cochlea, a snail-shaped spiral structure that is filled with fluid to aid in balance and hearing. In the fluid-filled spiral there are mechanosensing organelles of hair cells about 10–50 micrometers in length. These hairs capture high and low frequencies depending on their placement within the cochlea (higher frequencies at the start, and lower frequencies further inward of the spiral). They convert mechanical and atmospheric pressure stimuli into electric signals that then travel along the cochlear aqueduct, which contains cerebrospinal fluid, to the subarachnoid space in the central nervous system.

Simply put, sound enters the ear; vibrations are detected in the fluid by cilia and are converted into perception at the brain. You may also want to take note that we use this same process of capturing vibrations and creating an electrical signal, to then be interpreted through different "brains" of technology, as our signal flow of the mechanical side of our work as sound designers. Our ears are the best example of organic signal flow.

In the physics of hearing we don't remap every vibration on a one-to-one basis. That would be too overwhelming and chaotic for us to interpret. Evolutionarily, we hear what we need to hear in order to survive.

There are innate conditions to this selective hearing.

- Firstly, we have a specific range of frequencies within which we hear. We don't hear the highest frequencies that a bat produces when flying around on a quiet rural evening. And a train rumble to us is not nearly as violent as it is for an elephant in a city zoo that uses infrasonic (extreme low-end frequency) communication.

- Secondly, from our perceptible frequencies we selectively choose what we want to hear so that the aural world around us is not overpowering. When new meaning is not being introduced, we selectively choose to filter out what we don't need to hear.

Physics aids in determining what of sound is contained in the evolutionary response, and psychology aids In determining what of sound is contained in the associational response. The common denominator is perception.

Moving from the brain to the mind brings us to psychophysics, the study of the relationship between stimuli, the sensations, and the perceptions evoked by those stimuli.

Perception

The first step to the development and evolution of the mind is the activation of psychophysics in the brain. It is what makes an organism sentient. If you understand what you are experiencing around you, you can apply that understanding to learn and grow. This is how the mind evolves. And in our evolution our minds developed a complex way to interpret vibrations and frequency into meaning and emotion.

Everything in our world vibrates because where there is energy there is a vibratory region, some more complex than others but none ever totally silent. The brain seeks patterns and is continually identifying the correlation of sensation with perception of the energy that hits our bodies at a constant rate. When the brain interprets repetitive vibration, it creates the neural pathway of understanding around that vibration, which is why we can selectively block out sound we don't need to hear, e.g. the hum of fluorescent lights or the whir of a computer. But when a random pattern occurs, such as a loud noise behind us, we immediately adjust our focus to comprehend what made that sound, where it is in relation to us, and question if we are in danger.

Hearing is a fast processing system, as you see in Figure 1.2. Not only can the hair cells in your ears pinpoint vibrations, and specific points of phase of a vibration (up to 5,000 times per second), you can also hear changes to that vibration 200 times per second at a perceptual level. For comparison, vision's process to perception registers approximately 15–20 events per second. It takes a thousandth of a second to perceive the vibration in the inner ear; a few milliseconds later the brain has determined where the sound is coming from; and it hits the auditory cortex where we perceive meaning of the sound less than 50 milliseconds from when the vibration hit the outer ear.

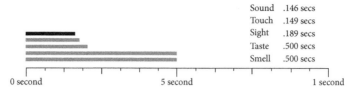

Figure 1.2 The time of the perception of the senses.

The importance of the link between vision and sound repeats itself as an indispensable factor in our work as sound designers. In our brain, at the auditory cortex, we identify tone and comprehension of speech, but it is not just for sound. There are links between sound and vision in sections of the brain to help with comprehension. For example, the auditory cortex can also help with recognizing familiar faces that accompany familiar voices.

The more we learn about the science of the brain, the more physical interconnectedness we find between the sensory perception functions. This is why when sound in theatre matches the visual aspects of what is seen, it can be an incredibly satisfying experience. It is the recreation of life itself, and when it is precisely reproduced it is as though we are actually living what is being presented in the production.

What is fascinating about the perception of hearing is that it does not solely occur in the auditory parts of the brain, but projects to the limbic system as well. The limbic system controls the physical functions of heart rate and blood pressure, but also cognitive function such as memory formation, attention span, and emotional response. It is why music can not only change your heart rate, as doctors in Italy experimenting with usage before cardio-thoracic surgery are finding, but also bring you back in time to a specific moment that contained detailed emotions. This link to the limbic system is one of the aspects of cognitive hearing we use most when placing music into a theatrical performance to support what is happening emotionally on stage.

Describing Sound

As a sound designer, you should have an understanding of what the collective unconscious experience is with sound. Any experience that human beings encounter can be reproduced on stage either in direct mirroring or in metaphoric symbol. Although this happens at the physical level of recreation because it is a dramatized telling of a story, the reproduction also resides at a metaphysical level within the overall event of the experience.

In order to understand the difference between the physical and metaphysical experience of sound, let's use phenomenology (a philosophy which deals with consciousness, thought, and experience). When we are able to break apart the experience of hearing sound to master control over it, we can use it as a tool to affect others. You want to learn sound's constitution in order to be able to control it.

In the beginning of your investigation into how sound works, you may come up against some obstacles. At first when investigating sound, it can be difficult to describe because of the lack of a clearly experienced relationship between subject and object. Secondly, if you are putting new language to something of which you have not previously taken note, you may not be able to find the words to describe it. Yet eventually, in time you will see that you will gain a deeper acuteness to your own reflection upon the sound experience, and your ability to describe it will increase.

All connoisseurs start somewhere, and when they begin they do not have the language to describe the experience. An accomplished wine taster forgets their earlier experiences when they could not tell the difference between grapes, regions, and years of vintage. And although not all wine experts' taste is the same, because their palate is particular and unique, they learn the detail of the qualities that speak to them in their own experience.

It is difficult to break down exactly the process our bodies go through to perceive sound. At its essence sound is not questioned and we do not normally critically examine what we hear daily. Through phenomenology we question with more existential language. And by defining the essence of sound, we take away what is familiar in experience in order to enrich the significance of its core. And hopefully we return to the whole experience again with deeper meaning.

You should analyze intentionally. As you describe experiences, take note of the details that create it and look for the intention of the meaning. This is at the center of an experience. At the edges of it is the horizon or limit. This limit creates a unity with the center of the experience because the center cannot be examined on its own, but must be understood within historical and cultural context.

In theatre, you always have an intention to your work, but it is normally based within the cultural and historical context of when, where, and to whom you are performing. Rediscovering the immenseness of the structure supporting the experience of sound adds to the flexibility of the human being as an artist. With more knowledge of how sound works, you can either play into the expectations of your audience or purposefully redirect away from the norm for effect.

Rediscovering sound means finding a meaning of what sound is in human perception. Traditionally, vision has been used to objectify while sound is used to personify. Phenomenology requires you to re-examine this through analyzing the experience. Instead of explaining what sound is, you describe it. Reflection in your mind can be described as an additional experience of the original experience.

For example, you're walking in the woods late at night. There is a lonely sound of wind in the trees, a cacophony of lively insects that surround you, and your feet are crunching upon the soft delicate forest floor as you walk. At night, in the darkness, you are strongly aware of the sounds you experience. Suddenly, you hear the howl of an animal nearby. It has the impression of being amplified. Fight-or-flight shock fills your body with chemical reaction. You cannot see this animal, but the more you listen intently for the additional sounds it makes, it becomes a more dramatic, fear-filled experience.

If you analyze this reflection of the experience of sound, you come away with how sound can give meaning to the invisible. You cannot see the wind, yet you can hear it. You do not see the animal, but you know it is there. Sound has the ability to create reality without vision, and gives that reality a personification. And the emotional response of the invisible is tangible through the lonely wind and being startled or surprised.

When describing sound we normally start with the sounds of objects. We know the difference between a car passing by versus a truck or motorcycle. We can discern the metaphysical texture of sound as to where and what an object is with extraordinary detail. Turning our attention to the existential level of the experience, spatial conditions appear. In order to find the intent of the sound, we must place it into a spatial context.

You will see that, with surprising accuracy, differences in size, shape, and material are discernable through sound. Our past experience with the vibration that an object makes very quickly sums up its properties. Its shape, size, and material is heard rather than seen.

The material properties that create the click of plastic are very different from something made of rubber. We can tell the fundamental shape by whether the object bounces or rolls. There is also a difference in hearing the shape of something that is flat like a domino, compared to something faceted like a die. The composition of the object creates richness in its sound texture. And finally, size is determined by the frequency of sound the object creates. A small ceramic vase falling to the floor is a very different sound from that of a large piece of furniture falling over.

Material and size are easier to interpret, but when we hear sounds experientially we cannot necessarily immediately identify an object's shape. Turning to the visual and auditory experience as a guide, sound and vision do not necessarily overlap. You may be looking over the table you're sitting at and see light coming in the window and remark on the time on the digital clock. But at the same time a radio is on in the other room and someone outside is mowing their lawn. Your visual input is very separate from your aural input.

The visual before you has an outline of shape and you can see it all as one visual image. You do not see beyond it. In this instance, you do not perceive shape from the sounds you hear, and certainly not their outline. With sound it is more about the relativity of how it exists in time—both in a sequential (relating to order of occurrence) and temporal (relating to time) aspect. Sound occurs linearly in space.

Instantaneous sound makes it more difficult to gather details because of its quickness, but when you combine duration with the temporal aspect of sound, you can better determine shape. If you bounce a ball, you may not understand the size of the ball. But if you apply time to the sound by rolling the ball, you can even discern the difference between round and oval. An egg rolling on a hard surface sounds different from a bowling ball. An object's size, shape, and material are more accessible when you have more time to experience the sound it creates. You do not need vision when you have time.

When the action of an object is instantaneous, the spatial significance is as important as vision in aiding comprehension. When a drop of water falls, it is a blur until it ends with the sound as it hits a surface. The understanding of the visual is vague until the motion stops with sound. And the amount of time it took for the drop to land is relative to the spatial properties that will help determine size and material.

An additional condition that adds comprehension to what you hear is the surface with which an object is interacting. When you roll a marble across a tiled floor, you comprehend the size, shape, and material of the marble. You also understand the tiled surface upon which the marble is rolling, due to the intermittent change of sound when it hits the grout.

How do we innately know all this? We have catalogued all of our aural experiences in our brain, and our mind has created associations to certain sensory perceptions by way of neural pathways. When they repeat themselves identically, they are mapped and remembered as tangible.

The more you take note of your experience with how sound affects you personally, the more vocabulary you will develop to help you describe the intention of your design. In time you will not remember the first steps because you will have the background of experience to support your choices.

Sound and Vision

The power of the visual dominates the definition of human experience. And even with the rise of modern metaphysics, a feeling of distrust of what is invisible creates an imperceptible realm of inaccuracy. In the past, few have tried to define how sound adds to experience.

The manifestation of hearing as part of human experience can be traced back to Pre-Socratic philosophy as early as 500 BCE, when Xenophanes described experience as the "whole he sees, whole he thinks, and whole he hears." The inclusion of sound at this time departs from the norm, and it could be argued that because we still do not see sound, we do not initially equate it to experience.

The ordinary listener completes endless auditory functions that require impressive delineation of what constitutes what they're hearing. When an ear is tuned to hear as a tool, it can be extremely powerful. For example, you know when your water bottle is almost full because of the pitch of the sound it makes.

As the water gets closer to the rim, with less air and more mass in the bottle, the sound of trickling water against the container increases in pitch as the tone of the body of water lowers in pitch. This is determined by the ratio of water to air in conjunction with the bounce of vibration of moving water against the container. But you didn't need to know the physics to understand when to stop filling the container. Your experience in the activity instinctually tells you what you need to know.

A car mechanic can hear exactly what is faulty in an engine by listening to it. This can more readily provide a clearer picture than having to find all the pieces that may be difficult to see. And as a trained listener, a musician must hear with extreme accuracy for tonal shift, dynamics, and timing.

If we start with a brain free of any characteristic or idea, it is experience that supplies all that there is for us to acknowledge. Primitive experience could be wrongly labeled as simple. Because if we don't delve into the complex, our definition of perception would be governed by what is unfelt and thereby consist of the abstract. It relies on ideas and not evidence. As we are now long past primitive in our hearing, dissecting what we now take for granted is part of our process to better know our craft as sound designers.

We know now the complicated intricacies that determine how we perceive, so therefore what is unfelt can be surmised or hypothesized. Once an experience is perceived and labeled, it gains meaning. The more you delve into how sound is created and perceived the more apt you are to create experiences that others will respond to subconsciously.

Most theatregoers do not recognize the sound that accompanies a performance unless they are specifically guided to notice it. We provide the perception of depth of the moment-to-moment reality by filling in the gaps of where the visual leaves off. In order to recreate true-to-life experiences, we have to supply the aural world in which the event exists physically or metaphorically.

If we do not normally take note of how we process sound in our lives and its existence in our experiences, we will not be able to ascertain its presence in a theatrical production as an audience member. And for most people, sound in theatre will be imperceptible because their ears are not tuned to know how they perceive sound. We, as sound designers, want to use that to our advantage. But we can only do that if we completely understand how human beings process sound ourselves.

Auditory Field

The situated context, and what is surrounding the occurrence of sound, is what is known as the auditory field. It is what is present and implicit, and yet not synonymous with the sound. It exceeds the sonic event, and yet it in itself is limited. It has a boundary or perceived horizon, and yet it absolutely does not encompass what we know as "the world."

An aspect we can determine is the sound that surrounds us in the auditory field. A way of defining this is what Don Ihde, in his book *Listening and Voice: Phenomenologies of Sound,* calls the "focus to fringe ratio." When listening to a symphony, you can choose to single out a single instrument over another. When walking down the street, you can focus in on a conversation over the noise of the city around you. What you choose to listen to becomes the focus, and the rest beyond that becomes the fringe. This all lives within the auditory boundary or horizon of the field.

But if I turn on an electronic audio recorder, it cannot perform the same function of selectivity and focus. It records everything in the field without any significance. That is why sometimes when playing back a recording, the fringe noise is equal to or overtakes what you had focused on with your own ears. The field in itself forms a shape of sound.

Taking note of the auditory field as a shape is an interesting concept for a sound designer to integrate into their design. When paired with the visual you can note that hearing is more omnidirectional than vision. And again pairing the sound with the visual, the scope and scale of your environment can be enhanced through sight because the visual boundary helps define the shape of the surrounding aural boundary.

But because we hear in 360 degrees, the shape of the field is dependent upon where we are within it. It can be imagined as a sphere with the human body positioned at the center. What is happening to the left, right, behind, in front of, above, or below is detectable because the auditory field surrounds the listener's perspective. Human beings use directional listening within omnidirectional hearing.

The sphere of sound around us can be extremely dramatic when sound is full within the field. The sound immerses, surrounds, and even penetrates the body. This is why when attending a symphony you can find yourself absorbed to such a degree that the distinction between the internal and the external is erased. However, even within this fullness, if someone were to cough to your right, you could locate it directionally.

Directionality and surround-ability exist together and they are co-present in our hearing. This dual dimension characterizes a specific richness to design that can manipulate an environment with a range of subtle to large gestures.

The existential properties of sound within a field are grounded in continuity. In experience, sound is perceptually present; you cannot escape it. You can leave an urban environment of loud traffic, sirens, and noise to escape to the quiet of a rural environment. But because sound is all-encompassing, it may be quieter than the city, but it is not silent. And even if you enter an anechoic chamber, you instantly hear the sound of your own body that is normally hidden in daily existence. Fields are never empty as sound is always present. Because where there is energy and movement causing vibration, there is sound.

So how does this apply to the sound designer and their artistry? Firstly, if we wish to recreate real-life experiences, we must know what the aural world of that experience entails. Secondly, if we wish it to be believable and not questioned, it must mimic the subconscious level of hearing that we as humans experience when we listen. Thirdly, we must understand how sound works in the space around us if we are to recreate different environments of the stories presented in a theatre venue. And lastly, as we add intention to our design, we determine what exactly the audience is to hear for the best support of the moment portrayed either physically or metaphorically.

Sound as Time in Space

Sound is a wave phenomenon. It travels through time. When describing sound, you speak in a linear format because one event follows another. It exists for a moment and then passes. It therefore delineates time by dramatizing what is taking place in the present.

The larger shape of the sound in our daily existence exists in a daily rhythm. There is marked repetition and difference between when the birds sing in the morning and when the insects and nocturnal animals make noise at night. In a city, there is a definite sound shift with rush hour versus overnight traffic. You can even track time in the onset of an HVAC system indoors. There is a daily rise-and-fall quality to the ordering of sound through time.

These structured rhythms of our daily chaotic aural life lend a feeling of security because of the constancy they create through repetition. We take their familiarity for granted because they are expected by us.

If we break it apart in time, we do not hear one instant followed by another, we hear the temporal span or the duration of the object that is creating sound. And that temporal span shows itself through our perception of how it passes into and out of our focus and retention. The Doppler effect, which changes the pitch of a sound an object makes as it passes, shows the temporal span in its unity even though the quality of the sound is different throughout.

What we grasp within the temporal span of the sounds we hear is dependent upon our focus. These temporal focal points give us a succession of events through time. For example, I can focus on the car as it pulls up in the driveway, the engine shutting off, the clinking of keys as someone walks to the door to ring the doorbell. Yet, what is not in my focus is all the while the washing machine in the other room is a constant mechanical bed of noise and the birds are chirping outside the window. Within the panorama of sound, we pick out the temporal directionality of focus through time.

And a general way to determine motion (such as the car pulling up in the driveway) in temporal duration is to notice if the clarity of sound is weakening or strengthening. As an object comes closer to us the detection of its vibration becomes stronger. And as it retreats from us, the detection becomes weaker. This gives us spatial awareness to our surroundings when it comes to objects in motion.

This focus, in an auditory sense, is the "now point" of time. It acts in a temporal manner just as a center focus of a visual picture does. It is the present moment.

Sound does not exist unless expressed across time, and sound waves travel through time at a perceptible speed. Sound is propagated in a room, and when it is cut off or finished, there is a collection of reflections that continue to live within the space until they run out of energy and dissipate.

It is not as instantaneous as light. Turn off a light and the room goes dark almost immediately. Stop sound and it continues to live. Sound is time. It takes time for sound to travel, so therefore we can gauge cubic space around us with time. This is the physical property of time and space with regards to sound waves.

The onset of sound is what we call our "source point." When it reaches our ears, that is the now point of time. The trailing off, which is based on characteristic aspects of the auditory field's structure, can be viewed as the horizon of the past. And since theatre exists in the now, we create the auditory focus in time for the audience.

When waiting for a specific sound you know is about to occur, your expectation is pushed to the future edge of the temporal span until you hear it. You take away all other background sound in order to perceive a specific vibration. Once you hear the sound you are expecting, you immediately change your perception to the active response of vibration, and you specifically minimize the listening to its reverberation. You try to remain as much in the moment of now as possible.

In a broad and open focus, such as when listening to a piece of music, each note in time will lend itself to the enrichment of the following notes. Because each note is equally as present as the next, it allows for the richness of a piece of music to evolve because each present note is also dependent on the last one.

What creates the richness of sound through time is dependent on the auditory field. You can focus on the duration of the sound's span determined by either the limits of the auditory field or the durational presence. Sound lingers, bounces, and reverberates. And the mixture of these textures in time gives consonance and dissonance to the moment of now.

Reverberation and Temporal Focus

The reverberation or the trailing off of sound is significant in determining the temporal focus. There is an initial onset of sound—the source—and then the time it takes to move in space.

- Firstly, the two voices of the source and its reverberation create a compound sound, a duet of distinct sounds working together to create space and meaning through time.

- Secondly, the source allows you to ascertain direction of where the object lives in space. It's the onset that is instantaneous. The continuous tone that follows travels as far as space can allow as it fills up around the object. What it does is give awareness of time and space as the duration lingers.

For example, listening to music fills the temporal span with both the onset and the reverberation of sound. It is analogous to vision in how you can take in an entire panorama of a landscape at once. It is full both in space and time. Where sound differs from vision is that you are immersed in the sphere of the sonic experience, and you cannot detect the spatial boundaries.

When listening to music, this filling of space surrounds, penetrates, and obliterates the sense of the internal and external balance. You don't primarily listen for specifics in music; in fact the appeal of music is to move away from components and take it in as a whole. You also don't normally acknowledge the practicality of space, direction, or shapes. There is too much sound occurring and that makes these focuses unclear.

The temporal edge, or the trailing off, of music is balanced with the nothingness of no longer being present. This clearer limitation is the horizon of sound. At the edge of the auditory field this horizon is delineated as temporal, and therefore sound affirms the time it takes to travel by diminishing in energy, and dissipating.

Auditory horizons have vague spatial significance. It is the threshold of your personal ability to hear. The way to determine the horizon is through strength and time. It may seem spherical in the sense that perceptually from our listening point the sound emanates outwardly, and we feel surrounded by the fullness of sound. The waves come into the present time and then fade away in time. At the end of our perception, there is a resistance offered that continually recedes from the center focus.

In a sense we await the coming of sound, it makes itself present, and the only way you can escape it is if you purposefully attempt to stop hearing it. Otherwise the sound continues as long as its strength through time and space allow its movement. What is present is found within the horizon and in this humankind lives within a sonic event.

Imaginative Mode

We as human beings don't solely hear sound; there is an additional arrangement in our minds that can create imaginative sound. This can be done on its own or with the addition of external sound. Because we are internal to our experiences, there is a self-presence of how we perceive sonic events. If we turn inward we can use auditory imagination to create sound in our heads. If I write the sound of glass shattering, you can create that sound by thinking of it as you read. I'm sure as you've been reading this book, you have been imaginatively creating sounds through the descriptions I have written.

The internal sound we can create through imagination can mimic or represent any external experience. It is said that Beethoven had the ability to hear an entire symphony in his head, and even after the onset of his deafness, his inner hearing did not fail; hence the 9th Symphony could be written without his ability to hear it. So that portends that the bounty of imagination is as complex as the perception of sound itself.

Imaginatively, our senses can be vividly presented and we can have a full experience of an event without any outside force. What is more difficult to determine is the structure of imaginative thought, because in its essence it is variable and easily changeable. As soon as you think of something, it is there.

If you imagine a bee buzzing in front of your face, it is similar to perceiving it in a real experience. But if you imagine that the bee flies around to be behind you, there are two modes of perception that you can have. You can experience it as you do in reality by hearing and feeling it behind you. Or, you can pull outside the experience to see it in your imagination as an observer to the event. You actually see the bee behind your head as if you are someone else. Imagination in this case exceeds perception.

The co-presence of the imaginative and perceptual modes is where theatre lives. We perceive the experience of watching theatre as our senses send signals to our brain. At the same time our inner imagination fills in what is either impossible to attain, or figurative or metaphorical in value, and creates a richer experience.

Sometimes it is the recognition of something that we know. Sometimes it is the experience of something that we have never witnessed before. It can be our internal voice that conveys meaning or it could be the lack of this voice that allows us to just be in the experience. It plays out in many different ways, and it is individual for all human beings. It is purposefully not something we control. All we can do as theatre artists is note how it affects each of us while creating the events, and try to evoke an intended common response.

What is happening is that the audience lose sense of their bodies. Just as when you sit in a chair lost in thought, your imaginative focus takes over. In the general sense your body disappears. The inner attention is the focus of the experience. But if there were to be an auditory interruption with a loud sound or something unexpected, the body would have a reaction and you would once again be aware of your body in space. When an audience is startled it reminds them that they are in a theatre experiencing an event because they are reminded by the reactionary response of their body.

When you read a book, you are seeing words, but what you see within the words is a different perception. The same effect happens when seeing a performance. At times you can wander off into your own thought because you are stimulated by what you are experiencing. These moments play upon the daily ordinary hallucinations of a synthesis of imaginative and perceptual co-presence, which is never exhausted.

While watching a performance, or listening to music, you may imagine colors swirling. You may feel a certain way that reminds you of something else. And at this time imagination takes focus over perception. If you try to concentrate on imagination and perception at the same time you meet resistance. This dance of the balance between perception and imagination is what occurs during a theatrical performance. What we strive for is the intentional harmony or dissonance between the perceived sound and the imagined sound. There have been times when I've used a low drone in a scene, and after it has stopped playing, the director will ask me if it's still running. This is because it is still imaginatively running for the director.

As sound designers we strike a balance of the internal and external through the support of the piece of theatre we are helping to create. For example, as the performance's voice singles out to a lone person on stage, a support of this idea could be to voice the music underscoring the event with a single instrument to give the same impression of soliloquy. Perhaps silence best equates what the feeling of this character alone on stage represents. Or we can even juxtapose the singularity by creating chaos around the character and thereby amplify the effect of aloneness.

It will depend on the intention of the piece of theatre, but the specific decisions you make should support in a metaphysical sense what you are conveying to your audience. You want to initiate imaginative thinking of the internal that helps support the external expression of the piece in a way that creates an emotional response. The artistic team works together to impress thoughts and ideas upon an audience.

Silence and Loudness

Silence and loudness are tools sound designers can use that rely on human beings' evolutionary response and perception.

We know that silence is an important element of the auditory horizon. And relative silence is what we actually hear. Because sound is in a sense given and then received, it could be said that silence is given in absence. It is an empty intention that gives the impression of being the opposite to sound. And because of this, the relative absence adds to meaningfulness of auditory experience. The rests or pausing in a phrase of music add more depth and meaning to the completeness of the experience.

Intentional gestures of silence are filled with their own significance. Any piece of music must be surrounded, and therefore grounded, by silence. It is what allows the music to express itself. This is why putting on headphones seems to give clarity to what you hear as it is cancelling out all other noise and creating a supportive silence.

If we await the coming of sound, and are grounded in a perceived silence, then silence could be the sound of time passing.

The absence of sound draws attention. If you've entered into a sound-deadened room, such as an isolation booth, you immediately remark about how quiet it feels without the reverberation of your own voice. After a few minutes, you start registering low-level vibrations, or perhaps a slight hiss that could be the molecules bouncing around in your head. Perhaps you tune into your own breathing or heartbeat, and suddenly it's all you hear.

It's then that we feel the need to have some sound in our environment; this shows how dependent we are on disregarded background noise. Once it's taken away, the brain is either waiting for what is going to happen next (in an environment someone else is controlling) or the brain will make its own noise such as singing or talking to yourself to help fill in what is missing (in an environment of which you are in control).

We can categorize sound into synchronous and non-synchronous, or asynchronous, sound. Synchronous sound matches what you see, such as the sound of footsteps to the person in front of you on the sidewalk. And asynchronous sound is what you hear without knowing what is making the sound, or anything not in your view. With so many synchronous and asynchronous sounds in our daily lives, the way to control the mind is to reduce the amount of stimuli inputs. We see this in meditation, yoga, and hypnosis.

The idea is that if you take away the distraction of sound for the mind, you can deepen the focus of thought. By simplifying the chaos, you are taking away the amount of data with which the brain has to work and placing that attention on what you specifically want your audience to hear, or the object of interest.

For example, when working with dynamics and wanting the audience to focus on the quietness of a house at night, you can shift their focus from a loud transitional moment to an object of interest such as a distant grandfather clock. It may not register at first as the ears have to adjust to the shift in volume and lack of complexity, but as the audience's ears accustom to the quiet, the clock becomes more pronounced. And because of this object of interest that you can hear from another room, the house seems even quieter than if it were silent because of the distance between the audience and the perceived asynchronous sound of the clock.

Sound designers use silence to focus the attention on specific moments in a production. Because silence is relative, it is the most dramatic when it comes directly after loud sound, but it can be used with subtlety as well. It can mimic the way a character selectively blocks out all other sound because of a heightened emotional state.

Let's say that two characters in love are on a subway platform, and it is full of people and the typical chaos that suggests the reality of the environment. Suddenly one of them begins to kneel down in order to propose marriage. Now, if we keep the din of the environment up it is similar to when a tape recorder captures all sound without any selectivity. But, if we take the point of view of the characters and fade the environmental sound around them, abstracting the reality of the space, we can focus in on them just as they are doing in their own minds. And consequently, we can hear the intimacy of this moment even though there may still be chaos surrounding them. The noise can return when the focus shifts back to when the other person gives their answer to the proposal.

In juxtaposition to perceived silence is loud sound, which plays upon the sympathetic nervous system of the audience's human body. The sympathetic nervous system is one of the two divisions of the autonomic nervous system, which regulates the unconscious actions of the body. The sympathetic nervous system's primary process is to stimulate the fight-or-flight response. A loud sound will stimulate not just the cochlea but also the entire inner ear. And the louder the sound, the less a human being is concerned with consonance or dissonance, or linguistic meaning.

After a really loud sound occurs, our focus is on our well-being in the situation. You physically manifest this by your motor controls being startled and producing sweat from the chemical reaction of fear. If the loud sound is repeated, a neural pathway within your audience's brain is built based on this experience, and the effect will diminish with use.

The guiding of your audience's emotion works because they are not in control of the sound around them. There is a link between executive decision-making regions of your brain and perception centers. This is why if you make the executive decision to tickle or pinch yourself, you will not react as strongly as if someone else does it to you.

You may notice it when you get into your car and start it up and the radio is blaringly loud. Then you remember that you really liked the song you were listening to last, and had made the choice to turn up the volume to a high level because of the joy loud sound can give you when you choose it. But now, that it's not in your control or your choice, the volume is extremely jarring when experiencing it after the perceived silence of shutting yourself within a car.

When designing for theatre, take into account the demographic age-range of the audience when determining the dynamic range of volume in your space. Younger people are used to and often seek loud music. They wear headphones and ear buds regularly, and their world is full of loud sound. Older people tend to choose specific moments to use loud sound for pleasure; and mostly loudness is sought after because their hearing has declined. When using loud sound for effect, it's in your best interest to keep your audience in consideration.

And a word of caution: exposure to intense loud sound can potentially alter your normal sensitivity, and as sound designers I would urge you to not over-expose yourself to loud sound. Protect your ears whenever in contact with loud sound.

Describing Music

We know that sound is the most powerful and common stimulus for emotional response, and when we rely on associational emotional response as a tool in sound design, this resides a great deal in our hearing of and association to music.

Music draws attention to itself, particularly music that is not sung. The meaning lies in the sound of the music, as we listen reflectively to wordless music. It enlivens the body because it plays upon a full range of self-presence. Music is felt in its rhythms and movements. The filling of auditory space equates to losing distance as you listen, and therefore creates the impression of penetration.

The sound of music is not the sound of unattended things that we experience in our day-to-day existence. It is constructed and therefore curiously different. Each piece of music, each genre or style is a new language to experience. Music comes to be from silence and it shows the space of silence as possibility. The tone waxes and wanes at the discretion of the musician, and composers can explore the differences between being and becoming, and actuality and potentiality.

In his book *Listening and Voice: Phenomenologies of Sound*, Don Ihde remarks:

> The purity of music in its ecstatic surrounding presence overwhelms my ordinary connection with things so that I do not even primarily hear the symphony as the sounds of instruments. In the penetrating totality of the musical synthesis it is easy to forget the sound as the sound of the orchestra and the music floats through experience. Part of its enchantment is in obliteration of things.

Music can be simply broken down into the idea that it is a score with instrumentation. It is a type of performance. And if we look towards how we respond to music, it can be found in the definition of each unique performance and its specific effect upon us. A score will tell a musician how to perform a piece of music, and they can play it note-perfectly. But one performance can vary from another because of the particular approach to the music by the individuals involved in creating it.

Because one cannot properly consider a work of art without considering it as meaningful, the art of music must then be defined as having meaning. To define it as meaningful would lead you to think that it is possible to actually say what a specific piece of music means. Everything is describable. But if you put into words the meaning of music, it almost seems to trivialize it because you can't seem to capture the entirety of its meaning.

What we can communicate when defining music is its characteristic. Most use emotion to do this. For example, the music can be sad. But is it the particular phrase in the music that is sad; or is it the orchestration; or is it a totality of the entire piece that creates the analogy? Or, more specifically, can it be the experience of hearing the music that creates the feeling of sadness? But even this is ambiguous, because if you come to a conclusion on a definition about how the music affected you emotionally, in describing it you still have to find commonality about the expression that was effective to everyone else who experienced it.

We can try to describe music in the sense of its animation. The properties of its movement correspond to the movement properties of natural expression. A sad person moves slowly, and perhaps this is somehow mirrored in the piece of music. The dynamic character of the music can resemble human movement. Yet this alone would also not fully explain what it is to experience sad music, because human movement implies change of location and musical movement does not.

Although music does not call for imaginative hearing or imaginative perception, it does call for imaginative introspection. This happens when a passage of music mimics behavioral expressions of feeling. And listeners can either imagine hearing the mimicked expression or they may be made aware of their own feelings.

There are two ways you can listen to music: within and without. Experiencing music from within involves an imaginative manner that reminds you of your own emotions. And experiencing music from without allows it to remain an expression that you're not experiencing as if it were your own.

When music accompanies an additional form of expression as it does many times in theatre, you can evoke the same two reactions from an audience. The first is that the audience empathizes with the experience; they feel an emotion that the performance is expressing (within). And the second is that they can have a sympathetic reaction; they feel an emotion in response to what is being expressed (without).

It's as if the music has a life of its own and has the ability to express itself. Whatever it expresses we react to as if it has the same qualities of being human. It's not as though we are imagining this in actuality. The music is not a living creature, but it does have a personality.

There is so much more to the experience of listening to music. There is a critical engagement between the active listening of the audience and the expressing of the musical performance. Perhaps it's the multi-dimensional aspect of musical expression, and its depth, that creates this engagement because we listen to different types of music in different ways.

What is so dynamic to music is that it can function as a metaphor for emotional life. It can possess qualities of a psychological drama, it can raise a charge towards victory, it can struggle with impending danger, or it can even try to recover a past lost. And it can describe both emotional and psychological states of mind. It is almost as if the experience is beyond the music even though we are not separated from it. Our inner response may divert in our imagination, but it is the music that is guiding us. That is why the experience of listening to music is often described as transporting us.

Music is perhaps an ordered succession of thoughts that could be described as an harmonic and thematic plan by the composer. And in this idea we supply an application of dramatic technique to music in order to create a conversation between the player and the listener. We use words such as climax and denouement with a unity of tone and action. We even use the term character. We develop concepts and use music as a discourse to express metaphor. But at times intellectual content is almost coincidental. We did not set up this conversation to be heard intellectually, its intention is to be felt emotionally. The composer and musician direct our aural perception as the listener.

Feeling Music

Seth Horowitz, who was recording music for his contribution to *Just Listen* (a film about sound), asked Dame Evelyn Glennie to define music. She stated that music is not something that you create and listen to with just your ears; you listen with your whole body. Evelyn Glennie is a marvelous percussionist who is mostly deaf and hears only a few high frequencies. Her music creates a sonic environment, because she does not hear in the standard way, she feels it.

Her perception of the vibration is kinesthetic. She feels the vibration from the stage through her bare feet; her instrument resonates at her legs, lower body, and neck; and she also feels the striking of the mallets through her hands, up her arms, and traveling all the way to her skull, thus creating a low-frequency resonance transferring through her body. These frequencies resonate her body through bone, tissue, and body fluid.

When I was on scholarship at Joffrey Ballet, we had a deaf dancer in our class. I was always amazed as to how he could know how the choreography fitted in time to the music since he could not hear it. I was so enthralled by this that I asked him how he was able to dance in time to the music. He said he primarily felt the low range of frequency of the piano and the rhythm in his feet, the middle range of frequency in his body, and the high range near his head. I began to listen in this way at age 14 and it has remained with me since. When I EQ in a theatre, I feel where those resonances hit my body. I know when a frequency is stronger or weaker by the way it hits my body.

In time, with experience, you will be able to discern the difference in feeling of a large-wave low frequency from a small-wave high frequency. If you continue to train your ears, you will eventually be able to fine-tune and know the exact frequency or at least the range of frequencies you are wishing to manipulate.

It seems that music should lend itself to a scientific explanation of mathematics, frequency, composition of tone, amplitude, and time; however, there is so much more to music than what can be studied. There have been interpretations of how different intervals in music elicit a reaction in the listener. And the main determination of emotional response comes from whether the interval contains consonance or dissonance.

Consonance is a combination of notes that are harmonic because of the relationship of their frequencies. Dissonance is the tension that is created from a lack of harmony in the relationship of their frequencies. The specific determination of these terms has changed throughout history with the exploration of new ways of playing music and it remains very difficult to come to a consensual meaning.

What is known scientifically is that the listener reacts with a different response to intervals that contain consonance rather than intervals that are dissonant. This goes further into the meaning of perception when we take into account the different emotional responses for intervals that are in a major key or in a minor key. This is why we tend to think of major keys as happy and minor keys as sad. However, keep in mind that both major and minor keys can contain consonance and dissonance.

Instrumentation

Every musical instrument creates its own harmonics based on the material of which it is made and how it is played (struck, bowed, forced air, etc.). And these harmonics add to the perception of consonance and dissonance. This is the reason why a violin will produce a different emotional response than that of a tuba. Each instrument has its own emotional tone; and when combined, the harmonics mix together in a way that creates a complexity of different emotional states.

When you place that complexity into a major or minor key using either consonance or dissonance and vary the speed and volume, you get music. A great composer uses each instrument's emotional tone, whether alone or in concert with other instruments, to convey what they want their audience to feel.

Rhythm

Rhythm can be defined as a temporal sequence imposed by meter and generated by musical movement. And yet not all music is governed by meters and bar lines. Arabic music, for example, composes its time into cycles that are asymmetrically added together. The division of time by music is what we recognize as rhythm. For a sound designer it is important to note that the other aspect of rhythm is not about time; it is the virtual energy that flows through the music. This causes a human response that allows us to move with it in sympathy.

Like speech or movement, music contains meter, stress, and accent. And the grouping of these is what gives a piece of music its movement, or language. It can contain suspension, giving a sustained moment to the expression. It can contain elements of syncopation, or it can pulse with regularity.

This is what can be discerned as the difference between rhythm, meter, and beat. The beat makes the rhythm possible. Meter is the frame from which rhythm grows. The rhythm is the nature of feeling.

Each culture depends upon its own interpretation of rhythm. A merengue will have a very different feeling from a Viennese waltz. The sociological and anthropological aspects to rhythm vary greatly, and rhythm is the lifeblood of how subgroups of people express themselves. It can be as broad as the rhythms of different countries, to the minuteness of different regions that live in close proximity. Rhythm is a form of expression and can be extremely particular depending on who is creating it and who is listening to it.

Non-Musical Sound

In speaking of music, I'd like to refer to what could be identified as non-musical sound. The putting together of sound that is not musical can be considered composing, and this non-musical sound can evoke feeling just as musical sound can. Sonic construction of non-musical phrasing pushes the boundaries of conventional musical sounds. And if music lies within the realm of sound, it can be said that even the active engagement of listening to compound non-musical sound can evoke an emotional response. It can be tranquil, humorous, captivating, or exciting. The structure and instrumentation of the composition is what will give the impression of metaphor.

We use non-musical sound a great deal in sound design as we are always looking for new ways of conveying meaning. And depending on the intention and thematic constructs of a piece of theatre, we create soundscapes from atypical instrumentation that are meant to evoke a feeling or mood when heard.

Association of Music

Music is one of the strongest associational tools we can use as sound designers. The most prevalent use of this is in jingles and theme songs. When you watch a show through its entire television life—for example the seven seasons of *The West Wing*—there is no denying that the opening theme music, written by W. G. Snuffy Walden, will become embedded into your consciousness.

One of the most often remarked upon associations is the use of John Williams's theme music to the movie *Jaws*. A single tuba sounding very much alone slowly plays a heartbeat pattern that speeds up until it's accelerated to the point of danger.

This is the perfect example of how repetition and the change of pace in music can cause your heart rate to speed up or slow down. It is why we feel calm with slower pieces of music, and excited with more complex or uneven tempos. The low infrasonic resonance of the frequencies created by the tuba imparts the feeling of danger approaching. When matched with the visual aspect of what you are trying to convey, a woman swimming alone in the ocean at night, the association is a very powerful tool to generate mood, feeling, and emotion.

Every action film is filled with loud, sudden, low-end noises mixed with fast-tempo rhythms that play upon your sympathetic nervous system's response. The association of the sad trombone pops up whenever something is disappointing because it is part of a collective association. The most common cellphone ringtones are easily recognizable quickly by a global community. If you play video games, the music that underlies the action can creep into your dreams. The success of an association is determined by how quickly you can form a bridge between a sensory stimulus and the emotion it elicits.

In sound design you also have the ability to practice mind control where you can transport your audience to a time and place they have never been, or to a specific time and place that supports the production. Have you ever had a moment when you are driving in a car and a song from when you were younger comes on the radio and you are instantly flooded with the emotions, sights, smells, and feelings of when that song first hit you and what you associated with it in the past?

When you're done reliving these sense memories, you've still maintained the action of driving safely and continuing the activity you were doing. But briefly your mind was taken over while your brain still functioned fully. The song controlled you temporarily. Music has the ability to transform your surroundings by changing the state of your mind.

In theatre, we transport an audience in their mind through sound even though the action of participating in a group experience is what they are actively doing. The association of music can help you as the designer to determine where you want your audience to go. Is it in the past, is it in the future, is it to a specific place, or is it internal or external? These are some questions that help you determine your intention as you build your design.

Theatre Artists

As individual theatre artists working together, you shape connections for an audience to larger, broader cultural experiences or to specific subcultures you are representing. Theatre artists use specialized skills and knowledge, professional discipline, and the understanding of sensory function to bind together with a shared identity of support, goals, and intention. And the aural subculture of the sound design field has a unique shared relationship to the rest.

The secret to the effectiveness of storytelling is emotion. Theatre looks at social considerations side by side with intellectual and artistic creativity. We use concepts of consciousness, sensation, perception, awareness, understanding, feeling, response, cognition, and illusion. And there is great depth as to how to use each one of these concepts.

We can divide these human experiences further by exploring the what, how, and the why:

What—categorizes observations to describe events
How—segregates the components of the process
Why—draws implications by broadening the scope of the questions raised

Answers to the question of:

What—provides the needed data in actuality
How—lends itself to discovering theories and models
Why—provides the foundation to the work

In theatre, sound designers want to create a reliable consistency to the repeatability of an audience reaction. We use a predictive skill towards social reaction to come to common yet specific conclusions of effect. We utilize the intensity and strength of what we are presenting. And we hope that the response is applicable to the audience's experience, thereby creating meaning through association. It is difficult to quantify sound's role in a theatre production because it is in conjunction with other disciplines where it is most effective.

Sound that is meaningful produces an emotional response due to what we perceive as the effect upon us. Emotions are expressed in body language and physiological changes. Changes to the body can be sensed and are a window into human reaction. All of this has evolved within the brain as it responds to stimuli without conscious awareness of it. You can actually see how an audience is responding through their body language.

The limbic system, which controls our basic emotions and cannot be specifically located in any area of the brain, controls the amount of arousal. It also is the place of association of stored memories and historical experiences. Therefore, we can conclude that the limbic system determines which aspects of the emotional response to the experience an audience will remember in the future.

What we want to do in theatre is construct the effect upon the audience. We can do that with a subliminal shifting of feeling or mood, or we can overwhelm the audience with immersion of sound. Both elicit emotional response. And when aural components are deliberate, detailed, and synchronous to intention, few will consciously recognize the motivation behind an emotional shift. The goal is to be in sync with all elements of the expression of the production so that one element is not singled out unless specifically intended.

Aural awareness remains subtle, often unconscious, and seldom recognized. And whether designed, or by accident, the aural space around us affects our mood and behavior.

Influencing Evolutionary Response

In a theatrical environment, the audience is listening with goal-directed attention, which focuses the sensory and cognitive skill on a limited set of inputs. Therefore, we as sound designers have the ability to shape the sonic journey and create specific selected frequencies and attenuation by making the environment as complex or pure as we determine in our design.

We use stimulus-based attention when we want to capture awareness and redirect focus because certain sound elements create triggers due to the lack of previous neural path routing. We create sonic environments by bringing attention to only what we supply; there is nothing for an audience to filter out, it is all on purpose.

When a sudden loud sound happens it makes the audience jump, and now if we add to it a low-frequency tone, the brain automatically starts creating subconscious comparisons because the input limitation is the only information the audience is receiving. We control what they hear and how they hear it.

Low frequencies have their own special response in a human being. There is an evolutionary reason as to why low frequencies immediately make the brain suspect there is danger nearby. Some have equated that hearing high-amplitude infrasonic aspects of an animal growl immediately forces humans into a fight-

or-flight response. More importantly though, loud infrasonic sound is not only heard, it is felt. It vibrates the entire body including the internal organs. Even with the subtlest use of low frequency, you can create unease internally.

There is also a factor in sound that can be used if it is specifically called for, and that is what we call negative valence or the feeling of annoyance, anger, or aversion. It happens with the idea of a false alarm. It is when the body is excited by a sudden loud noise that is intrusive but is not associated with danger. One example is when you click on a webpage and it announces a loud advertisement, causing you to immediately mute your computer or leave the page out of annoyance.

You were emotionally startled for something that posed no danger to you and you resent that your body had to react chemically. It has to do with not being able to source where the sound is coming from, recognize the voice or tone, and the sudden unexpected quality of loudness. The unexpected sound will startle an audience for this exact same reason.

In contrast, one of the most powerful tools for a sound designer is the ability to create the feeling of apparent silence. This is relative to the sound experience preceding and following the silence. It has its own emotional response because we are normally subconsciously subjected to constant background noise. The absence of sound increases attention and it can increase the ear's sensitivity.

The increase of attention because of silence has the same effect as the increase of attention from a sudden loud noise, with one exception: the detection of the absence of sound is slower. Perhaps this comes from the "silence before the storm" feeling of impending danger, alerting us that something is wrong because something is missing. Or it may come from how, in nature, crickets stop making noise when a predator is near.

There are biological reasons for the negative emotional reaction to sound or lack of sound. It would be safe to assume that fear governs survival, making you either stay and fight, or run away. And this learned evolutionary behavior comes from the need to survive and has dictated the commonality of our reaction to sound.

In comparison, there is no specific region of the brain that governs positive complex emotions derived from sound, making it more complicated to understand what triggers them. Positive emotions come from behavioral development. What makes one person excited could be boring to the next because it is less of a reactive emotion than it is one built from experience.

What's interesting in the differences of negative and positive emotional reactions to sound is that those that are perceived as negative are also perceived as being louder, even if played at the same amplitude. Perhaps this is because of universal sonic elements that imply that loudness equals intensity, low frequency equals power and large size, slowness equals inertia, and quickness equals imminence. These elements common to sonic communication are exactly what sound designers use to guide an audience's response to a specific storytelling journey.

Complex emotional response comes from complex stimuli, and in theatre the cleanest way to produce positive complex responses is to have multisensory integration. In simple terms, if the sound matches the visual in timing, amplitude, and tone, it produces a gratifying reaction even if the emotion is negative. This is because it activates more regions of the brain.

Sounds are processed faster if they are recognizable or commonplace because of previous neural pathways. And the strongest emotional response will come from human vocalization, both positive and negative. Hearing someone crying, screaming, laughing, or burping will evoke the strongest reaction in our brains because organic human sound is the most commonly heard. The frequency of the human voice is recognized in one of our most sensitive regions of the brain and it stands out from the rest of the frequencies because it's easier for us to hear.

We have heard the human voice in our daily existence and it is quickly discernable because we have created the neural pathway to recognize it. Because we process low-level sensory information such as tone and volume more quickly, we respond to the emotional content of the message before we understand the complexity of the language that is spoken. If our mother laughs at the other end of a crowded room, we will hear that frequency cut through the din of all other noise because the neural pathway of our mother's voice was set while we were in her womb.

The same happens in a theater. The actor's voices will be the first recognized sound that will cut through the aural landscape for an audience. It is the most prominent aural feature in plays with dialogue. And if you cannot hear the actors, it will lead to great frustration for those experiencing it.

Technological Manipulation of Music and Sound

Music has been made universal with prolific genres and styles and it is pervasive in our society. And recorded music allows for the distribution of music globally.

At the beginning of recorded music, it lacked a purity of sound no matter how good the reproduction. Live playing was recorded without thought to the auditory focus, fields, or horizons. Now, we approach recorded music with intention, knowing it is its own form of music that is separate from live music. The electronic elements of music no longer get in the way, they aid in creating a more dynamic production of music.

With a shift in musical technology, a deeper shift of insight and creativity can occur. There can be infinite flexibility and possibilities. Just as in the past, instruments needed to be invented, developed, played, and then tuned to create music, the same applies to technology. And although humans have been experiencing and producing music in diverse cultures since ancient times, this is but the next step in how we create music as artists.

Music's language is based on who is exercising control. The composer, conductor, and musician exercises control over pitch, timbre, dynamics, attack, duration, and tempo. There are attributes to the voice of the instrument and to the space within which it is played. The control is a manipulation of sonic events and their relationship to each other.

Mixing engineers manipulate the rules that influence these relationships within a subtle to broad range. And with the advent of technology, those composers and musicians who implement virtual instruments into their writing have a wider range of rules than could be historically produced in the past.

The creative application of spatial and temporal rules can be aesthetically pleasing. When sound or music elicits an aural image of space in support of the visual aspects, like it can in theatre, space is not necessarily a real environment. And it can be exciting when differences in aural and visual space coexist simultaneously.

Let's look at the manipulation of electric components of delivering sound. In the past, audio engineers would change, adjust, add, or remove components from their signal-processing algorithms. These would create accidental changes in the sound. The engineers would refine their understanding of the relationship between the parameters and algorithms of their equipment with the sound that was produced.

Now, aural artists with audio engineers can create possibilities of imaginative sound fields. This highlights the interdependence between the artists, both aural and engineer, with science. No matter how abstract or technical the specifics of the sound presentation, each complex choice has real implications to how it will be delivered as sound.

The mixing engineer can function as musician, composer, conductor, arranger, and aural architect. They can manipulate the music and the space wherein it lives as they distribute it to an audience. There are rarely any notations in musical compositions that contain specifics regarding spatial acoustics, and engineers have taken on the traditional responsibilities of the acoustic architect.

When an audio engineer designs an artificial reverberator to achieve non-natural reverberation in a space, the audio mixer then adjusts the parameters, and together they replace the acoustic architect who built the theater. Physical naturalness becomes then an unnecessary constraint and it is replaced through intention by artistic meaningfulness.

There is an art to engineering and mixing that should be explored to its fullest. What is possible with technology and the manipulation of sound to create new aural landscapes can be stretched to the limits of imagination. All of it, done with the intended desired effect, can have a strong impression upon an audience.

2
THE ART OF SPATIAL DESIGN

Space and Place

The acoustic study of a space is what can convert a space into a place. A space is a physical location. When you bring a consciousness to sound and listen within a space, a transformation begins to create a place. When we associate a space as a place, it is a way of seeing more attachments and connections to human associations. This is why we call an empty theater a space until it is filled with meaning, then that space becomes many different places in which to explore and live. Every setting we live in has an aural architecture, and how we perceive that is the phenomenon of auditory spatial awareness.

A sound designer owns the space as a vehicle of manipulating, controlling, and engaging an audience's spatial awareness. When configuring your space for theatre, the most important aspect to keep in mind is that you need to focus on the audience within the space. It's not necessarily about filling the entire room; it's about the understanding of where your audience is in the space, at what level their ears are, and if they are still or ambulatory. Your work is primarily for them.

The other needs of monitoring sound for those performing or running the show are also important, but for the artistry of shaping an aural experience for an audience, keep in mind how the sound waves are going to hit them. It's the listening experience of the audience that informs the personal and social context for them.

Primitive spatial awareness is hardwired into our genes; although rarely recognized, all human beings sense spatial attributes to the world around us. As we hear different sounds interacting with different spatial elements, we start to identify the multiple sources and assign a character to the space we inhabit. An urban environment of street noise bouncing, reflecting, and absorbed by the cityscape materials will sound very different from the aural personality of the intimacy of a small tiled bathroom.

We do not easily recognize that we are constantly reacting to the aural architecture of our environment as a sensory stimulus. For example, a room may feel cold or warm apart from its actual temperature because of the materials in the room. A large reflective space can appear lonely. The acoustics of singing in a cathedral can lift the spirit, while a room of meditation feels quiet and contemplative; yet both contain the element of a spiritual place. Aural architecture can give us social clues as well because the place we are in could feel public or private.

And again we come back to the pairing of the visual with the aural. Along with the feelings that embody different acoustic values to a room, there is an accompanying visual aspect. The aesthetics and symbolism combine when the eyes experience the visual architecture alongside what the ears hear as the acoustic architecture. What makes the acoustics of a cathedral seem vast is in part what the eyes see. With the empty space, and the time it takes for sound to reflect, the place around your body develops meaning.

This means that as sound designers we have a choice. Do we marry the visual to the sound or does it fit the story best to keep them incongruent? This is the essence of symmetry and conflict with what is the most useful expression in storytelling. If the story you are telling requires a conflicting emotional response, it may be best to think of how you could add that into the aural architecture.

Take, for example, a scene of an argument during a walk in the park. In a simplified sound design the automatic impulse is to place birds into the environment and create a peaceful outdoor place and leave it at that for the scene. But what if you take into account that this is a city park and there is traffic, people, perhaps a siren going past, and a sense of incongruous commotion? You are then adding to the story a complexity—that perhaps even the characters thought this would be a peaceful walk and yet can't get away from the world around them. This tension in the environment can inform their conversation. The intention is what is important. And in possible contrast to that, perhaps the story is best told to have a disruptive argument in a peaceful setting.

This is not about me telling you what is the best choice for a particular moment of sound design in theatre, but for you to think about the space becoming a place and to make artistic choices about your environment to best aid in the storytelling. The choice is about understanding the relativism of cultural context— how the sound is perceived and by whom, under what circumstances, for what purpose, and, most importantly, creating what meaning.

Ian Ritchie, in his book *Fusion of the Faculties: A Study of the Language of the Senses in Hausaland*, states that the Hausa people, who are one of the largest ethnic groups in Africa, recognize only two senses: seeing and experiencing. Vision is used only for the means of navigation, and the "experience" sense contains smell, taste, touch, hearing, emotion, and intuition. This is to say that hearing and thereby listening to the aural architecture influences how we experience events, aurally visualize the space around us, stimulate emotional response, experience the movement of time, and retain memories.

Four Aspects to Auditory Spatial Awareness

1 Social

Spatial awareness influences our social behavior with an emphasis on privacy or social interaction.

In the social aspect of auditory spatial awareness, we determine how we will act with others in an environment. If we are in a private space, such as a private garden, our body language and how we present ourselves will be at ease. There is no need to keep control of the appearance of oneself in this situation. In a public environment such as a community park, our bodies will perform in a different manner based on our own reactions to others around us. If we are in a business meeting, there is yet another different demeanor based on social norms of how to act to appear professional. When supporting an environment with sound design, you will be adding in the surrounding aural environment, and these environments in turn inform the actors to their settings more fully.

2 Navigational

Spatial awareness allows us to navigate and orient our way through space, by either supplementing vision or at times replacing it.

In the navigational aspect of auditory spatial awareness, we can determine where we are in space through our focus. Some animals, such as bats and dolphins, determine how far away they are from an object by measuring how long it takes for an echo of the sound they emanate to return. This is called echolocation. Blind people are now learning how to do the same. We determine the three dimensions of space and actually hear cubic dimension by how sound reacts around us. We can recreate that reality of cubic space in the sound for the audience for a more realistic experience, to inform beyond where the scenic elements end.

3 Aesthetic

Spatial awareness affects our aesthetic response to the space. As visual elements embellish a space for our eyes, aural elements embellish a space for our ears.

In the aesthetic aspect of auditory spatial awareness, we appreciate the quality of the way sound behaves in space. This type of space helps clarify specificity of sound. It is a space that does not feel noisy. A symphony hall with its near-perfect acoustic response is a glorious place to hear sound. And we can choose to be aesthetic with our sound or asynchronous, determined by our desired effect.

4   Musical

Spatial awareness strengthens our experience of music and vocal experiences by merging the source of the sound with the space to create a unified extension of the art performed.

In the musical aspect of auditory spatial awareness, we note how constructed sound such as music and voice react within a space. This, coupled with the aesthetic aspect, will define how the audience will respond to the sound.

All of these aspects come into play in a theatrical setting as the sound design grounds the production in the auditory spatial awareness. A theater has its own acoustic spatial properties. Changing the perception of them can be quite powerful for both the actors performing and the audience experiencing the production. If a scene takes place in a cave, you can help inform the actors how their voices respond as the sound bounces and echoes in the space. It will force them into the reality of place simply by applying the correct effect to the environment. The audience then feels as though they are in the cave with them, immersed in the scene.

The Architects

- **Aural architect**
  An aural architect is someone who is acting as an artist and a social engineer, selecting specific attributes of the space based on the desirable effect. This can be described in opaque language derived from the concepts, values, and vocabulary of a particular culture. The aural architect focuses on the way the listeners experience the sound waves in the space.

- **Acoustic architect**
  An acoustic architect is someone who builds, engineers, or implements the aural attributes selected by the aural architect. Acoustic design is the manipulation of spatial geometries and physical objects using mathematical equations and the science of physics. The acoustic architect focuses on how the physical properties of sound waves are altered by the space.

Sound designers think on the levels of both aural and acoustic architectural design to achieve their goals. What we do as designers is use technology to reproduce environments that are not normally amplified through a sound system. We look at situations such as a gun reverberating in the forest, which produces the emotional response of being in a scary or lonely environment, and then recreate it to give the illusion for the audience to have the same response.

Because modern culture is fundamentally focused on visual response, there is little appreciation to the value of the art of auditory spatial awareness. However, sound design can make a scenic design come to life and give more meaning to the visual sensory response by adding the spatial acoustics that accompany what we see.

We create aural richness when the physical design and the cultural context are combined. We can arouse anxiety or invoke tranquility; we can create isolation, frustration, fear, or boredom; we can promote socialization or isolation; and we can stimulate aesthetic pleasure. To be excellent at sound design is to be a student of the phenomenology of aural space.

Auditory Subcultures

Human beings are not homogeneous listeners when it comes to how they use their hearing skills; in other words, hearing is not uniform in structure or composition. It's only when listeners within a given culture share a similar experience or relationship to aural architecture that they then become an auditory subculture. These exist both within one culture and at times across many.

You can say that we as sound designers are an auditory subculture of aural architects, because we are attuned to an enhanced sensitivity that involves sound and music's evocation of emotion. Individuals who are blind, and must orient themselves within their environment based on sound, represent another example of an auditory subculture of listeners. And musicians attuned to sound from different countries would certainly possess different cultural reference points, and they too would be an auditory subculture.

A subculture is based on the experience of the aural and acoustic architecture, educational training, and cultural beliefs. And those that do not fall into a specialized awareness of auditory subculture are unlikely to show more than the basic attributes to the hearing of the space around them.

Auditory awareness of space includes detection of sensation, recognition of perception, and the meaningfulness of the effect. And active participation in either hearing or ignoring sound waves is needed to have an awareness of sound. As we did at the start of this book, closing our eyes and listening with intention, with training you can consciously choose how the audience actively participates or engages in their listening to determine the effect your design will have on a particular group of people.

Cultural Value of Acoustic Context

If we classify acoustic context into categories—natural, public and private, and man-made—we are determining the usage of space and its cultural value. People within these spaces adapt, and exhibit, their behavior according to the space they inhabit. When creating a space for the characters in our stories to inhabit, we want to keep these in mind as well.

- **Natural**
  The natural world is the environment surrounding us. Whether it is the sound of the ocean with a breeze and tropical birds singing, or a city street with all the levels of acoustic events that can inhabit it, it is the full sonic scope that shapes our world. It must be specific to the exact time of day and place you are representing.

- **Public and private**
  Within the natural world around us we can either be in a public or private environment. The aural architecture that exists within each space determines the impression of privacy or social interaction.

- **Man-made**
  In addition to the concepts of natural, public, and private acoustic environments, man has created internal and external spaces that are also public or private. These are made from many different materials and cause sound to react in specific ways.

And each of these examples has changed throughout history. Adherence to time period in respect to natural, man-made, public or private spaces is important because of the variance of cultural context through time. And especially in our present time, where we can determine our own personal acoustic experience, our auditory culture is such that we all can create an environment in which we are comfortable.

As a sound designer, if you are working in a contemporary time period, the addition of personal devices counteracting social engagement in a public space should be accounted for when creating your place. When people are isolated within their own environment because of technology, the perception of social sonic events loses its meaning. In current culture, we create a private environment within a public one with a loss of the intimacy and immediacy of social interaction due to individual preference.

Nature of Cultural Silence

In an environment, silence can convey more about social or cultural characteristics. Silence is an active choice we make as designers in creating an environment. There is a psychological complexity to silence that indicates not only a respite from natural and human activity, but also a state of calmness or composure. It can emotionally surpass speech, create respect for the environment, indicate an inner thought, or it may be a response to a social offense.

Choosing your silence is key as it creates an attunement of the audience's perception to what is happening on stage in a cultural context.

Aural Texture

Just as a visual space becomes unique with its individual embellishments of color and textures, an everyday aural space achieves a personality when embellishments are added. To add aural texture to create richness, let's compare it to a visual example. When a visual surface has uniform hue, intensity, saturation, and reflectivity, it will give the impression of visual banality. In contrast to this, wallpaper or a painted pattern creates a certain texture from a distance when you cannot determine details. It then creates a different texture when you get closer to the specificity of design.

The same can be said about sound. You are able to hear the specificity of design when you are at the optimal distance, and a different texture if you are farther away. The amount of detail is analogous to how close or far you are away from the sonic events. As you get closer, individual elements are elevated from the background noise and attention can be paid to specific sounds.

An aural soundscape is a highly detailed place and the more specificity you contribute to your design, the richer it will appear. Keep in mind that the sonic events that are closer have more strength, and those that are farther away are weaker. Add to this the intention and abstraction of point of view, of either being character driven or audience driven, and you can drastically change the aural qualities of your space.

Soundmarks

Barry Truax, in his book *Acoustic Communication*, defines soundmarks as "auditory counterparts of landmarks." They are sounds that have social, historical, or symbolic worth in an environment. Some examples of these are the sound of church bells, train whistles, and police sirens. Each soundmark creates an acoustic field based on the radiation of the soundwaves it produces, and the acoustic channel created is solely for those that live within the area of those soundmarks.

Take into account the geological make-up of the place you are in to create the correct version of the soundmark. A valley will condense soundwaves where mountains will cast acoustic shadows, and sound travels farther over water. And this aural environment brings a connection among those that experience it together.

For example, in *Long Day's Journey into Night*, the sound of the foghorn is extremely prevalent in the storytelling. There are seagulls, buoy bells, and waves during the day, and with the onset of night insects emerge as the play moves through time. Since the setting is based on the actual environment of New London, CT, it's important that it is represented correctly through its soundmarks. How fog dampens sound and how a foghorn or a buoy bell travels over water give the illusion of the setting around the house where the action takes place.

As the sound designer, it is up to you to create soundmarks that are unique to your production, either expressionistically or practically, to transport an audience to a location. When placing soundmarks into a space, be attentive to the specificity of the source of emanation and that it comes from the appropriate direction. And make sure to amend the source of emanation if the perspective has changed. Through this awareness, a sound designer can create small iconic references to create a cohesive design.

Subspaces

Usually we think of a theatre as one space, but to be more specific, it is made up of many different subspaces that have to be addressed independently in order to create the same experience for each audience member. Whether you are creating a conceptual sound design or sound reinforcement, all of your work will have intention or direction with the choices you make. A sound designer leads with the description of the aural imagination of an idea and then follows with the physicalization of it. When working in conceptual or compositional sound design, a subspace can be real, created, or imagined in the space.

The real subspaces of an audience are clear and can be arranged by seating structure. We can create within that a subspace of left and right if we so choose. We can use our imagination to create subspaces for any reason we need in support of the production.

We are working in a time where sound designers can have an amazingly wide palette where we can create many spatial characteristics. Whether the environment is in a perceived reality or contained within our imagination, whether we've experienced it before or it's of our own creation, sound designers transport an audience to an environment in a story.

In our work we take one reality of sound contained in our headphones during conception, present that sound in a new reality of a theatre venue, and play with the imagined space in its delivery to the audience. We create a map of the environment by stimulating imagination. We create the impression of what it is like to be in a certain time and place and then we bring that into the theater for others to experience. A theater space is a practical environment that helps us achieve what's in our mind's ear, and our aural tools reimagine the world around us.

You can do whatever you like as long as you can justify why you're doing it in support of the work presented.

Willem Tak, who was the lead sound engineer from the Philips Pavilion at the 1958 World's Fair, designed the aural architecture with this goal: "The listeners were to have the illusion that various sound-sources were in motion around them, rising and falling, coming together and moving apart again, and moreover the space in which this took place was to seem at one instant narrow and 'dry' and at another to seem like a cathedral" (as outlined in Blesser and Salter's *Spaces Speak, Are You Listening? Experiencing Aural Architecture*).

The Theater Space

In the space of a theater, we aim to create a neutral environment where we shape the audience experience by determining the places we create. In a theatrical venue we strike a balance between the noise floor of the space and the aural environment we wish to recreate. If we are to determine the selective sonic events that will happen within the space of a theater, our first task is to create as close to a perception of silence as we can with all of the equipment that is inherent in a theatre space.

Sound designers are in control of the creation of a sensory aural environment. The extremes in aural architecture range from a free field where sound can flow uninterrupted, to the nearness of reverberation in a small space. The perception of the sensation of walls close to you can be achieved by accentuating low frequencies and strong resonances. This gives the impression of confinement and of being enclosed. And in contrast, sound transparency makes your walls seem delicate or illusory and gives the impression that you can leave at any time.

An audience of listeners has varying awareness of their spatial surroundings; however, you can achieve a heightened awareness in even an average listener by choosing the unfamiliar, contradictory, and unexpected, because it will change the personality of what is common knowledge of a particular place.

Our senses are not scientific tools to measure space, yet the boundaries determined by hearing are as powerful as the boundaries determined by vision. Vision can approximate height, width, and length by organizing distance by relative size of objects. Hearing, on the other hand, gives us a sense of cubic space because sound travels in waves flowing around, through, and bouncing off objects.

Obviously, when seeing and hearing are complementary, the shape of the world around you is the most clearly defined. But what if you were to not have interdependent boundaries of sight and sound? Visual and aural boundaries are independent ways of enclosing a space; they do not need to be in accord with each other.

For example, glass is an aural boundary and not a visual one. Acoustically transparent material is a visual boundary and not an aural one. What I want to stress again is the intention in the illusion you wish to create. When you choose incongruity, you are working within an idea of abstraction. It is up to the sound designer to define the range of agreement and illusion in the aural soundscape.

Inconsistency between visual and aural boundaries is determined by virtual partitions. As darkness creates separation in a visual boundary, background noise creates separation in an aural boundary. Take, for example, talking to someone while traveling on a train. The sound of the train along the tracks, the other conversations going on around you, the announcements from the speakers, become inaudible as if in the next room. The conversation that you are participating in is what you hear because it is enclosed within the virtual aural boundary.

This appreciation of an imaginary acoustic boundary creates an ephemeral acoustic horizon. Beyond the horizon line, which is determined by the listener's point of view, any sonic event is too weak to be part of a shared communal experience. We know that every sonic event has an acoustic field; now add to that the idea that every listener has an acoustic horizon of perception. This is important in sound design to help shape the point of view in which the sound is heard, by being either character or audience driven.

When you have a place, such as a party, where there are multiple listeners with different points of view, the acoustic horizons converge and bump into each other, creating the inclusion or exclusion of listeners. By remembering that louder sounds will claim more space in a field, an aural architect can imagine and shape the interplay among each point of view and thereby create a more unified shared perception of a place. The sensitivity to this and what to focus the audience's attention on determines your intention as a designer.

We want to achieve a unity of acoustic science and social science in theatre because we are determining the audience's shared emotional response. An audience's reaction to space is directly related to the spatial acoustics, within the context of individual bias or personality. How each person individually thinks and feels about their response is not up to us, but the expression of the art and the impression upon the audience must remain consistent to the goals of the production.

Practical Application

Think of a theater space as a refashioning of the interaction within the environment to reach your goals as the sound designer. Break down the space into regions and concentrate on how you want the audience to hear for each specific production. The presentational frame speakers (commonly called mains), which usually are determined by the curtain line in a proscenium theatre, contain the left, center, and right speakers—or whatever is fulfilling the overall stereo effect of audio coming from the front in the space. This can range from simply three speakers to detailed line arrays (see Figure 2.1).

After that, the rest of your set-up is determined by intention. Because today's audiences have experienced audio in the cinema, entertainment in theatre tends to follow suit in order to create the same rich environment. The other speakers are traditionally called fills because they are filling in the rest of the space to create the literal and perceptive dynamic context and aural perspective.

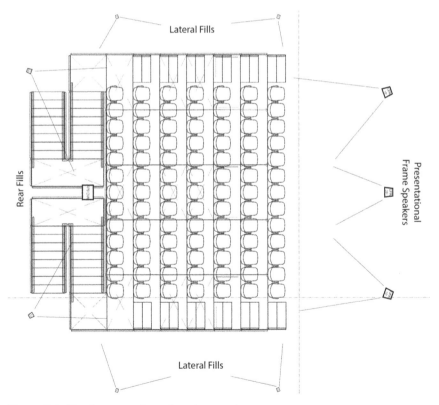

Figure 2.1 Simple surround speaker placement.

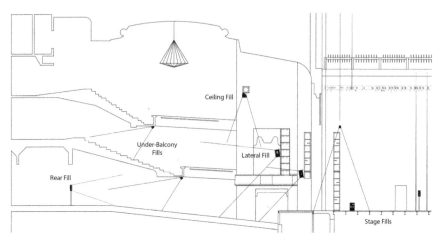

Figure 2.2 Simple fill speaker placement.

The house lateral fills, rear fills, ceiling fills, front fills, and floor fills create the full or surround-sound feeling for an audience. This can then be repeated on stage with lateral, rear, over-stage, and source-specific speakers to either monitor the actors or create your source points from within the production's visual perspective (see Figure 2.2).

In reinforcement design the zero point of your audio source is a requirement, and all speakers are set temporally from that. The zero point is the predetermined central point where the activity on stage takes place. All delay times for your fills are set to and referenced to this point. In conceptual design you have the ability to be non-specific; you may want to create a very diffuse environment. Changing or relocating the perception where the activity takes place on stage can achieve this.

Keep in mind that your zero point is a reference with time alignment to focus on-stage illusion. The challenge is then how the zero point affects the choices you make relative to the immersion of the audience. Connection to the zero point is a connection to reality. It's up to you to determine if you are working with abstraction or reality, or if you're representing the emotional or logical.

Temporal and Spatial Spreading

There are two ways to attribute sound spatiality—temporal spreading and spatial spreading. Temporal spreading is the way reverberation lengthens the time that the sound waves are traveling. And spatial spreading is the way the direction of the soundwaves get larger as they travel. In a highly reverberant space, such as an acoustically designed concert hall, a single note of a solo instrument lingers longer after the musician stops playing. Temporally the note is elongated, and spatially the reflecting surfaces multiply the soundwaves to a more diffused and larger envelopment.

There are two aspects to this sound: the original note and then the wave that hits the audience; although these individual concepts are not separate from each other because we use the original note as the locator of the sound's source. Sound originates in one place and the architecture of the room that encases it determines its spread. This is useful when determining the origin of sonic events and how sound would then move through the space you are creating in the theatre.

Reverberation

Reverberation can be aesthetically pleasing when used at an appropriate level. Excessive reverberation lessens the intelligibility of specific sounds, heightening the background noise level. Where deficient reverberation can make a space feel unresponsive and thereby "dead," excessive reverberation makes a space unpleasant.

Every space has its own reverberant profile, additionally determined by each listener's expectation and perception. Because we cannot determine direction when hearing encompassing reverberation, it creates a heightened state of alertness. The mood and emotion of the listener can be altered by how the physical space changes the way sound reacts within it.

Reverberation has an intricate pattern of behavior that at the onset becomes louder, then stays at a steady rate of sustain, before slowly decaying to silence. When controlling it, you can set the patterns of reverberation at every stage of its temporal presence. There is the initial onset of direct sound (dry) and then three divisions of reverberation that include attack, sustain, and delay (wet). In order to hear reverberation clearly, the direct sound must first stop.

If the original sound does not stop it is considered running reverberation. The proportion of direct to reverberant sound is apparent to everyone, yet the subtleties are apparent to only those who are trained to hear them. Spatial algorithms were created to supplement or replace acoustic spaces while recording. As a designer you can use these myriad variants to affect your sound and create whatever you like.

In Summary

As you can see, there is great depth to how human beings experience sound and how that perception gives way to meaning and emotion. The human body has evolutionary and associational responses to sound that evoke reactions. The intricacies of how this happens exist mostly subconsciously. And when creating theatre art, whose purpose is to evoke deliberate emotional response, we must understand how to construct sound and music to support the intentions outlined for the production.

We take into account how the body interprets vibration, perceives properties, creates meaning, and responds emotionally to sound and music. The science is the grounding layer to what then becomes the metaphysical. We move then into psychology of the individual and group, and how that influences the perceived effect. Who we are internally and externally defines the response to sound around us. And the next added layer on top of science is the cultural aspect and anthropology to how we as individuals relate to others in our environments.

We, as sound designers, consider all of this in order to create richness of design, reality of place, illusion of metaphorical ideas, and emotional content. Successful artistry in sound design is both instinctual and researched. And it is based on human reaction.

When moving forward through this book, experiment and try things like the first accidental findings of sound manipulation. You want to take note of your own personal responses and apply them in an instinctual manner. Playing sound for others will help you determine if you have achieved your intention, based on their reaction. It is a trial-and-error engagement until you have discovered the relationship between your intention and the end product. In time, you will understand how what you feel instinctually now has reason behind its effect on an audience. But most of all have fun. Playing with sound and music is enjoyable for all human beings.

Exercises for Part One

These exercises are meant to explore the reaction and understanding we have with sound. Some can be done independently, and some are best in a group to find commonality of response.

Exercise 1—Describing Sound

Procure a journal, and from this point forward, you will record the instances of sound that you experience. Note how they are manufactured, if they are organic in nature, how they affect you, and if there is an emotional or memory response.

Exercise 2—Sound without Vision

Materials—Shoebox and anything that fits in it and can make noise when the box is in movement.

Someone secretly places an object into the box and shakes and rolls it around, asking what is inside. The goal is to see if you can determine the shape of the object, the size of the object, and the material it is made from solely from the sound it makes. Describe why you come to your conclusion. And in the end try and name the object.

Exercise 3—Vision without Sound

- Play a horror movie and locate a scene that is full of fear, suspense, drama, etc. Watch the scene. Now rewind to the top of the scene again and watch with the sound muted. Note how the gratification in your response is different in each instance. How was the emotional effect different? Did it have the same impact on you?

- Now find a piece of dance that is choreographed to music. Watch it through the first time with music and then without. Notice if the movement without its support of music loses the emotional dynamic of association.

Exercise 4—Imaginative Sound

Imagine an experience you have in fact never done, e.g. skydiving, race car driving. Describe the experience through your senses. What do you hear, see, feel, taste, and smell? Take note which of your senses takes precedence in the experience, or if one is stronger than another. Note if you are experiencing it in the first-person perspective, or if you are an outside observer and watching yourself. If you switch this perspective do the imaginative senses go away? Note if there are any structures of focus, auditory fields, horizons, and spatial or temporal features.

Exercise 5—Perceived Level of Sound

- Have someone sit five feet away from you and have them tap lightly on the table every second. Play very loud music for thirty seconds and then slowly fade it down while the tapping continues. Note when you are cognizant of the tapping. How quiet does the room seem?

- Now play the loud music once more for thirty seconds and abruptly stop it while the tapping continues. Note again when you are cognizant of the tapping, and how quiet the room seems. Did you need time to adjust to hear the quiet sound after the loud?

Was there a difference to the perception in the relative silence?

Exercise 6—Frequency Response on the Body

Place yourself in a room where you have a speaker set-up that contains a subwoofer in addition to at least left and right speakers. Play a piece of music that has a wide range of frequency.

- Manipulate the EQ of this music to cut everything out but the low end. Play the music loudly with this new EQ and take note of how it affects your body.

- Then manipulate the EQ to remove the low and high end, leaving just the middle range. Take note again of now this feels as the sound waves resonate with the tissues and bones in your body.

- Lastly, change the EQ to reflect solely the high frequencies. Once more, notice if this EQ changes how you actually feel the music in your body.

Exercise 7—Aesthetic Response: Group Association

Take a moment to find the commonality of human aesthetic response by listing sounds that indicate season, time, religion, science, and feelings. You can make the lists out of anything you can dream up in human experience. When complete, compare your lists and note where there are commonalities to the perception of such broad topics.

Exercise 8—Aesthetic Response: Descriptions

Choose a piece of music randomly and play it. Notate your reaction to the music. How do you explain it? What is your focus? Is it an external explanation of the structure? Is it an internal explanation of how it makes you feel? Can you describe the musical movement or any emotions it evoked? Did it remind you of something else? Share your findings with the group and see if there are any commonalities in your description of the music and your response to it.

Exercise 9—Aesthetic Spatial Response

Make two columns. One list is for spaces that feel aesthetically pleasing, the other for spaces that do not feel aesthetically pleasing. With imaginative hearing, focus on how you feel and react as an aesthetic response to the perception of both lists. Write down your perceptions. Are there similarities within each column?

Exercise 10—Evolutionary Response: Temporal Expectation

- Choose a sound that you are going to hear. Have one person determine when they are going to make the sound without the others knowing. All must wait until the sound happens. Focus on the body's means of expectation of sound temporally, and then what occurs once you hear it.

- Next have one person choose a loud, sudden sound to play without anyone knowing when it will occur. Feel how the chemical reaction of flight or fight affects the body.

Exercise 11—Associational Emotional Response to Music

- Open up a music library or diverse song list. Put the play selector on random fire. Then hit play. Write down all of the emotional responses you get from listening to the piece of music and why. Then hit forward to the next song. Now, write down all of the emotional responses from the second piece of music. Are the intervals consonant or dissonant?

- Do this one more time, so as to get three different reactions to the music. Compare with others to see if there are any commonalities between the listeners or the songs themselves.

Exercise 12—Instrumental Association

As a group, think of someone you all know collectively. Based on their personality, assign an instrument that you feel gives the same perception of their individual qualities. Do this with a few examples, noting how each instrument has a personality that can be assigned based on how they are played. This is a great tool to use when determining how to choose instrumentation for thematic emotional journeys in a story.

Exercise 13—Resonance

- Find a metal container such as a bowl, goblet, or pan, and tap it with your fingernail or a hard object. You will immediately discern the metallic ring of its reverberation because of the resonant nature of the object. You gain a sense of the cubic space of its interior. How long does it linger; can you distinguish between the tap and the resonance?

- Pay attention to the event and deconstruct what you hear. Do you first hear the metallic clink hitting metal? Can you discern the reverberation that follows the onset of the tap once the objects separate? Notice how if you take just the tap alone and leave your finger connected to the metal object, you will fail to detect the interior cubic space of the object because there will be no resonance. It will be dampened.

Exercise 14—Immersion in Auditory Field

Choose a piece of music that has fullness to it, and is multi-instrumental and grand in scope. Play the music at a low level and notice from where the sound emanates and how it affects you. Now take that sound and amplify it so that it fills the room around you. Note now if you can discern from where the music is emanating and how it affects you. In which instance could you determine the auditory field? Could you delineate the horizon of sound? How did the extremes affect you physically and emotionally? Can you feel how you perceived the music externally and internally?

Exercise 15—Navigational Spatial Awareness

Stand in a room that has clearance between you and a wall in front of you. Begin reciting something you know by heart. As you speak, slowly walk towards the wall with your eyes shut. Are you able to determine where the wall is because of how the sound waves change as you get closer to it?

Exercise 16—Spatial Reverberation

Open a digital audio workstation (DAW) and bring in a piece of music that has a non-reverbed singular melodic line either in instrument or voice. While it is playing, apply a large hall reverb to it. Then change the reverb to a small room. Play around with the different reverbs and note the difference in the musical aspect of the sound when you add the space of reverberation. Does the lingering of notes or sound temporally enhance it, or not? Note the response you have emotionally with the subtle changes.

Exercise 17—Level of Reverberation

In your DAW, place a sound file of your choosing. Apply a reverb plugin to the channel. While the track plays, adjust your reverb output levels and listen to how it changes the initial sound or music. Note where the moment of aesthetic response is pleasant for reverberation and at what level, excessive or deficient, it becomes unpleasant. You will only learn through experimentation, so play around with the plugins you wish to learn, and listen with intent.

Exercise 18—Public vs. Private

List five locations that are public, and five locations that are private. Next to each one, write down what you imagine you would hear in those spaces. Note how the sound informs the social awareness and behavior in those environments. What is it that creates a public or private place? Is it the complexity? Is it the amount of noise?

PART TWO

CONTEXTUAL APPLICATION AND EXERCISES

This section of the book will bring the evolutionary and the associational response in human beings to a practical approach. In the following exercises, techniques will be practiced that can bring richness and specificity of intention to sound design.

3
EXERCISES TO DEVELOP ARTISTIC SOUND DESIGN SKILLS

Moving Forward

What I want you to start thinking about is how you are affecting each human being in the audience specifically. That specificity is the understanding of physiology, anthropology, sociology, and psychology of hearing. Once you open up your awareness to this broad concept with specific intent, you can then apply each of the tools laid out in this book.

I have outlined what I call "aural tools" to use in sound design that will enhance the artistry based on how you want your audience to respond. For me, these are the ways of thinking about sound when responding to a production in order to create a layer of aural support.

I will outline a definition of the tool, give you an example of theatrical application, and finish with an exercise and critical response questions to work with the idea. I have chosen to use Jeffrey Hatcher's play *Dr. Jekyll & Mr. Hyde* because of its rich detail of thematic expression.

EXERCISES

When creating content for sound design, the one suggestion I hear myself saying repeatedly is to "make your work specific and rich in aural quality." To be specific and rich means you understand the intention of effect you are creating for your audience.

You know the specifics of the following:

- Where—This can encompass many aspects of cultural context, geography, and spatial relationship.
- When—This can encompass history, time of day, or an event of time in one's life.
- Why—This answers the question of thematic motive.

- How—This is the means by which it will be accomplished.
- Point of View—This can encompass the playwright's, director's, designers', characters', and the audience's perspective.
- The Internal Event—the emotional state of the production, character, and moment.
- The External Event—the emotional state of the observer.
- Style of Presentation—The genre of an approach or method.
- Convention of the Execution of Design—The practical means to achieve your intention.
- Expression of Emotion Created by the Artists.
- Impression of Emotion Upon the Audience.

Sound design is best when this level of attention is brought to the smallest detail within a design. There should be a reason for everything an audience hears. If you cannot justify it within your intention, it will appear as though it doesn't belong in the production. And if you put something into a production just because you thought it'd be cool, it will only be cool if it works within the complexity of history, anthropology, psychoacoustics, psychology, and theatricality. Otherwise, you risk pulling your audience out of the story by drawing attention to something that is not synchronous.

Your intention can be to create an audience that is sympathetic, empathetic, or reacting in contrast to what is happening on stage. The variables change constantly and sound designers are contributing to the audience's perception. You want to add aural contextual detail to practical technical application to convey big ideas and minute subtleties.

The intention behind your work is where you want to focus. With every cue you create, you should be able to discuss at length your intention by keeping the above specifics in mind.

There is a function in your brain that peaks attention when there is an onset or offset abrupt change in amplification or frequency. You can use this if you want attention paid to the start or end of your cues. Keep this in mind, along with your intention, as you choose smooth fades or abrupt starts and ends.

Cues in these exercises are intentionally short; you typically will have very little time in a transition on stage to convey everything you need to impress upon an audience. You will need to accustom yourself to getting right to the point. There are longer cues, such as those for building tension, underscoring dramatic intent, showing passage of time, and portraying environmental soundscapes. These cues should contain the same richness as the shorter cues, with the same intention driving them.

Remember that musical association and the tonality of instrumentation guides human emotion more than soundscape. When approaching the emotional aspects of your cues, tonality along with pace will give you the most associated emotional response.

How to learn from the exercises in the book in three steps:

- Discussion of topic
- Time spent building cues
- Listening and discussing the intention and response of cues

All of the aural tools we are about to explore are used in tandem with each other. It's hard to divorce one specifically without using another. The goal is that you will develop an understanding of the work you are producing and know when you are using each tool for the effect you wish to achieve. There will be overlap as you go along, and by the end you will be able to point out each of these tools in one short cue.

Look at it like cooking: these are ingredients that when married together can bring complexity even in simplicity. The day's tool is the secret ingredient, but oil, salt, and water aid in the actual cooking method. Think of each tool as the focal point of the exercise and use the others to help support your intention.

Themes

When I use the term theme, I am focusing on what an audience can follow throughout a live production. These can be intellectual ideas, characters, animate or inanimate objects, locations, time periods, fantasy worlds, or anything of which you would need to remind an audience through repetition. The first question I raise in defining this in a play is, why does the audience need to be reminded of these themes? And the second question is, what is different this time around now that we have gotten to this part of the storytelling journey? As theatre is about storytelling, it is up to us to help our audiences enjoy the ride without questioning the journey.

Following a Theme

- First determine a theme's personality and how you can convey it in sound or music.
- Plot out the arc of this theme, its growth, and overall course throughout the play.

- When following a character, use the actor voice and behavior to aid in helping you determine pace, rhythm, and style.

- Use adjectives to help you determine the mood or emotion you wish to evoke.

Themes rarely remain exactly the same unless the purpose is to show no growth or change. Otherwise, it follows the storytelling to create a richer experience for an audience. Exact repetition for no specific reason will eventually lose its impact as the neural pathways of the audience get more accustomed to it, and could possibly annoy listeners through overuse.

Examples of Plotting Themes

Character
What conflicts occur within the character's psyche and do they change from it?
What external forces change the character?
What mood accompanies each moment you are supporting the character, e.g. power, growth, weakening?

Object
Who has it and does it get passed on to anyone else?
What is the meaning behind the object at every stage of the play?
Does the object have an innate sound of its own?
Is there an attribute that accompanies the object as it travels, e.g. urgency, sluggishness, importance, power?

Idea
What is the sound or music equivalent of this idea at the start of the story?
How does this idea change and grow, e.g. relevance to story, strength of message?
What mood accompanies this idea throughout the play?

Location
Is it a public or private space?
What is the cultural context of this place?
Is it natural or man-made?
What is different in the subsequent times you visit this location?
How does the mood and ambience change dependent on the other themes you are following?

Time Period
What is different the subsequent moments you visit this time period?
How do you travel in time, and what does that sound like?

What specifically is the key into this time period, e.g. instrumentation, digital vs. organic world?

How does the mood and ambience change dependent on the other themes you are following?

Fantasy or Abstract World

What is the complexity of this world and does it change the more you visit it?

What are the similarities and differences from the natural world?

What is different the subsequent times you visit this world?

What is the key into this fantasy world, e.g. specific abstraction, location-based, particular effect?

How does the world change dependent on the other themes you are following?

Theatrical Application of Themes

When you analyze a script, you look for the intended overall ideas, messages, and themes that the playwright intends to impart to the audience. *Dr. Jekyll & Mr. Hyde* is a play about dualities, and the more you understand the details of the psychology behind the decisions of the characters in the play, the better support you can be for the production and how it presents the themes.

Point of View

It's important to determine the point of view so that the audience can have empathy and understanding for certain characters' journeys throughout the story. Sometimes the point of view is a character and internal to the play, and sometimes it is the audience as objective observer.

Point of view is especially important when the production is presenting an event in which they want the opposite reaction from the audience. One simple example is when something tragic happens to a character and it can be viewed as comedic to the audience. In this case you would not support the character's tragic realistic point of view, it would be another's point of view of the circumstance that accentuates the humor.

In looking at *Dr. Jekyll & Mr. Hyde*, you need to understand the characters before you know how to present their points of view. You must understand their psychological arc, the challenges and conflicts, and their strengths and weaknesses. Additionally, you look at their place in the world that surrounds them and whether they engage or remove themselves from their community. How the world influences the characters, and how they manipulate their own world, is also part of the research. The best place to start in historical productions is conducting research into the time period and specific countries and regions.

Research

There is a great deal of research one can do in regards to the time period and setting of *Dr. Jekyll & Mr. Hyde*. For our sake here, I will give you a brief overall picture so that we can delve further into the specifics regarding how sound can support character and plot.

In 1883, London was the largest city in Europe. And although it contained many wealthy places, there were districts of extreme poverty and squalor. The middle class was beginning to burgeon while tens of thousands of people worked as domestic servants, or what was called the respectable working class. Industry and trade was growing as well, and were beginning to take structure in the city. The very first census of 1801 placed the population at around 1 million people. Fifty years later that number had more than doubled, and by 1911 there were more than 7 million people in the city of London. The infrastructure of the city was strained because of the rapid expansion of the population.

The air quality worsened in a coal-fired existence, and the disposal of urban detritus became more difficult. While the upper and middle classes were defining themselves, the very poor were at times indistinguishable from a criminal or dangerous class and the city made sure to delineate them geographically. The Public Health Act 1875 combined support for housing, sewage and drainage, water supply, and contagious diseases. It provided the most extensive public health system in the world for its time.

Because Dr. Jekyll is a physician and surgeon, research that speaks to the environment in which he works is crucial. At the beginning of the nineteenth century, Oxford had educated 75–80 percent of the working physicians in London; however, the kind of medical care you could receive would be sporadic in substance and incongruous in pathology. By the end of the century, when the play takes place, the number of educated physicians had dropped to 30 percent; this is because the quality of graduating physicians was higher. The emphasis in the field began to base itself in scientific inquiry and reputability, and only the students who could learn the scientific extent of the profession graduated.

In the middle of the century, bills were introduced into Parliament to regulate the qualifications of practitioners of medicine and surgery. By the 1880s there were finally a few physicians and surgeons that raised the level of respect for the profession. And in 1886, the Medical Act Amendment Act was passed, the goal of which was to reform medical education and thereby medical practice.

Themes in Practice

Looking at the themes that the playwright intends to convey, we turn from research of the time in which the play lives to the actual script itself. *Dr. Jekyll & Mr. Hyde* is a story that focuses on the dualities that exist within man's psyche and the consequences that can occur if you indulge in exploring them. This overarching theme can be explored and utilized in sound design by delving further into the thematic dualities and then designating how an aural representation can support these intellectual ideas on an emotional level. As you create lists to help you define how you want to approach sound, you can apply what you specifically wish to create in your design (Table 3.1).

When you map out the script with these dualities in mind, it can help you understand how you wish to approach the themes in the play aurally. It also helps define which themes stand out more than others, and whether or not you are in continuity or incongruous with your support of them. This also gives you vocabulary to discuss the intentions with your team to ensure that you are all working together collaboratively towards a single goal of presentation.

Table 3.1 *Intellectual Dualities and their Emotional Sonic Properties*

Intellectual dualities	Emotional sonic duality
Good vs. Evil	Organic vs. Inorganic
Human vs. Animal	Melodic vs. Tonal
Civilization vs. Barbarism	Structured vs. Asymmetrically Syncopated
Love vs. Hate	Consonant vs. Dissonant
Love vs. Fear	Natural Hearing Range vs. Infrasonic Frequency
Internal vs. External	Abstract vs. Concrete
Physics vs. Metaphysics	Sound/Music of the Time vs. Digital Approach
Conscious vs. Subconscious	Predictable vs. Unpredictable
Conscience vs. Morality	Solo vs. Orchestrated
Wants vs. Needs	Unresolved vs. Resolved
Public vs. Private	Complex vs. Simple
Upper Class vs. Lower Class	Stylistic vs. Raw
Life vs. Death	Major Key vs. Minor Key

The Main Character(s)

Dr. Jekyll is one of the most reputable physicians of his time, who looks forward in his profession and demands the requirement of scientific study in regards to pathology. It is still an experimental time for medicine and he is part of the community of physicians in London. He is a wealthy man with a servant, surrounded by colleagues and friends. He is part of society. Jekyll encounters the fight for reputability within his profession and is progressive towards experimentation. At the same time, he battles his own urge to understand the duality of man's primal urges and how it relates to societal norm.

I don't feel as though you can generalize Dr. Jekyll as a good or bad man; he is a man who is searching for something else. He has a want, which turns into a need, to explore the inner psyche of human existence. I feel this comes from having progressive thought in a society that represses it. There are certain things that a man in a high position within society cannot do, and that quest throws him deeper into the darker side of his own consciousness.

When Dr. Jekyll drinks his created tincture, his alter ego Mr. Hyde takes control of his mind and body and does what Dr. Jekyll would never do. Mr. Hyde lives with the extreme poor, criminal, and seedier side of the city. He appears physically different to those who know Jekyll, and the surrounding characters have the task of putting together the pieces of the mystery that perhaps Jekyll and Hyde are the same man. These two personalities that live within Dr. Jekyll mirror the two worlds that exist in London at the time.

The simplest introductory way into the dualities of the play is through the main characters themselves. Dr. Jekyll is also Mr. Hyde. In Hatcher's version of the story, this is additionally recognizable because others in the ensemble play Mr. Hyde alongside the main character of Dr. Jekyll. One man does not play both personas. In this telling, the embodiment of the two sides of the psyche is tangible in the separate role structure. You know physically when Mr. Hyde is intruding on Dr. Jekyll; and in reverse, when Dr. Jekyll is trying to control Mr. Hyde.

When developing the different thematic aural worlds of these two characters that live within one man, you can assign a theme to each. This will subconsciously aid in telling the story to the audience, so they know when one or the other has dominance at any moment. To help take the intangible to the tangible, the use of adjectives is helpful.

Dr. Jekyll Adjectives
Well-made, stylish, man of stature, amiable, sociable, analytical, progressive

Dr. Jekyll Sound/Music
Classical, of the period, major key, structured, metered, predictable, melodic, consonant

Mr. Hyde Adjectives
Smaller, remorseful, cruel, evil, mysterious, violent, chaotic, intermittent

Mr. Hyde Sound/Music
Avant-garde, not of this time, minor key, syncopated, unpredictable, harmonic, dissonant

In Hatcher's adaptation, multiple actors play multiple Mr. Hydes. Each brings his or her own energy to the role of Jekyll's alter ego. What this does towards supporting the themes of the story is it proposes the idea that we all have Hyde within us. That it is a manifestation in everybody's psyche to have dark urges. It creates a chorus-like effect when they act in unison, and it creates facets of a personality when acted separately. This disassociation physically from Jekyll allows the audience to separate the actions of Hyde from Jekyll and thereby empathize more with each character's struggle to maintain control.

How all this manifests in the sound design are the choices you make based on the point of view of the characters and how you want the audience to respond. Jekyll looks at a situation differently from Hyde. And later in the play when Dr. Jekyll speaks of a hypothetical patient who has symptoms similar to his own, his colleague Dr. Lanyon has yet another different perspective as well. What you want to focus on is the impression you wish to convey upon the audience. When you play different characters' themes, the audience will associate the point of view with that character.

After researching, finding music, or creating compositions and soundscapes that speak to what you hear when you put these adjectives together, then you can return to the script to determine how to use them to support the story.

Making a visual characterization or representation of sound helps to clearly define how you wish to approach opposing themes. You can place the timeline of what you are deconstructing on the x-axis, and any opposing theme on the y-axis. Then you determine when each theme gains control over the other. Comparing these graphs illuminates how the themes change.

Let's say you were to complete three graphs: one for the power struggle for control of Dr. Jekyll vs. Mr. Hyde, the second being Conscious Thought vs. Subconscious, and a third for Internal Journey vs. External. You can plot out how the aspects of your design change by visually seeing how each duality exists in relationship to the other dualities. You use the adjectives that determine the nature of your sound design to support the conditions that are changing the themes. And the graphs afford you the ability to map out your design prior to building the audio.

In Figure 3.1, you will see that in Act One of the play there is an alternation between Dr. Jekyll and Mr. Hyde, with Hyde becoming more powerful towards the end of the act. In Act Two, you can see when the two characters are simultaneously sharing the power as one person, and when they share the scene independently of each other.

This is a simple way to get concrete ideas into the seemingly elusive world of sound. The goal is to have intention behind your choices, and themes are a great place to start when creating the aural world of the performance. Once you have determined the what (the research) and the why (the analysis) of your themes, you can then concentrate on how (the delivery) you will present them to your audience with the intended effect.

The use of repetition with themes is a way of supporting the ideas of the script while upholding the cohesiveness of the style of the production.

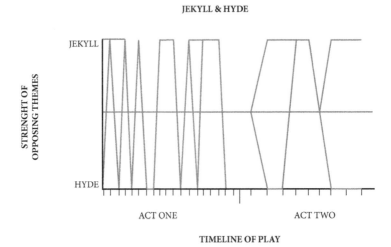

Figure 3.1 Mapping the power struggle between Dr. Jekyll and his alter ego Mr. Hyde.

EXERCISES

Imagine a moment you are supporting of a story of your choosing. Determine what theme you wish to focus attention on and its journey in the story. Use the previous examples of character, object, place, time, etc. Create one cue of introduction to the theme. Then create a second cue based on how the theme has changed in the arc of its story. Lastly, create a third cue to show whether the theme has a resolved or unresolved ending.

Each cue should be no longer than thirty seconds. Determine your genre, time period, and style. Determine the emotional response you wish to evoke from other listeners. Remember that music can highlight emotion quickly because of association, and use it wisely. Create a soundscape that has the specific range of physical and metaphysical properties.

Show distinct aspects to how the theme has changed with each cue. When your cues show a relationship in mood or aural temperament, they will be cohesive, and create a story.

Critical response to themes
- What type of theme are we following?
- What is the story being told?
- What genre, time period, or style is used?
- Is the cue cohesive and within the same design aesthetic?
- How does the theme change with each new cue?

- What mood or emotion is evoked?
- What tools in your digital audio workstation (DAW) were effective to create the journey of the theme?
- What is your intention? Was it conveyed to the listeners?

Repetition

The use of repetition is one of our most valuable tools as a sound designer. In theatrical storytelling, repetition is used for comedic and dramatic effect. It is used in every single one of our tools whether we are following themes, speeding up or slowing down time, showing growth in the arc of a character, creating a dynamic build, or reminding an audience of a setting. The goal of using repetition in theatre is to take the audience on an emotional path without thinking about the sound or why the sound is different.

The human brain creates neural pathways with repeated sound that eventually can be tuned out as unnecessary, which we then no longer hear. Bear this in mind when using repetition to tell the emotional journey. It's best to have a reason to repeat, but keep in mind that every moment in a story is different because the audience is discovering more information as they experience it. As you progress through the story take note of the variations in your repetition. It's the variations in the repetition that makes this tool effective.

Time
Evenly spaced repetitive punctuation creates the impression of marking time. It mimics the ticking sound of the second hand of a clock. If we speed up or slow down the repetition, it gives the listener the feeling of speeding up or slowing down time.

We can also aid in showing how the piece is moving forward and backward in time by using the same sound for the abstraction of the actual passage through time. We could even repeat the sound backwards to help tell the audience that we've gone backwards through time. If we are traveling to different time periods, repetition can aid in reminding the audience into which time period we have traveled, based on the components of the cue being repeated.

Place
We can remind an audience of the setting and where we are in the physical space of the story if we use the same sound when transitioning to an environment

we've been to before. The faster an audience knows where they are, the more engaged they will be in the story, because we've eliminated the need for them to determine where they are in the setting.

Character

We can show the emotional growth or decline of a character if we use a musical or sonic theme that complements or reflects their personal arc in the story. What happens to this theme to show the internal journey of the character is how you can portray this through sound.

Style

We can give an overall impression upon the audience of the change of mood and emotion within the style of the production. This is best shown in how the use of repetition changes throughout the entirety of the story. We can choose to remain in the same style or divert away from it for emphasis.

Emotional and Intellectual Themes

We can show both intellectual and emotional arcs through the use of repetition based on the changes that occur. Well-crafted sound design using repetition "helps the audience out." We free them from thinking too much about the mechanics of why they are feeling what they are feeling, or how they know where they are instinctually. Removing a step in the thought process for an audience helps them feel immersed in the story.

Theatrical Application of Repetition

The use of repetition aids in how aural themes remind the audience of where they are in time and space, the point of view in which they are experiencing this part of the story, and how the feelings and moods have changed from the last time it was heard.

When we meet Dr. Jekyll at the start of the play (after the prologue), he seems to be in control of Mr. Hyde. That, along with the fact that no one else in the story even remotely believes that the two are linked in any way, means that we are experiencing Dr. Jekyll the way he presents himself to society. The music and sound reflects this point of view at the start when referencing him or his setting. Based on the events that follow, the sound can show how his story changes by manipulating the subsequent cues that represent him. The journey Jekyll takes in the story is reflected in the changes that occur to your aural theme for him.

Because the two main characters psychologically embody the same man, you can follow the psychological journey through who is more dominant in each scene, and which of the personas has control. By the end of play, when Jekyll loses periods of time while living in his alter ego, Hyde is taking over inwardly and the design should support and reflect this idea.

You show the intellectual arc of this through the adaptation of what happens to your music and sound, knowing that your music and sound are affecting the audience emotionally. If we use the adjectives from our layout of the themes in the play, and their corresponding elements in sound and music, this is discernable through the "syncopated and dissonant" gradually overtaking the "structured and consonant" from the beginning to the end of the story.

If we return every time to Dr. Jekyll's house with the same genre of music, it will establish for the audience recognition of an unconscious guiding to a specific place. The metered, structured, and consonant tone of the music or sound will set the place quickly and they will not have to question where they are in time and space. It will tell the audience that we are returning to Dr. Jekyll's point of view.

Each time we return, however, we are further into the story and it is different.

Act One
Scene 2—Introduction to Jekyll and his colleagues
Scene 4—Jekyll in diary reflection upon himself, introduces the idea of the laboratory
Scene 9—Jekyll screaming into consciousness, first lapse in time, introduces the blending of the two characters
Scene 11—Jekyll in diary making the choice to go further into Hyde
Scene 16—Jekyll's impulse to dispose of Hyde, but changes his mind
Scene 17—Jekyll's Lab, first time we see the transformation into Hyde

Act Two
Scene 2—Inspector informs Jekyll of Carew's murder, Hyde bleeds through, and Jekyll commits again to abolishing Hyde
Scene 6—Jekyll's Lab, Jekyll/Hyde not present, Lanyon and Poole are searching his space
Scene 8—After Jekyll kills Lanyon, the reveal to Elizabeth that the two are the same man,
Scene 9—Jekyll carries Elizabeth to the Lab, Jekyll and Hyde in confrontation, Jekyll tries to kill Elizabeth but Hyde stops him, the full version of the prologue plays out

When a sound designer manipulates the theme to change according to the character's point of view, we give additional information about why, at this time, it's a different feeling when we return. Maybe the pacing has picked up. Perhaps Hyde's theme is bleeding into Jekyll's theme. By changing as we go along, the design never becomes rote and predictable. It is ever changing through time by supporting the emotional shifts in the story. The way to know how something has changed is to take what is a known constant and make changes to it as you go along.

If we begin first with a structured and consonant quality to the music that we bring to associate with Dr. Jekyll, when we repeat that quality later it will immediately remind the audience of him again. The subtle shifts in what is happening to him are introduced, and through repetition of what we will set up as the sonic association to Mr. Hyde, we mirror his character's psychological arc. So as Dr. Jekyll's repetition of theme goes from structured to unstructured, the addition of Mr. Hyde's dissonance grows within it.

If we remember that the brain makes pathways to know what to hear when we listen, we want to ensure that the information we are providing creates newness to our themes and supports the overall journey of story. It is through repetition that we acknowledge the changes occurring.

EXERCISES

The repetition within each cue is the storyline you are expressing and the qualities of repetition can demark time or emphasis. Create a cue using repetition to show one or more of the qualities listed at the start of this section. With each repetition a story should emerge as to why that repetition occurs.

For example, a train whistle repeated with a musical quality that gives the emotional feeling of anxiousness can show that a character is rushing for a train that is about to leave. With each whistle repeat the music can change in tempo, volume, pitch, etc. to show the urgency of the moment. And the repetition of the whistle can grow in abstraction to show the feeling of anxiety from the point of view of the character.

Develop a storyline you wish to convey; provide its setting, emotional quality, and think about the response you wish to evoke from the listeners. Use your imagination and concentrate on repetition.

Critical response to repetition
- How and why is the cue repeating?
- What is the story being told?
- What genre, time period, or style is used?
- Is the cue cohesive within the same design aesthetic?
- What has changed from the first to the last repetition?
- What is the mood or emotion evoked by the cue?
- What tools in your DAW were effective to create the repetition?
- What is your intention? Was it conveyed to the listeners?

Punctuation

Think of this tool as actual punctuation to the action that is happening on stage. First think about the difference between a period, comma, semicolon, ellipsis, tilde, or exclamation point. Then think about what their equivalent would be in an aural world within a theatrical setting. You use differences in punctuation to highlight what is happening in a theatrical manner.

For highly comedic value these would be emphasized and stand out on their own. But in a more subtle approach, punctuation can accent what is happening visually and can also begin and end cues for effect. Punctuation is short, to the point, and specific to the style and genre in which you are designing, and your punctuations should all live within the same aural world to create cohesiveness to your design.

The extreme of punctuation can lend itself to the element of surprise. As a part of our evolutionary process, any sounds that create surprise that are sharp, loud, ultrasonic, or infrasonic, affect the limbic system of the human body. All audience members will react to being startled.

Most importantly, remember that it's the use of association that creates a deeper meaning to the use of punctuation. And as always, you must have a desired intention to why you are using punctuation at every moment.

Comedic Effect

In *The 39 Steps*, the use of a repetitive orchestral "zing" punctuates the moment whenever a character says "the 39 steps." The repetition of this aural event is what creates the humor. There is also the possibility in this show to have cows and sheep punctuate lines during the Crofter scenes. When you have a show that is stylized in high comedy like *The 39 Steps*, the possibilities are endless because it is a show that contains a great deal of broad physical humor in the style of commedia dell'arte lazzi. Comedic punctuation is effective if it's based on the intentional timing of a line or the action contained in the blocking.

Subtle or Dramatic Effect

It's not as clear or definitive to identify the smaller usage of punctuation. Let's say you have underscoring for a love scene while the characters are speaking to each other. When they kiss you may want to punctuate the action as something that the characters were moved to do. If the characters are so transported that they go into their own bubble during the kiss, perhaps the appropriate choice is to punctuate with silence as if time has stopped, and then resume life around them when the kiss is over. If it's a kiss that feels like it's adding more complexity to the story, perhaps the appropriate choice is to add in additional sound or music accordingly. You must follow the story, style, and intention as to how you approach this or else it will seem superfluous instead of highlighting action.

Bumping In or Out of Transitions

Another use of punctuation is the beginning and ending of cues. If you need to punctuate to go into a transition, or if the lights are bumping into scene at the end of transition, you want to match what the lighting designer and you have discussed. If you have musical transitions, then your punctuation could be in the same instrumentation and key for seamlessness. If you have soundscape transitions, then your punctuations could be the shortest or sharpest sound you are using.

Theatrical Application of Punctuation

Punctuation exists in many forms for theatrical application. It can begin or end an auditory moment or stand on its own. The reasoning and intention is up to you to determine how best to affect your audience. As sound is in the role of support for the pacing of the action within a production, the way to determine how to best do this is to ensure that you match the timing of both the action on stage and how the lights are behaving in the space.

Punctuations could be sharp and fast, or soft and gentle. It is the job of the sound designer to bring us back always to supporting the intention of the moment both for the expression on stage and to the impression upon the audience. They can occur within scenes or within music or soundscapes. They help accent something that you wish to highlight. They can be infrasonic and exist solely in low frequencies emitted by a subwoofer, or they can be full sonic events with great detail.

We know that because of evolutionary response sharp, loud, and unsuspecting noises disorient a person because they are unable to identify what the sound is, or locate from where the sound is coming. Using this knowledge can enforce the horror aspect of *Dr. Jekyll & Mr. Hyde* by creating the shock and surprise of the story. It can also highlight the smaller moments of discovery as the mystery unfolds.

The precaution you should use when applying punctuation is to not draw attention to the sound unless that is your intention. So when it is a moment you want to punctuate that is not obvious to all who are watching and listening, you want to apply a subtler approach to not draw attention to the sonic element. When a moment is bolder, you can also be bolder to match, and thereby support the scope of the action.

Punctuation can be used frequently in Act One, Scene 17 of *Dr. Jekyll & Mr. Hyde*. This is the scene where Dr. Jekyll creates and drinks the tincture that turns him into Mr. Hyde. If you look at the script alone it seems as though Dr. Jekyll speaks about the tincture, swallows it, and then becomes Mr. Hyde. But in the performing of it, there are many small gestures that happen within the acting of the scene that are not expressed in the script. The actor must enter the stage, go to a box that contains the chemical liquids, pour them together to create the tincture, and then pause briefly before swallowing it.

In the production I designed, there was the added violence of the Hydes all coming onto stage and attacking Dr. Jekyll, as if to symbolize how transforming into Mr. Hyde was not a pleasant experience. After the attack, the cane is tossed from one Hyde to another in the symbolic reference of who has control.

Figure 3.2 shows the initial markings I made in my script. It doesn't have to be pretty, as I will outline later when explaining how to notate sound ideas in a script.

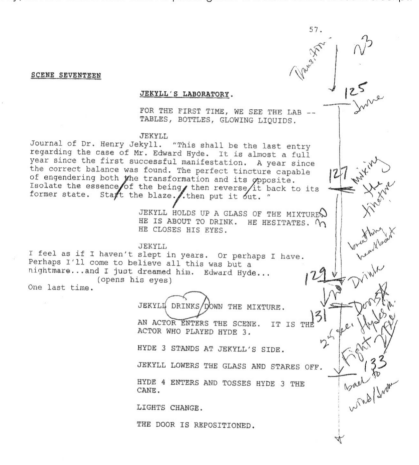

Figure 3.2 Act One, Scene 17 of *Dr. Jekyll & Mr. Hyde*. Reprinted by permission Paradigm Talent Agency on behalf of the Jeffrey Hatcher Copyright ©.

In the script you will see that I have a musical cue that transitions to a drone with ambience underscoring the dialogue. There can be a punctuation to mark that shift. Then you will see three distinct places in the script notated by hash marks, where the mixing of the tincture occurs. This is based on the action of the actor, and where he and the director felt it best to accent words with the creation of the tincture. With these three mixing cues, I punctuated the shift through the use of a sizzling sound effect. This showed that there was a change in complexity of the liquid mixture. With each of the punctuations I also combined additional layers of sound to reflect that it was growing with a life of its own.

I added more complexity to the suspenseful moment before drinking by adding in an almost imperceptible sound of breathing and a heartbeat to signify that this is going to be a visceral exchange in the body. When Dr. Jekyll drinks the tincture the sound goes almost completely silent before the onslaught of the Hydes. This is similar to a tactic used in horror films, to deceive the audience into thinking that perhaps it's not going to work this time.

Then there is a large punctuation as all the Hydes burst through the doors to attack Dr. Jekyll. Internally to the fight there are subtler hits using infrasonic frequencies to help immerse the audience by actually feeling each blow upon Dr. Jekyll. The last blow is the largest in dynamics, as if to signify that Hyde has taken over, and the Hyde theme has now replaced the Jekyll. Then there is the repetitive aural punctuation used by every cane toss delineated in the play to remind the audience of who has control.

If you look at the timings I wrote down in the margins, this entire event takes roughly a minute and a half. And in that short time there are at least fifteen punctuations that support the action of the scene.

EXERCISES

Create three punctuations that would belong in the same story, staying true to genre and style. First, think of a short and simple story. Then place it in a time period and assign a genre to it. Then think about your own personal style of how you would approach this genre, and choose what you are punctuating. Is it a comma or an exclamation point? Is it funny, scary, dramatic, or subtle? What story are you telling with each of these short cues?

The cues should be brief, but should be as rich as you can make them with the complexity of a multilayered approach. Even though the cues are short, that does not mean they are simple. The more thought and specificity you put into your cues, the richer your design. Think of it like an orchestra of individual instruments making up the complete sound you hear. The only difference here is that you don't have a lot of time to convey meaning.

Critical response to punctuation

- What form of punctuation is used, e.g. period, comma, question mark, exclamation point?
- What is the story being told?
- Are the punctuations within the same design aesthetic?
- Do the punctuations live in a time or place?
- What mood or emotion is evoked?
- What tools in your DAW were effective to create the punctuations?
- What is your intention? Was it conveyed to the listeners?

Dynamics

> The human ear is an exceptional sensory collector of vibration because of its sensitivity and the range of intensities to which it can respond. The human ear can withstand a great deal of sound pressure above the weakest vibration we can detect. The perception of apparent loudness can be considered a subjective quality because it's measured in relation to prior acclimation and harmonic content when switching between a moderate and a loud environment.
>
> Our ability to hear faint sound is not due to our ear's absolute sensitivity but more to the contribution of the amount of ambient noise in our environment. And any sound is dependent on the duration of that sound. Physiologically, the detection of dynamics is relative to many other circumstances in our environment, and dependent upon the person experiencing the sound and the distance they are from the source.

Within a theatrical environment, where we have control over what is heard and how loud or faint that sound is, we have the ability to shape the aural soundscape to our liking for whatever intention we need. Knowing that we are working in the quietest soundscape possible, even if that contains a noise floor due to equipment, we set the range of dynamics from that level to our loudest in the space.

The effect of dynamics upon an audience is the increase and decrease of sound using speed, volume, pitch, and complexity. Table 3.2 shows the effects increasing and decreasing these elements can have.

Table 3.2 *The effect of increasing and decreasing dynamics in a production*

	Increase	Decrease
Speed	Getting faster in time gives the impression of emotional urgency, excitement, and a rush to your climax. Physically time is speeding up.	Getting slower in time gives the emotional impression of regaining equilibrium from a faster speed or an abatement from normal speed. Physically time is slowing down.
Volume	Getting louder gives the emotional impression of imminence, power, and intensity. Physically something or someone is advancing in space.	Getting quieter gives the emotional impression of calm, softness, peace, or reservation. Physically something or someone is receding in space.
Pitch	Going higher in timbre gives the emotional impression of height, a degree of acceleration, weakness if faint, or superiority if loud. Physically it feels smaller.	Going lower in timbre gives the emotional impression of slowing down, a degree of deceleration, strength if loud, and inferiority if faint. Physically it feels larger.
Complexity	Increasing elements gives the emotional impression of complication, chaos, elaboration, or involvement. Physically it is more crowded.	Decreasing elements gives the emotional impression of depreciation, deterioration, and diminishment. Physically it is more solitary and sparse.

When to use either an increase or decrease in dynamics in theatre is dependent on how you want your audience to react in a moment. In a moment of build, you magnify what is happening to a point of climax. The climax can be signified by punctuation. After the climax comes the denouement of your sound. This can happen at any rate or duration you need to heighten a moment. But again, always make sure that your intention is clear.

However you choose to create your dynamics, most times you will decrease in the same manner in which you increase. So, if you were speeding up to your climax, you would slow down to decline. If the volume gets louder or the pitch goes higher to amplify a moment, it would then get softer and lower to return to the state at which you began. If you add to the complexity to the sound in order to reach your climax, you would take away the added components at the same rate you added them. Of course, this is not applicable if you are working in abstraction and need to vary this intentionally.

A slow increase in dynamics creates a dramatic tension, while a faster increase in dynamics takes an audience by surprise. A slow decrease in dynamics allows for breath in the denouement, while a faster decrease in dynamic return feels like an interruption. How you wish to move your audience should support the story.

Theatrical Application of Dynamics

Increasing and decreasing dynamics of volume, pitch, tempo, and complexity has varying avenues of reaction. When used in a purposeful manner, it creates the "ride" the audience is on as witness to the whole experience. This speaks to the overarching style and pacing of the production. It is not unlike a symphony where you have movements of big sweeping melody, single instrument solos, driving pace, and soft reflection all in one complete piece. When you have supported all the intellectual themes and emotional arcs in a cohesive manner, the impact of that work is most effective through your use of dynamics.

Increase of Dynamics

> Excites through abstraction
> Feels bigger as it fills the space
> Generates atmospheric closeness by encompassing the audience
> Affects the limbic system by raising heart rate and thereby effects a heightened emotional response

Decrease of Dynamics

> Excites through abstraction
> Pinpoints focus by clearing the aural environment of complexity
> Creates space around the audience by removing atmospheric pressure
> Offers relief by easing the heart rate and emotional response

Choosing when to implement how an increase or decrease in dynamics affects an audience is dependent once again on the story being told. Increases and decreases can be used separately throughout the production or used sequentially in direct opposition to each other. When one is used directly after the other you are highlighting the difference between them more greatly because of their proximity in time. And again, the use of punctuation (bold or subtle) to start, transition, or end a dynamic shift is also possible to accent the exact moment of change.

A slow dynamic shift has a different feeling from a fast dynamic shift. When you take time to show the difference in dynamics, the audience has more time to reflect on what has just happened and to understand what is about to occur. When you have a fast shift in dynamics, it takes the audience by surprise both in time and meaning.

Imagine taking someone by the hand to guide him or her across the street. By slowly taking their hand and walking, the person you are guiding is aware of his or her surroundings and can garner meaning from the experience. If you quickly grab their hand and run, they are less apt to take in all the information of their surroundings and to understand the need to move so fast.

When you highlight time for an audience, you can create suspense through understanding; and in counter to that, you can create surprise by not allowing the audience time to process the information.

You can get as detailed as you need to help your thought process behind your design. You can map out how you see the dynamics unfolding through the entire play, separate acts, individual scenes, internal emotional shifts, external action, or your designation of sound cues. The amount of detail you need to help you understand how the sound waves fill a space, and therefore affect an audience, is going to vary from person to person.

The use of dynamics is mapped out by sound cue in Figure 3.3 representing Scene 17—Dr. Jekyll mixing the tincture and becoming Mr. Hyde. The level of increase begins to rise when the mixing of the tincture occurs with Q125, Q127, and Q129. There is a fast increase when the Hydes burst in the door with Q131 for the fight, the last blow landing on Q133, before leveling back almost to where the sound started with the cane toss at Q135. Volume and complexity were the focuses I chose with this scene; I needed the most dramatic effect for how heightened the action was on stage.

Sound design can be intangible because you cannot see it. By mapping the dynamics visually, it can help you gain better insight as to how the design is going to feel in the space. I think of the line on the graph as my actual level of support. If the action or volume increases on stage, the line shifts underneath it to support it. The success of the support you lend is dependent on your understanding of the script.

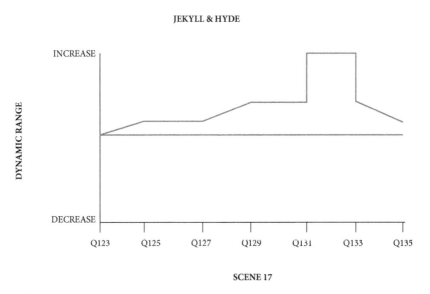

JEKYLL & HYDE

Figure 3.3 Dynamic range of Act One, Scene 17.

EXERCISES

Think of a heightened moment in a story you wish to support, concentrating on the emotional content of why it stands out. Whose point of view is this moment coming from? How does it affect the characters involved? How does it affect the audience? Set this moment into a time period and determine the style or genre you think will tell this story best. Magnify this moment with the use of speed, volume, pitch, complexity, or a combination to achieve your intention. Create a complete increase, punctuation, and decrease cue lasting no longer than thirty seconds.

Some examples could be the emotional lead-up to a kiss and its after-effects, a car physically speeding up to a crash and how the sound dissipates after, or even a cultural group responding to a football team about to score. You determine the event, define all its parameters, and then represent them aurally in the three steps of increase, climax, and decrease.

Critical response to dynamics
- Is there a sense of an increase, climax, and decrease in the cue?
- What is the story being told?
- What genre, time period, or style is used?
- Is the cue cohesive and within the same design aesthetic?
- How do the use of speed, volume, pitch, complexity, or a combination create the increase?
- Does the decrease use the same technique as the increase in the reverse direction?
- Does the punctuation of the climax live within the world of the increase and decrease?
- What mood or emotion is evoked?
- What tools in your DAW were effective to create the dynamics?
- What is your intention? Was it conveyed to the listeners?

Ambience

Soundscape is the auditory equivalent of a landscape. A soundscape represents sonic events that currently exist in a specific place. Birds singing, babies crying, cars passing by, and people talking are examples of dynamic actions that create periodic vibrations. A soundscape needs events to produce vibrations and therefore can never be static by definition. Only through the illusion of theatre can we consciously choose to create a static state in an environment.

Spatial Quality to Soundscape

To give an example of how a space effects its contents, think once again of how the note of a violin can be elongated by the aural architecture of the concert hall. The environment embodies the sound of the note and gives it a personality. By the mere act of reflection and absorption, there is a constant dialogue between the sonic events and the response of the environment they are in.

In fact you must take into account interference, shadowing, dispersion, diffraction, and reverberation as well. To aurally visualize a space you need to think of the interdependency between spatial objects, physical surfaces, and the passing energy that contains a wide range of sound.

Public and Private Space

When you have your windows open on a summer day, the activities in the public environments surrounding your house permeate into the private space of the house's interior. The open window merges the visually and socially defined areas into one aural experience. Public life has entered into private life. When working on a play you must take into account the public environments around the private: when they bleed into consciousness and when they disappear.

Creating Background Noise

In order to create background noise for theatre, recall how we as human beings selectively hear. We only want to hear background noise when it is important to the storytelling. Otherwise it would act in the manner that you want the audience to selectively hear.

Therefore, when creating your cues you want to ensure that nothing is punctuating your ambience without purpose, as it may steal focus within the identity of the soundscape. Keep the volume at a consistent level as to not attract audience attention by a change in attenuation. And ensure that there is nothing overtly discernable to detract away from what is important on stage. Your cue must be long enough to cover the entire scene, as it will be notIceable if you loop shorter segments to make up the length of time.

One helpful action to aid in building soundscape environments is to lower the volume to the approximate level it would be played in the theater when listening back in your headphones. When the volume is lower, anything that has the possibility of being obtrusive will be evident. The goal is to have a rich environment that mimics your intention of what the audience selectively hears.

Theatrical Response of Ambience

For the ambience in *Dr. Jekyll & Mr. Hyde*, the time period represents the past. And the sound designer must do research and apply imaginative listening to approximate what it would have sounded like in a specific time and place. Looking at photographs, paintings, and films of the past help to fill out what lies in your imagination. First act as the observer of the image and then place yourself as an experiencer of the sounds contained within it.

Look for the following:

- How many people are in the environments? Since we know that London was overcrowded with people at this time and more so in the lower-class neighborhoods, there will be a different aural landscape to a public place based on class.

- Are they public or private spaces? What are the differences between the noise levels of the street where Mr. Hyde almost attacks the little girl to the internal office of Dr. Lanyon?

- What size is the space? If indoors, how tall are the ceilings? How large is the room? Is there a lot of furniture? If outdoors, how open is the space? Are there man-made buildings and organic material like grass and trees?

- Is the space indoors or outdoors? Does the outside world intrude into the indoor space or is it aurally separate?

- Are there animals?

- How much is manufactured by man?

- What is generating noise?

By separating all of these instances that can occur in an ambience, you can then build the environments in which the characters live.

If you have to imagine and build something that is more about the quality of an ambience, then that decision will come from the collective consciousness of the demographic of your audience. For example, when creating the lab where Dr. Jekyll works, you can rely upon past portrayals of scientific or medical labs. You are looking for what an audience associates with that particular environment.

A laboratory in the genre of monster movies generally has a bubbling aural bed, or could have sporadic electricity-arcing sounds. An audience member who hears that when the story transitions into Dr. Jekyll's laboratory will immediately know that there is scientific experimentation occurring and that the lab is active, because they have heard it before with a specific common association.

EXERCISES

Create two contrasting environmental ambience cues at one-minute lengths. As with the other exercises, give special attention to story, time period, time of day, genre, and style. However, now consider the spatial qualities to the environment and whether this is a public, private, natural, or man-made space. Again, complexity in design makes your work unique and rich.

Some examples of contrast when creating the two cues are time of day, public or private, natural or man-made, city or rural, or even time period. Pick two opposing environments or themes that will evoke an opposite reaction from your listeners.

Critical response to ambience
- What is the environment for each of the cues?
- Is there a story being told?
- What genre, time period, or style is used?
- Are the cues based in reality, imagined, or metaphorical?
- Are the cues cohesive and within the same design aesthetic?
- Are the cues contrasting in environmental ambience?
- In each of the cues, is it a public, private, natural, or man-made space?
- What mood or emotion is evoked and are the cues in emotional contrast to each other?
- What tools in your DAW were effective to create the ambience?
- What is your intention? Was it conveyed to the listeners?

Drones

A drone is a continuous humming-like sound usually mechanical in nature, which sustains sometimes for minutes at a time. Drones can also be melodic, either in consonance or dissonance, depending once again on the intention of emotional response to the story being told.

There are many sound-effect libraries that contain drones. Finding one in a library and plugging it into your show is not a specific way to approach the intention of your design. Once again, you must think about where you are, the mood, feeling, emotion, point of view, abstraction, repetition, style, genre, time period, etc. A drone should be so specific to the individuality of the idea and feeling that it is most appropriate to use for the intention of that particular moment. There can be many different classifications of drones.

Creating a tension drone in sound relies on the reaction of the limbic system as our fight-or-flight response is triggered. We know that low infrasonic sound triggers a human being to sense danger. If our intention is to create a sense of danger, then a low infrasonic drone will be effective. A high-pitched drone can be piercing and annoying, and it too can create a fight-or-flight response if used with an element of surprise.

Drones can be soothing, such as the sound of white noise that some people use when they need help to fall asleep; a two-toned harmonic sustain can feel angelic. The use of drones in theatre can be at times overly utilized, so I caution you to use your best judgment to use this tool specifically to support your storytelling. Keep in mind the importance of why the drone begins and ends. What is the motivating factor that needed the support of sustaining a hum or tone?

When your drone matches the amount of complexity in an event, the more distinct and unique is your expression of a moment. As with any aural environment, there are many instances of sound happening at once. Within the tonal quality, whether mechanical or melodic, it is possible to have other sounds that add to the information of the environment you wish to convey. Within an ambience of a dungeon, you may have a drone that contains drips, reverb, something that mimics distant screams, etc.

Just as when working on ambiences, create your drones at the volume level you need to hear. And then lower the volume to see if it still has the same effect and impact on the listener. You will notice that anything that stands out by punctuating the steady nature of the drone will stick out when you lower the volume.

Usually, you do not want to draw attention to the intellectual aspects of the drone, but more often you wish the audience to feel it. It's important to stress that this type of cue is a sensed or felt support cue to a motivating factor either in dialogue or action. Be sure you create the desired effect by not distracting the listener into hearing the sound cue but focusing them more intently on how the story is making them feel.

Because of the mapping of neural pathways, it takes approximately five to seven seconds for a constant sound to become common knowledge and for a person to stop listening to it. The change of attenuation or frequency will be what alerts the listener to the sound again.

If you begin a drone in silence, the audience will hear it. This signifies that there is something to pay attention to that is about to happen. If you begin a drone masked by words or action, it will be more of a subconscious response that something is different without the audience knowing why it feels that way. The same applies for when you choose to take a drone away from the listener. If you allow for the hearing of the fade to relative silence, the audience is aware of the denouement. If you mask it behind language or dialogue, the audience simply feels that the heightened moment is complete.

Theatrical Application of Drones

When preparing the drone aspects for use in your sound design, you want to ensure that you are using them for the feeling they evoke and the reaction you wish to attain from the audience. Drones can range from complex to simple in their organization and can be utilized on their own or as beds to other sonic events. The disposition, or how they relate to the elements they support, is the focus of why you would choose to use a drone in sound design. They will be congruous if they remain true to the time period, mood or feeling, or energetic flow of a design.

Because *Dr. Jekyll & Mr. Hyde* is a psychological story using dark horror as its vehicle, the sound design wants to evoke feelings such as fear, shock, surprise, tension, suspense, repulsion, etc. We know that human beings have a fight-or-flight response when it comes to infrasonic frequencies and that they will generate an ominous feeling of tension. We want to use this information to add to the excitement of the story.

Because Hatcher has written Mr. Hyde as played by separate actors, we are able to track Mr. Hyde as a complete entity with his own separate emotional arc. If the sound design uses low-frequency drones whenever Mr. Hyde appears on stage, it will create an association with Hyde that is evil and frightening.

The horror events of the story are presented in the heightened realism component of the play's structure. The use of a drone to create a bed under these scenes guarantees not only the intended emotional response, but also presents a component of the play's structure as set apart from the rest by keeping a specific sonic element present for the entirety of the scenes that contain Mr. Hyde.

In opposition to the low-frequency tension of horror, and because we are working with dualities in this play, you can choose high-frequency, piercing, and disruptive drones to complement the infrasonic. This frequency of drones can make one feel like they have a headache or simulate ringing in the ears. It could be used when Dr. Jekyll is finding it hard to keep Mr. Hyde out of his psyche. You want to always lend support to the theme of duality in this play, so having Mr. Hyde as low frequency and Dr. Jekyll as high frequency is a subconscious way to reinforce the intellectual idea. This creates a separation between the two personas, and through association the audience will begin to recognize one from the other.

EXERCISES

Create a drone no shorter than one minute and no longer than three minutes. If you choose to begin your drone without punctuation, be sure to fade it in so that it has the impression of coming out of nowhere. Be clear in its distinction and relativity to your story, point of view, genre, style, time period, and abstraction. Do not use any increases or decreases in dynamics, or internal punctuations. Make sure that it has a setting, and concentrate specifically on the mood and feeling of the emotion you wish to evoke. And again, play the cue at the appropriate level for it to be heard in the theatre to distinguish its effect.

Critical response to drones

- What type of drone is the cue—mechanical or melodic, consonant or dissonant?
- What is the story being told?
- What genre, time period, or style is used?
- Is the cue cohesive and within the same design aesthetic?
- What are the components of the drone?
- Is it as effective at a quieter level?
- If there are minor punctuations, do they work or distract from the drone?
- What mood or emotion is evoked?
- What tools in your DAW were effective to create the drone?
- What is your intention? Was it conveyed to the listeners?

Time

In sound design, we sometimes need to manipulate time to tell a story. We may travel through time periods, show passage of time, stop time, jump time, speed it up, or slow it down. Manipulating time is an abstraction of something that is an accepted norm of our existence. We live in a linear world and theatrical storytelling relies on a timeline of experience that produces discoveries.

Whether the story adheres to a natural timeline is up to the author or playwright. When a story is best told by manipulating time, sound can be a very strong design element in highlighting this movement and helping the audience understand what is happening by supporting the changes that occur. This is best done through abstraction or the breaking of set rules.

Speeding Up and Slowing Down Time

To give the impression of speeding up or slowing down time, sound designers manipulate the differences in the acceleration and deceleration of pace and the rise and fall of pitch. The rate of the speed is completely dependent upon the moment you need to support. The style, genre, time period, point of view, and why time feels like it's speeding up is based solely on the individual story and production.

Stopping Time

In order to show how time stops, you must take into account: the emotional reason, the feeling and mood, the perspective of the point of view, the genre and style of your design, and the event itself. For an audience to feel as though time is stopping there should be a certain feeling to the moment directly before the event.

- The precursor to the event can be slow, normal, or fast in speed and dynamics. And it can be constant or sporadic temporally.

- The climax is a punctuation of the actual stopping of time. Then there is a suspension of the moment where time has stopped.

- Finally, the recovery afterwards is in reverse to how you got to this moment. For example, if you accelerate to the punctuation, you decelerate out of it. If you decelerate into the punctuation, you accelerate coming out of it.

The dynamics of pitch, speed, and complexity apply here as well, and should consist of everything you need to convey in those very few seconds. For an audience, stopping time is a surreal event but one that we have all experienced at one time or another.

The most common stoppage of time is when there is impending danger such as a car crash, or any emotional or heightened moment. Many people who have experienced car crashes will remark that at the point of the crash everything went into slow motion and stopped. This is because the heightened event was so great emotionally. Some will even remark that every detail of the event came into view. You want to play into the human existence of when it feels as though time has stopped, and mimic the pacing of those moments for your audience.

Traveling through Time

When traveling forward or backwards in time there are many elements that can contribute to why and how an event is taking place. Your interpretation should show whether it is an internal emotional traveling, an external structure of the story, or both.

You want to be clear in the aural properties to present whether it is more of a wormhole progression or a jump-cut to another time period. You should know from whose point of view it is perceived, and the emotional aspect behind the reason for the change. And finally, you want to make sure you convey whether you are traveling forwards or backwards in time.

If it happens more than once in the play, determine the convention that remains consistent to telling the audience how it happens and how it is different each time around. It can be as specific as literal sound effects, broadcasts, and music to show not only the journey through time but also where you start and end on that journey. Or it can be very abstract, as to the feeling and emotion that focuses on the propulsion of the event and point of view. Often, it is both. The more specific you are in regarding how you convey traveling through time, the less the audience has to think about what is happening and can go on the journey with you.

Passage of Time

Many times in theatre, usually in a transition between scenes or moments, we need to show passage of time. You have to convey that time is passing and yet not make it seem to the audience that they are just waiting for thirty seconds watching nothing. From the sound design perspective you want to mark time and give the impression of whether time is passing slowly, normally, or quickly. How this is shown is through a consistent rhythm or pace to the cue.

The world the passage of time lives within is reliant on the cohesiveness of your design and conventions, whether it is musical or soundscape in nature, what time period or genre you're in, or the style in which your design lives.

Because your audience is only listening to your design and not actors' dialogue or plot, you have their full attention. Choosing specifically what you want them to hear and how you want them to hear it will aid the perception of the passage of time.

When you take into account what needs to happen during this passage of time, you can add details that support individual ideas. You may want to show an emotional change, or specificity to the physicality of space, or even events that happen that are integral to the storytelling yet not portrayed by the actors.

These are mini-stories that can be conveyed and each will have their own particular journey of dynamics, mood, and pace.

Theatrical Application of Time

Time period is very important, and your soundmarks should reflect the time period in which the play exists. Remembering your soundmarks is important. Big

Ben in London can be used, but it would be heard through heavy fog and smog. There are no cars, but you would hear horse and buggies. The doorbell would be a twist bell or pull bell. If you do not stay true to the time period, the sound will be pulled to the forefront and take focus because the audience will be trying to justify the anachronism.

In the play, Dr. Jekyll loses time when Mr. Hyde has gained more control and power. This is mostly apparent in the words of the script, but there is the action of one character becoming the other and back again that must represent that time has passed for the transition.

Since it is ultimately Dr. Jekyll's journey, this is interpreted from his point of view. It is as if he travels through a wormhole to become Mr. Hyde, and then he comes back to consciousness through that same wormhole in reverse. In the play, it takes place in a moment; but in reality, he loses hours upon waking.

In order to portray this instant psychological and physical journey through time, you can use the aural elements that constitute the scene where the audience is shown how Dr. Jekyll becomes Mr. Hyde through the drinking of the tincture.

To create the faster shift into Mr. Hyde, you can use the suspenseful drone, the subtle punctuations of the mixing of the tinctures, the increase of heart rate and breathing, and the low frequency of Mr. Hyde overtaking the sound, ending with a punctuation—all within seconds. This becomes the transition that can be repeated and amended, as the audience now knows it as the shift into the alter ego.

To show that there is a shift of time in the transition out of Mr. Hyde to wake back up as Dr. Jekyll, you could do this in reverse. You can begin with punctuation, and this time use the high frequencies of Dr. Jekyll overtaking Mr. Hyde's low end, and then end it with the subliminal breathing, heart rate, or tincture sounds as the high frequency (that equates a headache) slowly dissipates as if waking from a dream.

The script and direction dictate how long the time passage is; what we have to highlight is the information about the shift.

EXERCISES

Create three cues showing stoppage of time, traveling through time, and passage of time. Each should be no longer than thirty seconds. Determine the story you are telling, the time period, style, and genre of your design and take into account from whose point of view the audience comprehend what is occurring. Be sure to use the other tools of theme, repetition, dynamics, punctuation, ambience, and drones to help you tell your story.

A marked repeated tempo using punctuation will help show time—choose the speed of your time.

The dynamics will govern the response—choose when to heighten the dramatic effect.

Follow the themes of emotional or physical change—choose the events within the passage.

The music you use will be associated with the mood you intend.

Critical response to time

- Why and how is time manipulated?
- Did the cues speed up, slow down, stop, and show passage of time?
- What is the story being told?
- What genre, time period, or style is used?
- Are the cues cohesive and within the same design aesthetic?
- How do the cues portray the sense of time?
- What mood or emotion is evoked?
- What tools in your DAW were effective to create the Time?
- What is your intention? Was it conveyed to the listeners?

Concrete vs. Abstract

I like to start with the concept that we have two worlds that exist simultaneously. The world outside of us is what we perceive through our senses, and the world within us is what constitutes thought, perception, imagination, feelings, and emotions. If the world outside of us is concrete, then the world inside of us is abstract. We can fluctuate between acknowledging these worlds in our day-to-day existence, but they are both active simultaneously.

We can be walking down the street and simultaneously daydreaming about a future hope at the same time. We may not notice the cars passing, or the other individuals on the sidewalk when we are deeply invested in the fantasy. And staying within our metaphor, there are moments of reality that will pull us out of our minds as well, such as almost bumping into another person on the sidewalk. It's important to understand how abstraction helps us to transition between these two worlds so that we can represent them sonically to support a theatrical performance.

Abstraction relies on ideas not events. It is a byproduct of a process that is governed by rules and classifications of the literal. You can form an abstraction by filtering out aspects that are relevant to a particular purpose. You then eliminate or change characteristics that are perceived to be real or concrete. If we choose to break the rules of what is perceived as real, we delve into the world of abstraction.

For example, let's say that a drinking glass falls off the table and shatters on the floor. If we filter, eliminate, or change any aspect that is relevant to the reality of the event, we have abstracted it. We can create an abstraction based on an idea by possibly delaying the time the glass reaches the floor, changing the sound it makes, adding reverb, or slowing it down. We can change the rules, or classification, of the literal and create an idea from an event with the use of a wide range of expression.

The world of abstraction is a fun place for a sound designer. We can express magic, terror, joy, horror, or anything we can interpret through our imagination and intention that determines the abstract temperament of a particular world. It's a temperament that is not necessarily affixed, and in time it can grow to be more extreme or bizarre. It is based in the emotional world of the story instead of the physical world in which the story lives.

When transitioning between the two worlds of concrete and abstraction you can also include a change in the feeling of time; it may feel like time stops for a moment and then speeds back up. There may be a punctuation to mark that moment of change. There can be an increase in dynamics before the change and decrease after it. But before or after the transition live two distinct worlds: concrete and abstract.

The concrete, real, or natural world is exactly how it sounds; it is the literal world around us, and the commonality within the definition of how it sounds to all human beings. The natural world contains synchronous sounds like birds in the trees, the radio in the room, the crowd to our left or right, or anything that you would hear in a particular environment. The abstraction of those sounds, perhaps asynchronous in nature, is left to the circumstance or heightened event for which the abstraction takes place.

The abstract world is what I like to refer to as the world of manipulators. In our DAWs it is found in the functions of reverb, distortion, compression, delay, pitch, time, etc. What these have in common is that they warp sound into the perception of being something more than its original form by changing its natural rules.

Reverb automatically evokes a dreamlike state or memory. Distortion makes it seem like something is chaotic in your mind. Changing pitch and time alters the perception of the circumstantial because time behaves in a linear fashion. And frequencies are dependent on size and shape.

Play with size, distance, duration, timbre, pitch, or anything else you can dream up to create dynamic dimensions to your sound; however, make sure that you do so with a specific intention in mind. You can model reality or create fantasy; either way you are the creator of the virtual space for the listener.

Theatrical Application of Concrete vs. Abstract

Knowing that both concrete and abstract can live together in the same moment, as well as independently, in *Dr. Jekyll & Mr. Hyde* we must focus the choice of how to use this tool in a way that supports the theme of dualities once again.

The most prevalent duality in which we can use this concept is by focusing on internal dialogue vs. external appearance. Another focus can be the duality of the past told in memory vs. the present events in the storyline. Yet another can be the animalistic impulsive behavior of Mr. Hyde vs. the control that Dr. Jekyll wishes to have over his life. Again, it comes down to your intention in how sound is to support the play.

The switch between the themes you are supporting is where you create abstraction in your concept. Abstraction is a change in the rules of the natural world. What is expected is changed in some way by values such as time, pitch, volume, distortion, etc. It is up to the circumstance to determine the best way to effect change to abstract.

For example, in *Dr. Jekyll & Mr. Hyde*, the effect of reverberation can add to the ghostly inner mind dialogue that Mr. Hyde embodies within Dr. Jekyll. Placing microphones in the space that then can add additional reverberation for when Mr. Hyde is talking to Dr. Jekyll gives the impression that Hyde is internally part of Jekyll because his voice has a reverb effect on it. Also, knowing that reverberation gives an audience the impression of memory, the use of a reverbed microphone in scenes set in the past signifies the memory of an event because it sounds different from a dry reality.

It can be as evident as highlighting the switching of the actors playing Mr. Hyde. On page 70 in the script, Jekyll is reading a letter. Other actors take turns as Mr. Hyde to read the letter to him as if it is Hyde that reads the letter in Jekyll's head. This is a change that supports the theme of the internal and external and who has control over Jekyll's mind.

Along with the choice of reverberation that is applied whenever the Hydes speak, the switching between the characters could be supported as well. One way to do this is to start with the Hyde drone acting as a bed creating emotional tension, and then add reverb signifying Jekyll's internal thought through the additional shaping of the space. And when the switch of the Hydes occurs, use a punctuation to accent the actors' movement and voice. These are ways that take the abstraction of multiple characters playing one alter ego, and create a structure in which they all have a voice and clarity of where they are in Dr. Jekyll's head.

A more subtle approach to supporting changes in a psyche through abstraction is how you effect the end of the transition into Act One, Scene 9. This is when Dr. Jekyll returns to consciousness with a scream that he believes comes from someone else when it was actually his. He later describes that he was having a nightmare. The transition into the scene can reflect his nightmare and then the waking from it with an abstracted ending. If we have chosen the low frequencies for Hyde and the high frequencies for Jekyll, the waking from this dream can be a quick dynamic shift between the two to simulate a high-frequency scream at the end. Perhaps even the reverb, which supports the Hyde aspect of his personality, lingers as the abstraction needs time to dissipate.

There are many abstractions in theatre because in its true essence theatre is not real. The fighting that happens on stage is a simulation of a fight; no one is really in danger. The audience accepts this as the rule of theatre, and we can use the accepting of the rule or counter it at will. But the accepted construct of theatre is that realism is in actuality surrealism. It is a telling of a story with people portraying characters on a set that is not the actual structure it represents. The audience concedes to this as the way theatre is portrayed, and sound is given equal if not more leeway where abstraction is concerned.

Because sound relies on the physiological, psychological, sociological, and anthropological existence of emotional response, its very nature can be determined as abstract. If you, as a sound designer, can create the division between the concrete existences of human experience with that of the abstracted emotional ideas of thematic structure, you will be able to create a rich journey that feels common and yet unique to the story you are telling.

EXERCISES

Create two thirty-second cues: one transitioning from abstract to concrete
                                      one transitioning from concrete to abstract
Some examples may include the following:

Waking up from a dream—choose the dreamlike state of the abstraction, how the shift occurs, and then the concrete world that follows.

Slipping into a bath after a long day—choose the concrete world that the character wishes to escape from, and then the mental abstraction of what it is like to melt into a hot bath.

As with the cues preceding this one, remember to take into account the story, themes, emotions, repetition, dynamics, punctuation, and time that this all exists within. Determine a genre or style, time period, and setting and then create the event of the switching between the concrete and abstract.

Critical response to concrete vs. abstract
- What is the story being told?
- What genre, time period, or style is used?

- Are the cues cohesive and within the same design aesthetic?
- Is it necessary to be abstracted to tell the story and why?
- What mood or emotion is evoked?
- Which direction does each cue travel: concrete to abstract or abstract to concrete?
- What tools in your DAW were affective to create the cue?
- What other tools were used, e.g. themes, punctuation, repetition, dynamics, time control, ambience, tension?
- What is your intention? Was it conveyed to the listeners?

4
HISTORY EXERCISES USING TOOLS

Because theatrical storytelling is reliant on time period to show its relevance to a modern audience, we must be able to research music and sound through time. This means sound designers understand who the composers of the time are, how music was created, when and how it was possible to record and duplicate it, and how the general public was able to experience it. We must understand its historical context as to how genres developed and how music spoke to the people of its time.

We will use the tools outlined previously, of themes, repetition, punctuation, etc., to help us through this journey. The aural tool notated for each exercise, as the "special ingredient" to the cue you are creating, does not mean that the other tools are not present; it means that the specific tool will be the focus of the cue.

These exercises help to facilitate efficient and specific historical research with quick cue building. Eventually, the goal is to have each of these exercises completed in one three-hour sitting, and to have the student learn how to work in a rich manner quickly, efficiently, and historically accurately.

Each exercise consists of finding an image that was created in a specific time period. The musical research supports the emotional element in your representation of that image. The visual and musical elements must be of the same time period; however, if for the support of the story, the country of origin need not be consistent with both the aural and visual.

You can add in any additional sound effects or soundscape as it fits your intention. As each exercise contains a "special ingredient" from your toolbox, as you move through the timeline you will build upon the last so the goal in the last exercise is to have as many as possible of the ingredients used in support of your storytelling.

To give you a brief idea of the music in each time period, I will outline composers you can research, styles and structures that were prevalent, and how human beings heard this music. It is a way to show you how music has grown in time based on style, community, consumerism, and distribution.

Note that this is in no way a comprehensive study of what could amount to volumes of historical research of music. This is simply a starting point from which you can begin more specific research of your own. I will be outlining how music was recorded and distributed, who had access to it, and what it sounded like at the time. Studying this and gaining all the details of how music grew through time could occupy years of study.

When creating cues for your exercises in this section, use the music of the time period listed. You will see that there are many genres of music in even a twenty-year span. And as we get closer to the present day, the subgenres explode with the ability to obtain music globally. Keep in mind that there are aural listening subgroups that reflect culture, class, geography, and age. Know who is listening to the music you choose and what the point of view is in the image you are supporting.

For example, the reason why this is important is that one person's reference to 1980s music may not be another person's reference to the decade. The 1980s saw a large splintering of genres, and specificity is needed to understand the subculture that is listening. After you determine that, you have to understand how to apply it to a collective visual representation.

The only way to attain specificity is to do a lot of research and to know how listening to music evolved. This is just a slice of what you could delve into. I'm sure there may be genres and bands that I've missed because my perspective is based on being an American born in the 1960s.

As an artist who uses other artists' creations to inspire your own work, it is best if you understand how and why that artistry was cultivated.

Music in the 1600s

Baroque Music (1600–1750)

It was during the seventeenth century that the system of modes that were developed in the Dark Ages and Middle Ages finally diminished in popularity. By adding accidentals to these modes the major and minor key system was developed.

The seventeenth century also saw the invention of several new forms and designs in the structure of music:

- Opera
- Sonata
- Oratorio
- Suite
- Fugue
- Concerto

The orchestra started to take shape, mainly in the string section, and the violin became the dominant instrument and thereby the most important in creating drama. Pieces were commissioned by royalty and music moved away from the sacred into the secular environment for those from society's higher classes.

Composers of note	Nationality
Vivaldi	Italian
A. Scarlatti	Italian
D. Scarlatti	Italian
Corelli	Italian
Monteverdi	Italian
Bach	German
Handel	German
Couperin	French
Lully	French
Rameau	French
Purcell	English

Monody

A monody is a single voice line supported by an instrumental bass line, upon which chords are constructed. In opera of this time, the voice line follows the natural rhythm of speech in words. This style of writing for the voice (half-singing and half-reciting) became known as recitative.

The only notation the composer wrote down beneath the melody was a bass line to be played by a low stringed instrument, such as a cello. This is called the basso continuo, but the composer expected another continuo player on harpsichord, organ, or lute, to build up chords upon the bass line.

As these chords had to be improvised, the player has to be very skillful. The figures below the notes indicate which chords to play, and this is called a figured bass.

Early Opera

- The first opera was written in 1597: *Dafne*, composed by Peri. It is comprised of choruses, dances and instrumental pieces, all performed by a small orchestra, and it contains both music and drama.

- One of the first truly great operas was composed by Monteverdi in 1607, and is called *Orfeo*. There is a lot of instrumental ritornello. Ritornello is Italian for return, and refers to when a section of the music returns to be repeated. Before each verse of the aria, or song, we hear an instrumental ritornello.

The Italian Overture
Scarlatti's operas often begin with the Italian overture, delineated by the following pacing: quick, slow, then quick. And Scarlatti designed the arias in his operas in da capo form, i.e. ABA. Another name for this is ternary form.

The French Overture
Lully's operas begin with a French overture whose pacing was as follows: slow, quick, then slow. This is in direct response to the Italian overture as it is the exact opposite. Each country wished to be distinct.

Baroque Opera in England
One of the great English operas of the seventeenth century is *Dido and Aeneas*, composed by Purcell.

Oratorio
Originating from around the same time, oratorio is vocal music that at first is very similar to opera. It contains arias, choruses, and recitatives, and they are acted out with scenery and costumes. The main difference is that an oratorio is based on a sacred story. Eventually oratorio performances ceased, and were performed in musical presentation only. Handel's *Messiah, Samson*, and *Israel in Egypt* are all oratorios.

Passion
A passion is a special oratorio telling the story of Christ's crucifixion. Besides recitatives, arias, and choruses, Bach also included settings of chorales. These are considered hymn tunes.

Cantata
Bach composed more than 200 church cantatas (cantata means sung). These are for soloists and choruses, accompanied by the orchestra and continuo, and are a miniature version of oratorios. An example is *Number 140*, by Bach, based upon the chorale *Sleepers, Wake*.

Instrumental Music

During the Baroque period, instrumental music became as important as vocal music.

Fugue

A fugue is a piece that is contrapuntal, or in counterpoint. It is based upon the idea of imitation. It is usually written in three or four parts, called voices, and these are referred to as soprano, alto, tenor and bass. The detailed structure of a fugue can be rather complicated. The entire piece grows mainly from a single brief melody line. This is called the subject. Then it is repeated by the other voices in turn in their corresponding voice. The most famous collection is the *48 Preludes and Fugues* by Bach.

Chorale Prelude

These are usually for organ, and most of them were composed in Germany. It is based on a chorale and could be in fugal style, or based on a set of variations.

Suite

A suite is a collection of music for dance for one or more instruments. Many were written for harpsichord.

They consist of the following:

- A German allemande — in 4/4 time, at a moderate speed
- A French courante — in 3/2 time, at a moderately fast speed (the Italian version is a corrente)
- A Spanish sarabande — in a slow triple time
- A gigue — usually in compound time

However, before or after the gigue a composer might introduce dances such as the minuet in 3/4 time — a slow and stately waltz, a bourde, a gavotte, or a passepied. Sometimes a suite began with a prelude or an opening piece. The pieces were usually in the same key, and in binary form (AB). French composers, however, often wrote in rondo form (ABACADA, etc.).

Baroque Sonatas

Sonata means sounded, to be played. Many Baroque sonatas are for two violins and the continuo (usually cello and harpsichord). Composers called these trio sonatas. There consist of only three music lines — with the harpsichord playing the figured bass. And a violin was sometimes replaced with a flute or an oboe.

There were two types of sonata:

- The sonata da camera (chamber sonata: camera is Italian for chamber). These were played in people's homes. The continuo would be played by harpsichord or lute.

- The sonata da chiesa (church sonata: chiesa is Italian for church). These were played in churches. The continuo was played by organ. These were far more serious than chamber sonatas.

Composers of sonatas:

- Purcell

- Corelli

- Bach

- Handel

- Scarlatti

- Couperin

Concerto Grosso

This is a musical composition that consists of solo instruments accompanied by a larger orchestra. A small group of soloists could be usually two violins and a cello (called the concertino) and the orchestra of strings were called either the ripieno or the tutti (meaning everyone).

Solo Concerto

This grew out of the concerto grosso, and is defined by a single instrument solo accompanied by a string orchestra. There are solo sections and tutti sections. The quick movements were often in ritornello form: tutti 1, solo 1, tutti 2, solo 2, tutti 3, solo 3, etc.

Vivaldi wrote more than 500 concertos, both concerto grossos and solo concertos, with his most famous being *The Four Seasons*.

Orchestra

During the Baroque period, the orchestra started to take shape. The string section became a self-contained unit. To this composers would add other instruments in ones and twos: flutes, recorders, oboes, bassoons, horns, and occasionally trumpets and kettledrums.

There was still a continuo. There was a lot of contrast, especially in the dynamics. And sometimes there were also echo effects through repetition.

The Main Characteristics of Baroque Music

- The basso continuo (figured bass)

- One mood throughout the entire piece

- Important string sections

- Modes were replaced by the major/minor key system

- Many different forms are used (e.g. binary, fugue)

- Many types of music, e.g. the chorale, opera, the dance suite

- Energetic rhythms, long melodies, many ornaments, contrasts (especially in dynamics, but also in timbre)

American Music

1640—The Bay Psalm Book, Cambridge, Massachusetts, is the first book printed in British Colonial America. The entire Book of Psalms is translated into English meter, indicating a dominance of religious music.

Circa 1700—Black slaves include songs based on Old Testament stories in their worship services and this marks the beginnings of negro spirituals.

Circa 1775—British soldiers sing "Yankee Doodle" to mock colonists; Americans adopt it as their own.

Circa 1776—"Johnny's Gone for a Soldier," an adaptation of an Irish folk tune, proves popular during the American Revolutionary War.

Music in the 1700s

The Baroque period ended in 1750 with the death of Johann Sebastian Bach. The reason the period ended at that time is because Bach became the epitome of Baroque music and was considered impossible to follow. He had set the standard for Baroque music and what followed that time is considered the Classical period. There is a great deal more to know on this subject, and it can be engrossing reading to see how music evolved through time.

Events of the 1700s

- John Eccles is appointed as Master of the King's Musick in London.

- William Croft returns to the Chapel Royal, where he had been educated, as a "gentleman organist."

- William Corbett becomes director of the New Theatre at Lincoln's Inn Fields.

- Johann Sebastian Bach becomes a chorister at St. Michael's Church, Lüneburg.

- Tomaso Albinoni is employed as a violinist by Fernando Carlo, Duke of Mantua.

- An inventory of musical instruments kept by Prince Ferdinando de Medici provides the first evidence for the existence of the pianoforte.

Classical Music of the 1700s

- Arcangelo Corelli—*12 sonate a violino e violone o cimbalo (op. 5)*
- Godfrey Keller—*The Royal Trumpet Suite*
- Antonio Caldara—*Maddalena ai Piedi di Cristo*
- Tomaso Giovanni Albinoni—*Sinfonie e Concerti op. 2*

Opera of the 1700s

- Carlo Agostino Badia—*La costanza d'Ulisse*
- Henry Purcell—*Dido and Aeneas*
- Alessandro Scarlatti—*Eracles*

Publications

- Jacques Boyvin—*Traité abrégé de l'accompagnement*

Notable Dates

1714   Carl Philipp Emanuel Bach born
1732   Franz Joseph Haydn born
1750   Johann Sebastian Bach dies
1756   Wolfgang Amadeus Mozart born
1770   Ludwig van Beethoven born
1788   Carl Philipp Emanuel Bach dies
1791   Wolfgang Amadeus Mozart dies
1792   Gioacchino Rossini born
1797   Franz Schubert born

As you can see, music was taking structure through opera and orchestral pieces. There were positions in the church and in courtly commissions. The time represented an exploration of music within a specific structure.

EXERCISES

1600–1800   Special Ingredient—Themes and Repetition
Find an image in artwork that spans from 1600 to 1800. Look closely at the themes in the image: character, object, idea, etc. Take the listener on a journey of point of view through repetition of themes. Examples may include repetition of movement, change in a character or idea, or a reminder that the listener needs to

understand the visual mood or emotion evoked. You want to either support or juxtapose the image with your sound. Remember that you can use all the tools in your toolbox to help you. The cue should be no longer than thirty seconds.

Critical response

- What are the themes present?
- Is there a story being told?
- Does it complement or juxtapose the visual?
- Is it in the appropriate genre, time period, or style?
- What mood or emotion is evoked?
- What tools in your digital audio workstation (DAW) were effective to create the cue?
- What tools from your toolbox were used?
- What is your intention? Was it conveyed to the listeners?

Music in the 1800s

Music from the 1800s is known as Romantic music. The Romantic era was a period of great change and emancipation. While the Baroque and Classical eras had strict rules of balance and restraint in terms of structure, the Romantic era moved away from that by fostering artistic freedom, experimentation, and creativity.

During this era, the emotional and expressive qualities of music were valued over technique and tradition. Composers, at times, used this expressive means to display nationalism. In the late nineteenth century, there was an expansion in the size of the orchestra and also in the role concerts played as part of urban society.

American Music
"The Star-Spangled Banner" (1814)

Operas
La Boheme—Giacomo Puccini
Madame Butterfly—Giacomo Puccini
Tristan und Isolde—Richard Wagner
Aida—Giuseppe Verdi

Ballets
Giselle—Adolphe Adam
The Nutcracker—Pyotr Ilyich Tchaikovsky
Swan Lake—Pyotr Ilyich Tchaikovsky

Other

Symphonies, sonatas, and waltzes are very popular during this time.

Composers

- Ludwig van Beethoven

- Carl Maria von Weber

- Franz Schubert

- Adolphe Adam

- Frédéric Chopin

- Giuseppe Verdi

- Richard Wagner

- Pyotr Ilyich Tchaikovsky

- Johannes Brahms

1800s History of Recorded Music

In mid nineteenth-century France, Leon Scott invents the phonautograph. This new machine makes it possible to translate the changes in air pressure onto a smoked cylinder. A stylus captures the impression of sound onto a membrane, although it is not able to reproduce the sound it transcribed.

Twenty years later Charles Cros, a poet and inventor also from France, invents photographic color processing. He proposes that Scott's invention would be improved by photoengraving onto metal instead of a membrane. This would allow the replaying of the original sound by retracing what is etched.

In the same year, American inventor Thomas Alva Edison discovers a way of recording and replaying sound and applies for the US patent. This patent covers all "sound writers" and "talking machines" as phonographs. His phonograph etches upon tin-foil cylinders. A year later he considers the process of Horace Short's invention of the steam turbine to use as a compressed amplifier to overcome the lack of volume. And ten years after this patent, he files for another to convert the recording cylinder from tin foil to wax coated.

After ten years, Emile Berliner, an American of German origin who recorded "The Lord's Prayer" in 1884 (which is still preserved by the BBC in London), develops a method of recording laterally onto a disc instead of the cylinder. He also invents a way to reproduce copies of the original disc.

The year 1888 begins the commercial exploitation of the phonograph and dictating machines because of the interest of Jesse Lippincott, a financier. Edison's rivals, Chichester Bell (Alexander Graham Bell's brother) and Charles Tainter, develop the Graphophone at the Volta Laboratory. It is a vast improvement upon the mechanics of the Phonograph due to its ease of operation and fidelity of reproduction.

The Phonograph and Graphophone are still a novelty but are in intense competition with each other for the popular market. The Phonograph shows itself to be more popular and the New York Phonograph Company opens the first recording studio.

Primitive forms of the jukebox that are displayed in amusement arcades become incredibly popular in the United States. This creates a demand for entertainment recordings, e.g. comic monologues and music.

By 1885, entertainment in the form of recorded music is firmly in place for public consumption. This creates an incentive for more research and investment in the record business.

A year later, Eldridge R. Johnson designs and manufactures the spring motor used in clockwork. This invention installs F. Seaman's National Gramophone Company in New York as yet another rival to both the Phonograph and Graphophone.

EXERCISES

1800–1900   Special Ingredient—Manipulation of Time
                   Find an image from the time period and create a cue that
                   manipulates time. Take the listener on a journey of speeding up,
                   slowing down, stopping, jumping, or showing passage of time.
                   Remember to use abstraction, themes, repetition, punctuation, and
                   dynamics to help you create a supporting aural world to the image
                   or one that contradicts it. Keep in mind how music was recorded
                   and manufactured and who is listening to specific styles and genres
                   of music. The cue should be no longer than thirty seconds.

Critical response
- What manipulation of time is present?
- Is there a story being told?
- Does it complement or juxtapose the visual?
- Is it in the appropriate genre, time period, or style?
- Is the appropriate technology highlighted?
- What mood or emotion is evoked?
- Are the technological sound aspects represented?

- What tools in your DAW were effective to create the cue?
- What tools from your toolbox were used?
- What is your intention? Was it conveyed to the listeners?

Music 1900–1920

Early Jazz and Ragtime

- Originated at the beginning of the twentieth century in African American communities in the Southern United States.
- Influenced by African and European music traditions.
- Ragtime was a popular Jazz style in the early twentieth century.

Popular ragtime musicians:

- Ernest Hogan
- Vess Ossman
- William H. Krell
- Scott Joplin
- W.C. Handy

Orchestral
In the early twentieth century, symphonies, orchestras, concertos, and string quartets, were a continuation of the Romantic style. They were, however, larger, better funded, and better trained.

Composers

- Ralph Vaughan Williams
- Claude Debussy
- Giacomo Puccini

    ○ *Tosca* (1900)

    ○ *Madama Butterfly* (1904)

During this period the First World War took place. With any advent of war in a society, music plays a large function in both support and escape. The songs from the First World War enhanced the beginning of popular music that was no longer orchestrated or commissioned. This was aided by the publishing of sheet music, which was first seen between the late nineteenth century and early twentieth century. The pianoforte was present in the homes of those who could afford the instrument, and this boosted the sales of sheet music.

Popular Songs Sung by the Soldiers of the First World War
"Pack Up Your Troubles in Your Old Kit Bag"
"Keep the Home Fires Burning"
"It's a Long Way to Tipperary"
"If You Were the Only Girl in the World"
"Oh! It's a Lovely War"
"I Wonder Who's Kissing Her Now"
"Lorraine My Beautiful Alsace Lorraine"
"Roses of Picardy"
"Over There"
"For Me and My Girl"
"Daisy Bell"
"When this Lousy War is Over"
"Old Gallipoli's a Wonderful Place"

1900–1920 History of Recorded Music

In the early 1900s, E.R. Johnson trademarks His Master's Voice (HMV), and Berliner and Johnson together create the Victor Talking Machine Co. The method of reproduction moves from the metal etched process back to a thick wax coating. This leads to rival companies almost destroying the recording industry because of possible patent infringement.

Opera and classical music is recorded onto twelve-inch single sided discs, forty of them in the case of Verdi's *Enani* (released by HMV Italiana). The Victor Company's Victrola comes into the public market and Victrola becomes the popular term for phonograph.

With the invention of the diode thermionic valve and triode, the possibility of electrical recording is now possible, although it is in an experimental stage. Edison continues to use the cylinder machine but the disc is strong competition; and with the first jazz releases using the cylinder technique to capture its sound, it helps to stave off the end of cylinder use. Precision clockwork gramophone motors commence with manufacturing by the British Crown Jewelers.

The first million-selling disc is Paul Whiteman and His Orchestra's *The Japanese Sandman* and *Whispering*. This begins the popularity of owning discs, which boosts the industry throughout the decade.

EXERCISES

| 1900–1920 | Special Ingredients—Drone, Ambience, and Tension |

1900–1920 Special Ingredients—Drone, Ambience, and Tension
Find an image of the time period that evokes an emotional mood or response. Take the listener on a journey that expresses the underlying current of the emotional space the visual is expressing. Remember to use abstraction, themes, repetition, punctuations, dynamics, and manipulation of time to aid in the support of the visual expression. The cue should be no longer than thirty seconds.

Critical response

- What elements of drone, ambience, or tension are used?
- Is there a story being told?
- Does it complement or juxtapose the visual?
- What mood or emotion is evoked?
- Is it in the appropriate genre, time period, or style?
- Does the cue speak to the appropriate aural subgroup?
- Are the technological sound aspects represented?
- What tools in your DAW were effective to create the cue?
- What tools from your toolbox were used?
- What is your intention? Was it conveyed to the listeners?

Music 1920–1940

Jazz

Jazz had a reputation of being immoral, as older generations saw it as a threat to old values in culture. This theme of generational judgment continues through time in regards to popular music.

Popular jazz artists:
Kid Ory (1886–1973)
Louis Armstrong (1901–1971)
Jelly Roll Morton (1890–1938)
Earl Hines (1930–1983)

Swing

Swing became popular in the 1930s. Swing bands usually featured soloists who would improvise a new melody over the arrangement.

Popular bandleaders:

Duke Ellington (1899–1974)
Benny Goodman (1909–1986)
Glenn Miller (1904–1944)

European jazz
The end of the First World War marked the start of European "jazz," influenced by Americans' love of jazz.

Popular groups:
Original Dixieland Jazz Band—came to England in 1919
Quintette du Hot Club de France—considered one of the most significant continental jazz group in Europe, founded in France in 1934

Broadway
You can see the influence of jazz on Broadway musicals as well. And moving away from vaudeville, theatre musicals gave composers a place to create full stories with music. These were very popular, and Broadway music, such as the song "Summertime" from *Porgy and Bess*, would find itself back in the jazz canon with a different interpretation.

Popular shows:
Porgy and Bess—George Gershwin, 1935
Show Boat—music by Edna Ferber, lyrics by Oscar Hammerstein II, 1927

Orchestral
Jazz had a great influence on orchestral music during this period.
    Paul Whiteman (1890–1967)—commissioned Gershwin's Rhapsody in Blue to play in his orchestra

Neoclassicism

- A style of music popular between the two world wars
- Influenced by music of the eighteenth century, Baroque, and Classical periods
- Seen as a reaction against Romanticism

Igor Stravinsky—Russian composer who made neoclassicism popular in the 1920s:
Symphonie de Psaumes (1930)
Pulcinella (1920)
Octet (1923)

Modernism
This style of classical music is characterized by a desire for progress and science, surrealism, anti-romanticism, political advocacy, general intellectualism, and breaking with the past or common practice.

Arnold Schoenberg—German composer who developed the twelve-tone technique of composition in 1921:

Pierrot Lunaire (1912)

Third String Quartet (1927)

A Survivor from Warsaw (1947)

American Folk Music

Folk music has no nameable origin. It is more of a tradition than entertainment. There are folk songs that date so far back that they are considered oral histories. In America, songs by traditional folksingers such as Leadbelly and Woody Guthrie tell the sort of stories that often don't appear in history books.

From its origin, folk music has been the music of the working class. It is community-focused and has rarely had commercial success. It is something anyone can understand and in which everyone is welcome to participate. Folk songs range in subject matter from work, war, economic hardship, and civil rights. Of course, there are also songs of nonsense, satire, and love, but its focus was more political.

From the onset of American history, folk music appears at times when people need it most. The earliest folk songs rose from slave fields as spirituals: "Down by the Riverside," "We Shall Overcome," etc. These are songs about struggle and hardship, but are also to inspire hope. They come from the need of the worker to know there was more to the world than the hardships of the time.

Music of the Great Depression

Woody Guthrie—"This Land Is Your Land"

Pete Seeger—"Which Side Are You On?"

Henry Warren—"Forgotten Man"

Aaron Copland—"Fanfare for the Common Man"

1920–1940 History of Recorded Music

In 1922 both Belgium and France apply for a French patent, as England also begins developing a system for constant linear speed recording. While the popularity of live radio, the recording industry begins to dip economically, Victor and Columbia release the first electrical recordings in the United States. These first recordings are successful and all other recording companies begin to release their own. HMV releases their first electrically recorded symphony.

In Chicago, Bartlett Jones is granted a US patent for stereo recording by using a dummy head to simulate how people hear. The most popular talking movie, *The Jazz Singer* is released in 1927, although it is not the first movie with sound.

Companies begin to shift in 1928 as The Radio Corporation of America (RCA) procures the Victor Talking Machine Company, and HMV and Columbia

Graphophone Co. join to form Electrical and Musical Industries (EMI). In 1931 Edison dies at the age of 84, and EMI receives a patent for a technique that is the basis for present-day stereo recording.

From 1930 to 1940, the manufacturing of magnetic tape is introduced into the recording industry. BASF supplies 50,000 metres of recording tape for large-scale experiments by AEG, who gives the first demonstration to the public at the Berlin Funkausttellung.

The first recording of a full symphony orchestra is recorded by BASF engineers using a Magnetophon. It is Mozart's *Symphony No. 39* with the London Philharmonic Orchestra conducted by Sir Thomas Beecham, and it is still in existence today.

In 1938 experiments begin to help solve issues of recording multi-track optically and magnetically onto 35mm film stock.

EXERCISES

1920–1940   Special Ingredient—Dynamics and Punctuation
                 Choose an image of the time period that evokes a dynamic shift in theme, emotion, or event. Remember to use the other tools in your toolbox to help support the visual with a rich aural soundscape.
                 The cue should be no longer than thirty seconds and show a clear increase, punctuation, and decrease to dynamics.

Critical response
- What dynamics are present?
- Is there a story being told?
- Does it complement or juxtapose the visual?
- Is it in the appropriate genre, time period, or style?
- What mood or emotion is evoked?
- Are the technological sound aspects represented?
- What tools in your DAW were effective to create the cue?
- What tools from your toolbox were used?
- What is your intention? Was it conveyed to the listeners?

Music 1940–1960

1940s
This period contained the Second World War, and again music was used for nationalism, support, or escapism of the war.

Rock and Roll

Strands of American music combined to form what would eventually be coined "rock and roll." The style had developed by 1949, and quickly became popular nationwide. It really took off in popularity in the 1950s. This rock style incorporated an electric guitar version of the Chicago blues, jazz, country, folk, swing, as well as other types of music, and was greatly influenced by bebop jazz and boogie-woogie.

Jazz

At the beginning of the decade, big bands dominated popular music. It was mostly associated with the cinema of the time and the war. Many would go out to escape their lives and listen to jazz publicly. It was widely accepted by all races during this time.

Bandleaders:
Glenn Miller, Tommy Dorsey, Duke Ellington, Benny Goodman

Eventually, many of the singers with the big bands struck out on their own.

Singers:
Bing Crosby, Frank Sinatra, Ella Fitzgerald, Billie Holiday

Bebop

Bebop and rhythm and blues grew out of the big band era toward the end of the decade. Beginning in New York City, it contained complex harmonies and chord changes, dissonance, syncopation, and edgier improvisation. It soon became associated with the civil rights movement and other African American social movements.

Musicians:
Charlie Parker, Thelonius Monk, Dexter Gordon, Miles Davis, John Coltrane
Bebop underwent numerous evolutions in the 1950s, and styles like soul jazz, cool jazz and hard bop emerged from it.

Cool Jazz

After Miles Davis' *Birth of the Cool* (1948), a smoother form of jazz based on Lester Young's swing tenor sound developed.

Musicians:
Chet Baker, Dave Brubeck, Stan Getz, Paul Desmond, Gerry Mulligan, Claude Thornhill

Cajun Music

The 1940s saw a return to the roots of Cajun music. The earliest traditional Cajun music began before the twentieth century in Louisiana, but this time marked the beginning of what would be known as the Cajun Renaissance, which came to fruition in the 1960s.

Musicians:
Iry LeJeune, Nathan Abshire, Lawrence Walker, Aldus Roger

Zydeco
Clifton Chenier, a Creole, began playing this updated form of French music. Zydeco was briefly popular among some mainstream listeners during the 1950s.

Musicians:
Boozoo Chavis, Queen Ida, Rockin' Dopsie, Rockin' Sidney

Classical
Because Classical composers tend to evoke the emotional zeitgeist of an era, European composers added jazz tonalities and introduced Classical dissonance to their music. American-born composers remained more traditional and evoked nationalism.

European composers:
Bela Bartok, Arnold Schoenberg, Paul Hindemith, Kurt Weill, Nadia Boulanger

American composers:
Aaron Copland wrote *Rodeo* (1942) and *Appalachian Spring* (1944).
William Schuman wrote his symphonies *#3* (1941) through *#7* (1949).

Radio was a lifeline for Americans in the 1940s, especially during wartime, providing news, music and entertainment, much like television today. Radio programming included soap operas, quiz shows, mystery stories, children's hours, fine drama, and sports. Kate Smith and Arthur Godfrey were popular radio hosts. Radio faded in popularity as television became prominent. And many of the popular radio shows transferred onto TV.

1950s
This decade saw the birth of rock and roll, with Bill Haley's *Rock Around the Clock* becoming popular in 1955.

The feel-good innocence of a lot of this decade's music comes directly on the heels of post-war optimism in America. The young people of the time hadn't struggled through the war years. They were looking for something more exciting.

Some of the music associated with the 1950s was actually recorded in the 1960s. For example, "Blue Moon" by the Marcels, as well as the "girl groups," are from the 1960s. When you look at the actual dates, musically the styles tend to break off mid-decade. Songs from 1955–1964 are very much alike. Things don't change much until the British musical invasion of the United States and the US military invasion of Vietnam, which includes the period of 1964–1974.

Rock and roll, rhythm and blues, love songs, jazz (first Newport Festival), calypso (Harry Belafonte), and musicals were all popular. The music was relatively apolitical. Record sales rather than airplay began to determine the popularity of a song.

Hit makers:
Patti Page, Nat King Cole, Teresa Brewer, Tony Bennett, Doris Day, Eddie Fisher, Frankie Laine, Dean Martin, Peggy Lee

Popular groups:
The Platters, Les Paul and Mary Ford, Ames Brothers, Four Aces, Buddy Holly

In 1956, Elvis became the first rock star with hits "Don't Be Cruel," "Heartbreak Hotel," "All Shook Up," and "Can't Help Falling in Love." Black recording artists Chuck Berry ("Johnny Be Good") and Fats Domino ("I'm Walking") became rock and roll stars overnight.

American Bandstand became a venue for the musicians and singers of the time to showcase themselves on television. The show had an audience of 20 million teenagers and 20 million adults.

Stars that were discovered on American Bandstand:
Bobby Darin, Frankie Avalon, Connie Francis, Fabian

The Grand Ole Opry and Your Hit Parade are popular TV shows, sponsored by Lucky Strike cigarettes. This allowed the introduction of new music to the viewing audience.

Broadway and movie musicals played an important part during this decade.

Broadway musicals:
Guys and Dolls — Frank Loesserth
The King and I — Rodgers and Hammerstein II
The Pajama Game — Adler and Ross
Bye Bye Birdie — Strouse and Stewart
My Fair Lady — Lerner and Lowe
West Side Story — Bernstein and Sondheim
Gigi — Lerner and Lowe
The Sound of Music — Rodgers and Hammerstein II

1940–1960 History of Recorded Music

In 1941 the recording sessions for the soundtrack of Walt Disney's Fantasia, conducted by Leopold Stokowski, are hailed as a technical and artistic triumph. Glenn Miller sells over a million copies of "Chattanooga Choo Choo" and is awarded the first ever gold disc.

The FM radio frequency spectrum, which ranged between 42 and 50 MHz, is changed to between 88 and 108 MHz by the Federal Communications Commission. This wider range helps avoid interference and more radio stations emerge.

Polyvinylchloride (PVC) is developed by the oil industry and is suitable for making gramophone records and recording tape with low surface noise. This new substance makes it possible to create pressings of microgroove long-playing records, and the Columbia Broadcasting System team develops this further.

By 1949 the 10-inch (or 12-inch) records at 33 1/3 rpm are available for purchase. RCA then releases the first 7-inch 45rpm microgroove disc to the market. And because the first transistor is demonstrated creating a revolution in recording equipment design and performance parameters, popularity of playing and recording music extends to the domestic market. All of the advances above lead to the record companies adopting new standards to improve sound quality in 1950, and the production of the 78rpm shellac disc begins to be discontinued.

The link between film and sound continues as Cinerama presents mult-track replay to the public. This increases the excitement in popularity and leads to more research. What follows is the possibility of recording right-hand and left-hand signals simultaneously on separate tracks on quarter-inch magnetic tape. Because of this, stereo LPs are available. And when records are released, they are issued in both monaural (mono) and stereophonic (stereo) versions.

EXERCISES

1940–1960   Special Ingredient—Thematic Cohesion
                   Find an image of the time period that allows you to make thematic
                   parallels that are consistent in their agreement. Take the listener
                   on a journey that shows cohesion of all the elements used in
                   complete support of the visual. Remember to use abstraction,
                   themes, repetition, punctuations, dynamics, manipulation of
                   time, or a combination of these. Take note of the possibilities in
                   stereophonic sound, and the specific genres that were using it
                   in their recorded music. The cue should be no longer than thirty
                   seconds.

Critical response
- What are the themes present?
- Is there a story being told?
- Does it complement the visual?
- Are the themes cohesive?
- Is it in the appropriate genre, time period, or style?
- What mood or emotion is evoked?
- Does it speak to the appropriate aural subgroup?
- Are the technological sound aspects represented?
- What tools in your DAW were effective to create the cue?
- What tools from your toolbox were used?
- What is your intention? Was it conveyed to the listeners?

Music 1960–1980

In the late 1960s and early 1970s, rock music developed different subgenres. Teenagers were in control of what was popular based on radio play and record sales. The British Invasion in 1964, when the Beatles came to America, marked a strong shift in what what was popular in the music industry.

Beat

Beat groups characteristically had simple guitar-dominated line-ups, with vocal harmonies and catchy tunes. Beat music uses driving rhythms, which the bands adopted from their rhythm and blues and soul music influences.

- Beat music is a pop music genre that developed in the UK in the early 1960s.
- Also known as Merseybeat, it originated around the Merseyside area of Liverpool.
- Beat music is a fusion of rock and roll, doo-wop, skiffle, rhythm and blues, and soul.

Popular beat acts:

- The Beatles
- The Searchers
- Gerry and the Pacemakers
- Cilla Black

Rock

- Rock music is a loosely defined genre of popular music that developed during and after the 1960s.
- It has its roots in 1940s and 1950s rock and roll and rockabilly, rhythm and blues, country music, folk music, jazz, and classical music.
- The typical configuration of a rock group is a quartet consisting of an electric guitarist, lead singer, bass guitarist, and a drummer. Additional electric and acoustic guitars were eventually added, as were other instruments, such as the organ or piano.

American Folk Rock

The folk scene that arose in the United States and Canada in the mid 1960s was made up of folk music lovers who liked acoustic instruments, traditional songs, and blues music. The music usually contained a socially progressive message.

Popular artists:

- Woody Guthrie—considered the pioneer of early folk
- Bob Dylan—best known as a protest singer for the civil rights movement and Vietnam War:
  - "Blowin' in the Wind" (1962)
  - "The Times They Are a-Changin" (1964)

Psychedelic Rock

Psychedelic rock is a style of rock music that is inspired or influenced by psychedelic culture.

- It attempts to replicate the mind-altering experiences of hallucinogenic drugs.
- The first use of the term "psychedelic" in popular music is by the group The Holy Modal Rounders in 1964, in the song "Hesitation Blues."

Popular bands:

- Jefferson Airplane
- Grateful Dead
- Big Brother & the Holding Company
- The Beatles with the release of their album *Sgt. Pepper's Lonely Hearts Club Band*
- The Rolling Stones with the release of their album *Their Satanic Majesties Request*

Progressive Rock

- Progressive rock came into most widespread use around the mid-1970s.
- Progressive rock bands push rock's technical and compositional boundaries by moving past the standard rock-song structure. Bands leave the formulaic three-minute rock songs to venture into longer, increasingly sophisticated songs and chord structures.
- Progressive rock often incorporates elements from classical, jazz, and world music and experimented with full orchestration.

Popular bands:

- Pink Floyd

- The Moody Blues
- Procol Harum

Hard Rock and Heavy Metal

This subgenre is marked with highly amplified, guitar-driven hard rock with aggressive vocals.

Popular bands:

- AC/DC
- Grand Funk Railroad
- Led Zeppelin
- Deep Purple
- Queen
- Alice Cooper
- Judas Priest
- Aerosmith
- Black Sabbath
- Kiss

Punk Rock

- Punk rock developed between 1974 and 1976 in the US, the UK, and Australia.
- Punk rock bands typically create short songs that are fast, and hard-edged. They contain stripped-down instrumentation, with often political, anti-establishment lyrics.
- Punk embraces a "do it yourself" ethic, with many bands self-producing their recordings and distributing them through informal channels.

Popular bands:

- The Ramones
- The Sex Pistols
- The Clash
- Patti Smith

Motown

Motown Records is a record label originally based in Detroit, Michigan. Founded by Berry Gordy, Jr. on January 12, 1959, as Tamla Records, the company was incorporated as Motown Record Corporation on April 14, 1960. The name, derived from the words "motor" and "town," is also a nickname for Detroit.

Motown played an important role in the racial integration of popular music, as it was the first record label owned by an African American. Its primary feature was to showcase African American artists who achieved crossover success. In the 1960s, Motown was the most successful proponent of what came to be known as the Motown Sound, a style of soul music with a distinct pop influence.

In addition to the songwriting prowess of the writers and producers, one of the major factors in the widespread appeal of Motown's music was the use of a highly select and tight-knit group of studio musicians. They were collectively known as the "Funk Brothers," and they recorded the band tracks of the Motown songs.

Studio musicians of the Motown Sound:

Keyboardists:
Earl Van Dyke
Johnny Griffith
Joe Hunter

Guitarists:
Joe Messina
Robert White
Eddie Willis

Bassists:
James Jamerson
Bob Babbitt

Percussionists:
Eddie "Bongo" Brown
Jack Ashford

Drummers:
Benny Benjamin
Uriel Jones
Richard "Pistol" Allen

The story of the band's career and work is told in the 2002 documentary film *Standing in the Shadows of Motown*. Much of the Motown Sound also came from overdubbing and duplicating instrumentation. Motown songs regularly featured two drummers, either overdubbed or in unison, as well as three or four guitar lines.

Disco

- Disco is a genre of dance music that originated in and was initially popular among African American, gay, and Hispanic communities in the United States in the late 1960s.

- In 1974, New York City's WPIX-FM premiered the first disco radio show.

- Musical influences include funk and soul music.

Popular disco artists:
Bee Gees, Diana Ross, Donna Summer, The Jackson 5, Sister Sledge, ABBA, Village People

Funk

African American musicians blended soul music, jazz, and rhythm and blues into a rhythmic, danceable new form of music. Funk highlights a strong rhythmic groove of electric bass and drums as it de-emphasizes melody and harmony. Unlike rhythm and blues and soul, which feature many chord changes, funk songs are often based on an extended vamp on a single chord.

Like much African-inspired music, funk consists of a complex groove with rhythm instruments such as electric guitar, electric bass, Hammond organ, and drums. Funk bands also usually have a horn section with several saxophones, trumpets, and in some cases, a trombone. The horn section periodically plays the "hits" of punctuation in the rhythm.

Funk performers:
James Brown, Sly and the Family Stone, George Clinton, Parliament-Funkadelic, Curtis Mayfield, The Meters, Bootsy Collins

Funk bands:
Earth, Wind & Fire, Eric Burdon & War, Tower of Power, Average White Band, The Ohio Players, The Commodores, Kool & the Gang, Cameo

Funk music was a major influence on the development of 1970s disco music. And funk samples were present in most styles of house music and early hip-hop music.

Classical Music

Composers at this time were coming from a dissonant expression into an experimental phase. And minimalism was the reaction to all the chaos that came previously. Since recording techniques were becoming accessible, studios were willing to allow artists to experiment with cutting showing the process. Music at this time felt like it was meant to be experienced.

Minimalism

- Originated in America as experimental classical music
- Any music that works with limited or minimal materials
- Also known as "process music"—music that arises from a process, and more specifically, music that makes that process audible
- Most often heard in constant harmony

Popular artists:
John Adams, Wavemaker, Philip Glass, Steve Reich

Karlheinz Stockhausen—a German composer widely acknowledged as one of the most important, but also controversial, composers of the twentieth and early twenty-first centuries. He is known for his groundbreaking work in electronic music, aleatory (controlled chance) in serial composition, and musical spatialization.

1960–1980 History of Recorded Music

Mono has been almost completely replaced by stereo recording and studios upgrade their equipment with multi-track tape recorders. What began as two-track or three-track recording, could now extend from the one-inch eight-track tape to the two-inch sixteen-track tape. And in 1963 Philips introduces the Musicassette at the Berlin Funkausttellung.

Two years later, pre-recorded Musicassettes are released to the public. And although they did not rise in popularity yet, they were simple to use. Philips does not protect its proprietary technology and allows other companies to license its use. Because of that, pre-recorded eight-track cartridges are sold for the automobile market. For the first time, the public could hear pre-recorded music while driving.

Ray Dolby introduces the Dolby Noise Reduction (DNR) System for film sound engineers, who have been using sophisticated technology to achieve noise reduction. This then becomes industry standard in recording studios as well.

The Phillips compact cassette becomes the standard format for tape recording and by 1968 approximately eighty-five different manufacturers sell over 2.4 million cassette players worldwide. Four-channel records (quadrophonic) are available to the public, but confusion over incompatible systems and the weak economic climate prove it to be an unenthusiastic venture.

In 1977, 100 years after Edison's idea that every home would contain a talking machine, the average home has two or three. Cassette tape sales accelerate and it begins to challenge the disc as a playback format. Record companies begin releasing recordings in both disc and cassette format. This leads to Sony developing the Soundabout cassette player (later renamed the Walkman), whose innovative headphones are capable of producing quality sound with the smallest signal from the amplifier. Self-powered by batteries, this made pre-recorded music, light and portable.

In 1978, the development of the compact disc by Philips Industries is announced. And as recording becomes a more complicated process, computer memory is brought into the studio.

EXERCISES

1960–1980   Special Ingredient—Thematic Antithesis
                   Find an image of the time period taking into account what is, and is
                   not, harmonious in the theme or action. You can either take the listener
                   on a journey that shows lack of cohesion in the elements of the visual,
                   or the sound can act in complete antithesis to the visual. Remember
                   to use abstraction, themes, repetition, punctuations, dynamics,
                   manipulation of time, or a combination of these. Noise reduction
                   has played a large role in the sound quality of recorded music. And
                   remember to associate the correct genre to the subgroup that would
                   listen to it. The cue should be no longer than thirty seconds.

Critical response
- What are the themes present?
- Is there a story being told?
- Does it juxtapose the visual or is the sound in contrast to itself?
- Is it in the appropriate genre, time period, or style?
- What mood or emotion is evoked?
- Does it speak to the appropriate aural subgroup?
- Are the technological sound aspects represented?
- What tools in your DAW were effective to create the cue?
- What tools from your toolbox were used?
- What is your intention? Was it conveyed to the listeners?

Music 1980–2000

Now is when music starts to really fracture into many different subgenres based on the reaction to other genres that preceded them. I cannot fully explain here the depth you can achieve when you start to acknowledge the music of this time. I will lightly touch on styles that stand out for me as someone who lived through this period.

To start with I want to break down roughly the beats per minute (bpm) and how music genres lived within this metered time.

Dance and Urban bpm Breakdown

60–80 bpm—dub
80–130 bpm—ska
80–110 bpm—hip-hop
120 bpm—disco
110–130 bpm—house (128 bpm 2009)
125–150 bpm—trance
130–148 bpm—techno
144–190 bpm—jungle
190 bpm and up—no man's land because you are now doubling

Electronic music that permeates within this:
Breakbeat (big beat UK) 110–130 bpm
Garage (a subgenre of house) 130–150 bpm
Dubstep (a techno version of dub) 140–160 bpm

Techno

- Techno is a form of electronic dance music that emerged in Detroit during the mid to late 1980s.

- Though many styles of techno now exist, Detroit techno is seen as the foundation upon which a number of subgenres have been built.

- The initial take on techno arises from the melding of Eurocentric synthesizer-based music with various forms of African American music.

- Add to this the influence of futuristic and fictional themes that were relevant to life in American late-capitalist society.

- Juan Atkins, an American musician, is widely credited as the originator of techno music.

Rap and Hip-Hop

Hip-hop started in the Bronx and Brooklyn boroughs of New York in the 1970s. Records were easily accessible to the public and featured youths rapping over others' music. Both rapping and breakdancing were ways of battling it out on the street. The groups were in teams called "crews" or "gangs" of rappers.

For me, in my central New York suburban neighborhood, my first introduction to rap was "Rapper's Delight" by The Sugarhill Gang. It was the first rap single to get into the top 40 Billboard chart. It uses the track "Good Times" by Chic as its foundation. The Sugarhill Gang never had another US hit, but they did release a few songs that were popular in Europe.

In the early 1980s, after Blondie's "Rapture" was a hit on the radio, rap became mainstream and branched out to rapping over original music. For example, one of the biggest developments for rap music in the 1980s was the use of the sample and sampler. And the Akai MPC60 is still used in some hip-hop today, although upgraded.

Boasting of being cool (Big Daddy Kane, UTFO, and MC Shan) slowly starts to meld into a tougher persona (LL Cool J, Run-DMC, and Ice-T), which then builds to a more violent message (Ice-T, NWA, Tim Dog, and Boogie Down Productions).

From this point rap generates what we now know as gangsta rap. And it remains popular from 1986 to 1992.

As a reaction to this, groups form to combat the more negative associations with rap: The Native Tongues, De La Soul, A Tribe Called Quest, the Jungle Brothers, Queen Latifah, Monie Love.

Ironically, a group not involved in any of this becomes the biggest-selling rap group—the Beastie Boys. They are three white college students at New York University, that go out on the road as the opening act of Run-DMC because they share the same producer, and by the end of the tour they are headlining. Their *Licensed to Ill* becomes the biggest-selling rap album of that time.

Because of this, others came in (Vanilla Ice, MC Hammer) to become the more stylized, entertainment version of hip-hop. This idea of feeling as though rap is selling out makes the gangsta rappers go harder.

Through the rest of the 1990s, Dr. Dre and Eminem characterize the popularized version of gangsta rap, and Native Tongues break up. Then ensues the East/West Coast war about who's tougher in the gangsta rap scene.

After the death of Tupac in 1996, and Biggie Smalls in 1997, rap slowly goes into commercial decline. Hip-hop acts are still successful but they seem to be similar permutations of the same aesthetic, with the exception of a few alternative groups such as Outkast.

Teen Pop
1980s

- Teen pop is a subgenre of pop music that is marketed and oriented toward teenagers.

- Teen pop covers genres and styles such as pop, dance, and rock.

- The first major wave of teen pop occurs in the mid to late 1980s, with artists such as Debbie Gibson, Tiffany, and New Kids on the Block.

1990s

- In the early 1990s, teen pop still dominated the charts until grunge music crossed over into the mainstream in North America by 1991.

- Teen pop remained popular in the UK, with acts including the boy band Take That. They remained popular until the mid-1990s when Britpop became the next major wave in the UK, eclipsing the style in a similar manner to how grunge did in North America.

- In 1996, the girl group Spice Girls release their single "Wannabe," which made them major pop stars in the UK, as well as in the United States the following year. In their wake, other teen pop groups came into prominence, including Hanson, the Backstreet Boys, *NSYNC, and All Saints. Other teen bands, mostly popular in the United States in the late 1990s, include pop princesses such as Britney Spears, Christina Aguilera, Mandy Moore, and Jessica Simpson. Clean-cut boy bands such as the Backstreet Boys and *NSYNC mirror the female success.

- The demise of late 1990s teen pop was due to several factors: promotional oversaturation of teen pop music in 2000 and 2001; the public's changing attitude toward it, deeming teen pop as inauthentic and corporate-produced; and the transition of the preteen and teenage fan base of these teen pop artists during 1997–1999 to young adulthood (and the accompanying changes in musical interests).

New Wave

In the late 1970s there was punk rock, which was the direct reaction to all that was considered the leftover rock of the 1960s, which was the soft rock of the 1970s. In other words, it's a direct reaction to complacency. Punk rock is popular from 1976 to 1980, and out of that comes people who want to perform modern forms of music without being aggressive, and who wish to incorporate other styles of music.

Technology introduces the synthesizer, which comes into mass usage. This starts a large genre, which is everything that is not punk or dinosaur rock, called new wave. New wave has many different subgenres:

- Synth pop (Human League, Thompson Twins, Flock of Seagulls)—uses synthesizers and is somewhat dance oriented.

- Post-punk (Gang of Four, Echo and the Bunnymen, Siouxsie and the Banshees)—has a rock aesthetic. Guitars are less aggressive, and music is more broken down.

- Goth (Bauhaus, The Cure, Sisters of Mercy)—known for gloomy, dark lyrics and the fashion statement of wearing all-black with white make-up.

With the emergence of MTV (Music Television), bands became more theatrical in their approach so they could become more popular using a video image. It's not that the music was groundbreaking; their image is what they became known for. Because of their good looks, bands such as Adam and the Ants, Duran Duran, Spandau Ballet, and Culture Club became teen pop, even though that was not their goal.

The popularity and mass audience of MTV creates a generation of people that now see starting a band as totally accessible. What began to take place was that a lot of college and high-school students started their own bands, creating music that was initially called college rock. It slowly became referred to as progressive rock before finally, in the late 1980s, being termed alternative rock.

The most notable rock band from that time, which starts off the decade with the release of album *Boy*, is U2. They hail from Ireland and can be categorized as rock, alternative rock, and post-punk rock. They are still very active today. U2 has released thirteen studio albums (six of those in the 1980s and 1990s) and are one of the world's best-selling music artists of all time, having sold more than 170 million records worldwide.

The bands that at that time typified alternative music include R.E.M., Let's Active, and the B-52s. Athens, Georgia is where this subgenre started to take root. As synth pop and good-looking guys on TV became the new mainstream, the reaction of these bands was to not focus on looks and to create music that does not sound synth-poppy. The lyrics were mumbled, and the guitars had a jangly sound.

Also in the late 1980s to the mid-1990s, hair metal began to share the airwaves (Ratt, Billy Squier, Loverboy, Def Leppard).

Grunge

Grunge developed out of Seattle, Washington, which is isolated in many ways from a lot of touring musicians because it took too long to travel there. Local musicians took up playing in bands and created this hybrid of punk and heavy metal.

Suddenly, in 1991 Nirvana put out *Nevermind*. And it's just the right combination of punk rock of the 1970s and jangly guitars of the 1980s, with a catchy hook. It completely overtakes all the hair metal and synth pop of the 1980s. And so begins the rise of the next wave of alternative music (Nirvana, Pearl Jam, Stone Temple Pilots).

Bands that have lived in complete obscurity emerge. And in 1991 comes Lollapalooza as Jane's Addiction's farewell tour. It becomes a clearinghouse of all the bands playing alternative music and generates the alternative culture of the 1990s (Smashing Pumpkins, Hole, Nine Inch Nails).

Shoegaze

- Shoegaze is a subgenre of alternative rock that emerged from the UK in the late 1980s, which grew from bands including the Cocteau Twins.

- It lasted until the mid 1990s, reaching its critical peak in 1990 and 1991.

- The British music press names this style "shoegazing" because the musicians in these bands maintain a motionless persona during live performances; they stood on stage and stared at their effects pedals or the floor.

- The shoegaze sound is typified by significant use of guitar effects, and indistinguishable vocal melodies that blend into the creative noise of the guitars.

- Few shoegaze bands were dynamic performers or interesting interviewees, which prevented them from breaking through into markets in the United States.

- In the 1990s, shoegaze groups were pushed aside by the American grunge movement.

- My Bloody Valentine's 1991 album *Loveless* is often considered the pinnacle of shoegaze.

Indie Rock

Indie rock is a reaction to the grunge and alternative music of the 1990s. Lollapalooza spun out and was temporarily over, Kurt Cobain was dead, and bands had retreated or gotten into drugs. Many people viewed the commercialization of alternative music as something of which they wanted no part.

Out of that grew indie rock, which is a loose term that can encapsulate many different artists. It includes a wide variety of bands attempting to make music that is not traditionally rock oriented. It is sparser and deliberately not commercial sounding. There is no goal of mass success.

- It primarily refers to rock musicians that are or were unsigned, or have signed to independent record labels, rather than major record labels.

- Indie rock artists place a premium on maintaining complete control of their music and careers, releasing albums on independent record labels (sometimes their own) and relying on touring, word of mouth, and airplay on independent or college radio stations for promotion.

Math Rock and Post-Rock

Tiny factions, but their overarching goal was to create interesting music that is not for mass consumption.

1980s

- UK: indie music charts have been compiled since the early 1980s. Initially, the charts featured bands that emerged with a form of guitar-

based alternative rock, particularly artists such as Aztec Camera and
Orange Juice.

- Some definitive British indie rock bands of the 1980s were The Smiths,
The Stone Roses, and The Jesus and Mary Chain, whose music directly
influenced 1990s alternative rock movements such as shoegaze and
Britpop.

- United States: music commonly regarded as indie rock is descended
from an alternative rock scene largely influenced by the movements of
the 1970s and early 1980s and their DIY ethic.

- The late 1980s band the Pixies is said to be the main influence in 1990s
indie rock.

1990s

- In the 1990s, as the alternative genre became commercialized as
mainstream success and the meaning of the label "alternative" changed
away from its original, more counter-cultural meaning, the term
indie rock was used to refer to the bands and genres that remained
underground.

- A few of the defining artists of 1990s indie rock were Elliott Smith,
Guided by Voices, Pavement, Sebadoh, The Grifters, Liz Phair, The
Elephant 6 Recording Co., Modest Mouse, and others, who placed
a premium on rough recording techniques, ironic detachment, and
disinterest in selling out to the mainstream alternative rock scene.

Britpop
Britpop is a subgenre of alternative rock that originated in the UK.

- Britpop emerged from the British independent music scene of the early
1990s and is characterized by bands influenced by British guitar pop
music of the 1960s and 1970s.

- Britpop groups brought British alternative rock into the mainstream.

- The movement developed as a reaction against various musical and
cultural trends in the late 1980s and early 1990s, particularly the grunge
phenomenon from the United States.

- In the wake of the musical invasion into the UK of American grunge
bands (in particular Nirvana), new British groups such as Suede and
Blur launched the movement by positioning themselves as an opposing
musical force. Others including Oasis, Pulp, Supergrass, and Elastica
soon joined these bands in the genre.

- Britpop bands relied on catchy hooks and wrote lyrics that were meant to be relevant to British young people of their own generation.

- Britpop bands conversely denounced grunge as irrelevant and having nothing to say about their lives.

- The emphasis on British reference points made it difficult for the genre to achieve success in the United States.

Classical Music

Classical music moves from minimalism to the postminimalism and totalism. These two styles paralleled each other in their emergence.

Postminimalism

- Postminimalism refers to works influenced by minimalist music

- Postminimalism was a main feature in many popular bands and artists including Kraftwerk, David Bowie, Brian Eno, and Neu!

Writer Kyle Gann has employed the term more strictly to connote the style that flourished in the 1980s and 1990s, which was characterized by the following:

- A steady pulse, usually continuing throughout a work or movement

- A diatonic pitch language, tonal in effect but avoiding traditional functional tonality

- A general evenness of dynamics, without strong climaxes or nuanced emotionalism

- An avoidance of obvious or linear formal design

Composers:
John Coolidge Adams, William Duckworth

Totalism

- Totalism is a term for a style of art music that arose in the 1980s and 1990s as a developing response to minimalism. It paralleled postminimalism.

- In the early 1980s, many young composers began writing music within the static confines of minimalism, but they were using greater rhythmic complexity, often with two or more tempos audible at once.

- The term totalist refers to the aims of the music. They were trying to have enough surface rhythmic energy to attract unsophisticated listeners, but also to contain enough background complexity to satisfy connoisseurs.

Composers:
Mikel Rouse, Michael Gordon, Trance, Kyle Gann

1980–2000 History of Recorded Music

In 1981 the Walkman II is available for public consumption and has 50 percent fewer moving parts. It becomes the most successful audio product of the post-war period. A new cable channel MTV begins transmitting video versions of popular songs and becomes essential for promotion of recordings. And research between Philips and Sony in Japan brings the compact disc (CD) system to the audio industry in order to produce a commercial digital playback record.

In 1982 *Thriller* by Michael Jackson sells 40 million copies worldwide and becomes the most successful product in the history of sound recording. And compact disc hardware and software, which launches from Japan and eventually the UK, is hailed as the most important development in recorded music. This establishes the CD as the finest music carrier available. And after slow initial sales, within the year 1986, 50 million discs are sold. This puts the sales of the CD above the LP for the first time in history.

Sony develops digital Audio Tape (DAT) in the United States. This uses the cassette format to record digitally with a smaller profile. To prevent digital copying, the DAT hardware manufacturers agree to install Serial Copy Management System (SCMS) in all equipment.

What follows are advancements in the CD and cassette formats. Compact Disc Interactive (CD-I) is marketed as an entertainment system to consumers. Based in CD-ROM (Read-Only Memory), CD-I systems play audio, film, and other media such as computer games and illustrated encyclopedias.

Philips has the Digital Compact Cassette (DOC), which is compatible with magnetic cassette equipment. But because they were unable to reach agreement over the format of digital recording technology, Sony introduces the MiniDisc (MD). This brings together the ease of recording with a Musicassette with reproduction quality of a CD. But even as all these new formats arrive onto the scene, it does not diminish the popularity of the CD.

In 1996 at the Consumer Electronics Show in Las Vegas, the first Digital Versatile Disc (DVD) is introduced. It is a faster CD with a larger capacity, capable of containing audio, video, and computer data.

Music piracy on the Internet, which uses the MP3 format, is looked at as a cult activity. Manufacturers begin to place watermarks that can not be heard onto CD albums in case they were uploaded onto the Internet. Specification for the Secure Digital Music Initiative (SDMI) is published, which aims to provide a legal alternative to music that has been pirated.

EXERCISES

1980–2000   Special Ingredient—Concrete vs. Abstract
Find an image of the time period looking beyond what the visual entails. The artwork need not be abstract. Take the listener on a journey of point of view through abstraction. Examples may include going into the mind of a character, or the overall impression of a public scene, or perhaps singling in on a visual aspect or character represented. The cue should be no longer than thirty seconds and have a clear catalyst that forces sound into abstraction. Students may choose to return to reality afterwards if it supports the visual.

Critical response
- Is there a story being told?
- Does the abstraction support the visual?
- Is it in the appropriate genre, time period, or style?
- What mood or emotion is evoked?
- Does it speak to the appropriate aural subgroup?
- Are the technological sound aspects represented?
- What tools in your DAW were effective to create the cue?
- What tools from your toolbox were used?
- What is your intention? Was it conveyed to the listeners?

Music 2000–2010

What you will see happening at the turn of the century is the simultaneous coexistence of many styles. Artists were looking for a new way to approach music, and they used the influence of past genres to create new ones. This time period saw a huge increase of different styles in music and this is mostly due to the ease with which music could be created and obtained globally. The human race's ability to hear any music we wished, at any time, changed our perspective of music and how we used it in our daily lives.

The amount of music was exploding across the globe. There is no way for me to capture it all here, so I will give some examples of the variances.

Hip-hop

- Hip-hop dominated popular music in the 2000s.

- Eminem is considered the biggest hip-hop act of the decade as well as the best-selling overall music artist.

Artists:
50 Cent, The Black Eyed Peas, Kanye West, Nas, Jay-Z, Missy Elliott, Ludacris

Alternative Hip-Hop
Throughout the 2000s, alternative hip-hop contained philosophical, positive, and complex lyrical subject matter, while denouncing materialism, fashion, and money. Branching out of slam poetry, this subgenre also includes a lot of spoken word.

Artists:
Mos Def, The Roots, Atmosphere, Aesop Rock, Common

Southern Hip-Hop
Artists:
Lil Jon, T.I., Flo Rida, Rich Boy, Rick Ross, Young Jeezy, Lil Wayne

Auto-Tune became popular by mid 2007, beginning with hip-hop artist T-Pain. It was used as an effect in songs rather than a major replacement of the standard human voice.

Rock
With the increasing popularity of hip-hop, rock experienced a diminished presence on mainstream music charts by the end of the decade. High-profile rock stations like K-Rock in New York City and WBCN in Boston changed their programming to other formats. New York City, which once was the leading market of rock, was reduced to only one modern rock station, 101.9 WRXP-FM.

Alternative Rock, Indie Rock, Garage Rock, and the Post-Punk Revival
A new group of bands, which drew inspiration from post-punk, and new wave, emerged into the mainstream. They were variously interpreted as part of a garage rock, post-punk, or new wave revival. These attempts to revive the elements from the 1980s and 1990s came from many different countries. Because of this, the bands cited diverse elements from traditional blues, through new wave, to grunge.

Detroit:
The Von Bondie, Electric Six, The Dirtbombs, The Detroit Cobras

New York:
Radio 4, Yeah Yeah Yeahs, The Rapture

Social networking sites emerge, such as MySpace and Purevolume. They enabled the amateur artist to promote their music. And because of the internet, many unsigned artists were discovered and listened to in alternative communities.

Two of the most successful bands from these scenes are The Strokes, who emerged from the New York club scene with their debut album *Is This It* (2001) and The White Stripes, from Detroit, with their third album *White Blood Cells* (2001).

Post-Grunge

After the first wave of post-grunge bands lost their popularity, a new sound emerged. They took post-grunge into the twenty-first century with commercial success, abandoning most of the angst and anger of the original movement. They wrote more conventional anthems, narratives and romantic songs.

Artists:
Puddle of Mudd, Foo Fighters, Creed (Christian rock influence)

Indie Rock

The rising popularity of internet radio led to high album sales for indie rock, despite little radio play. Bands including Modest Mouse and Fleet Foxes released albums that broke into the mainstream and gave indie rock recognition. MGMT, LCD Soundsystem, Grizzly Bear, and Vampire Weekend gained popularity around the world, including the United States.

Hard Rock and Heavy Metal

The popularity of metal music carried over from the bands of the late 1990s, such as Korn, Deftones, Limp Bizkit, Slipknot, and Coal Chamber. This evolved in the early 2000s with the similar genre, rap rock, bringing in a wave of new rock artists.

Artists:
System of a Down (alternative metal influence), Evanescence, Staind (post-grunge influence), Papa Roach (hard rock influence), Disturbed, Linkin Park (alternative rock influence), Limp Bizkit

Emo

Emo eventually broke into the mainstream in the 2000s after having been a reaction to the hardcore punk of the 1980s. The new emo had a greater appeal amongst adolescents than its earlier incarnations. Emo music in the 2000s is characterized as having confessional and expressive lyrics. It eventually became a term to describe the fashion or behavior of a culture that is shy, emotional, or sensitive.

Artists:
Jimmy Eat World, Good Charlotte (pop rock influence), Fall Out Boy (punk rock influence), My Chemical Romance, Panic at the Disco

The 2000s saw older bands releasing successful new albums. This is partly due to new interest of a younger audience attracted to vinyl, but mostly represented a revival for their original fans. There no longer seemed to be the stigma that older rock and roll bands are past their prime.

Artists:
AC/DC, Guns N' Roses, Metallica, Aerosmith, Bon Jovi

Metalcore

Metalcore evolved from a wide genre that was influenced by extreme metal and hardcore punk. The rise of metalcore led to increased popularity of every other subgenre of heavy metal, including death metal, black metal, and thrash.

Artists:
Killswitch Engage, Underoath, Bullet for My Valentine, Avenged Sevenfold

Innovations in the 2000s included the advent of technical death metal, folk metal, and deathcore.

Pop-Punk

Successful pop-punk bands in the 1990s, such as Green Day, Weezer, Blink-182, and The Offspring, also continued their success during the 2000s.

A second wave of pop-punk bands emerged in the 2000s, such as New Found Glory and Sum 41, who have a sense of humor in their videos and a more radio-friendly approach to their music. More recent pop-punk bands include Simple Plan and All-American Rejects. They have a sound that has been described as closer to late-1970s and early-1980s hardcore.

Pop

Teen pop bridges between the 1990s and 2000s, and only lasts until the start of the decade. Modern R&B and hip-hop pushed it out of popularity around 2001.

Artists:
Britney Spears, Christina Aguilera, P!nk, Mya, *NSYNC, Westlife

A new girl teen pop rock movement began. Avril Lavigne was arguably the first and lead artist to take this new direction in pop music, with hits such as "Complicated" and "Sk8er Boi."

Artists:
Michelle Branch, Vanessa Carlton, Hilary Duff, Selena, Ashlee Simpson, Demi Lovato, Katy Perry, Taylor Swift

- Janet Jackson, Kylie Minogue and Madonna experience revived success.
- Justin Timberlake garnered much acclaim with his album *Justified*.

- *American Idol* winners became a big part of the American pop sound. Kelly Clarkson experienced huge success and tons of hit radio singles beginning with a pop sound and then transitioning back to her roots in country.

- Lady Gaga overtook the later part of the decade and revived the electronic influence of pop music that had not been prominent since 2000. Her debut album, *The Fame*, is released on August 19, 2008.

- In 2001, Michael Jackson releases his final studio album, *Invincible*. He dies in June 2009, evoking the largest wave of public mourning since the death of Diana, Princess of Wales in 1997.

- Children's music rises significantly in sales, especially with Disney (The Cheetah Girls, *High School Musical*, *Hannah Montana: The Movie*, and the Jonas Brothers).

It was fashionable to sample songs from the 1980s or remake them during this time:

- Rihanna's "S.O.S." (sampled Soft Cell's "Tainted Love")

- Flo Rida's "Right Round" (a reworking of Dead or Alive's "You Spin Me Right Round")

- Aaron Carter's "I Want Candy" (originally written by Bow Wow Wow)

- Britney Spears' "My Prerogative" (Bobby Brown) and "I Love Rock 'n' Roll" (Joan Jett)

- Fall Out Boy's "Beat It" (Michael Jackson)

Adult Contemporary
After 9/11, adult contemporary music emerged, featuring songs with appropriate, positive and uplifting lyrics containing love and hope. This led to adult contemporary stations substituting the words "soft-rock" with "lite-rock," which has a more modern-edged connotation. Norah Jones is considered the best adult contemporary jazz singer of the decade with 37 million records sold worldwide.

Artists:
Coldplay, Daughtry, Gavin Rossdale, Sara Bareilles, Colbie Caillat

Contemporary R&B
The popularity of contemporary R&B is seen during the 2000s with the global success of established artists such as Beyoncé, Mariah Carey, Jennifer Lopez, and Usher.

- Alicia Keys is considered the greatest singer of R&B of the decade with 30 million records sold worldwide.

- Beyoncé Knowles is the best-selling female performer of the 2000s, selling over 75 million records.

Country
Country slips out of mainstream popularity in the early 2000s, due partly to the public retirement of Garth Brooks and partly to a growing discontent among some traditional country music fans and artists over the perceived direction and sound of the genre.

Country Pop
This subgenre, which has its roots in the Nashville Sound of the late 1950s and early 1960s, continues to flourish in popularity.

Country acts:
Shania Twain, Dixie Chicks, Lonestar, Martina McBride, Tim McGraw, Faith Hill, Keith Urban, Rascal Flatts

Many non-country artists enjoy success in country music: Hootie & the Blowfish, Kid Rock, Sheryl Crow, Robert Plant, Jewel, Jessica Simpson, Bon Jovi, Miley Cyrus (mostly part of the teen pop genre with roots in country).

Despite the fact that country music songs have long been crossing over into pop radio (and charting since the start of the Billboard charts in 1940), some critics contend that the pop-oriented sound was little more than repackaged pop music.

However, traditional country music retains a large following during the decade, thanks to the ongoing successes of veteran artists such as Reba McEntire, Brooks & Dunn, Toby Keith, and Kenny Chesney, and newer artists such as Paisley, Blake Shelton, and Billy Currington.

Many legendary country music figures die during the 2000s: Waylon Jennings, June Carter Cash, Johnny Cash, Buck Owens, Hank Thompson, Porter Wagoner, and Eddy Arnold.

Electronic Music
In Europe, trance is very popular in the early part of the 2000s but it diminishes towards the middle of the decade. Hard house arrives directly after trance in 2001.

As a reaction to this, ambient chillout music achieves mainstream popularity with the successful marketing of compilations. The genre even is used in television commercials and soundtracks.

Disco house and funky house, which were popular in the late 1990s, continue to be successful through to the mid 2000s. And electro house, developed around 2006, rounded out the electronic sound that begins to merge with other genres such as hip-hop as the decade moves forward.

Electro-pop and nu disco increase in popularity in North America and become equal to hip-hop and R&B as the dominant genres of music.

Artists:
Hellogoodbye, Timbaland, Aly & A.J., Moby, The Crystal Method

Dubstep

This genre is characterized by a tempo between 130 and 145 bpm, heavy sub-bass, and a distinct, precarious bass line. It uses more sampling than previous electronic styles and often has a "dark" sound. While a very new genre, it is particularly popular in Southern California.

Jazz

- Jazz musicians such as Dave Brubeck, Wynton Marsalis, Sonny Rollins, Wayne Shorter, and Jessica Williams, continue to perform and record.

- A number of young musicians emerge, including the pianist Jason Moran, vibraphonist Stefon Harris, trumpeter Roy Hargrove, and bassist Christian McBride.

- Pop singer Christina Aguilera's album *Back to Basics* is intended as a reference to the 1920s, 1930s, and 1940s-style jazz music.

- In addition, a number of new vocalists achieve popularity with a mix of traditional jazz, pop, and rock forms: Diana Krall, Norah Jones, Cassandra Wilson, Kurt Elling, and Jamie Cullum.

Reggae and Dancehall

Newer charting acts such as Elephant Man and Sean Paul achieve mainstream success in the United States.

Reggaeton

Reggaeton gains mainstream exposure and massive popularity in North America due to its blend of reggae and dancehall, hip-hop, contemporary R&B, and electronica, as well as adding the influences from Latin America such as bomba, plena, salsa, merengue, Latin pop, cumbia, and bachata.

The UK and Europe

Rock bands:
Coldplay, Franz Ferdinand, Keane, Radiohead, The Verve

Indie rock and indie pop bands:
Arctic Monkeys, Kaiser Chiefs, The Libertines, Editors, Lily Allen, Kate Nash, Florence and the Machine, The Ting Tings

Post-punk bands:
Bloc Party, Foals, Editors, Oasis, Sleepy Hollow

Synth pop acts:
Hot Chip, Junior Boys, The Veronicas, Ladyhawke, Ladytron, Little Boots, La Roux, Telefon Tel Aviv, Lights, Phoenix (French), Cut Copy (Australian)

Pop singer-songwriters:
Dido, David Gray, James Blunt, James Morrison, KT Tunstall, Amy Macdonald

Grime:
This is a distinctly British version of hip-hop that became popular, with notable artists Dizzee Rascal and Tinchy Stryder achieving success.

Girl groups:
Sugababes, Girls Aloud, t.A.T.u.

Reality music shows:
Popstars, *Pop Idol*, *Fame Academy*, *The X Factor*

Eurovision Song Contest—from this contest, the most famous singer from the 2000s is Helena Paparizou from Greece.

In 2004, O-Zone (a Moldovan pop music trio) has a hit song, "Dragostea Din Tei," that becomes a European hit that featured prominently in many other countries as well.

Soul singers:
Amy Winehouse, Joss Stone, Natasha Bedingfield, Corinne Bailey Rae, Adele, Duffy

Electronic music:
Daft Punk (France) became one of the biggest European electronic music acts of the decade.

Artists:
ATB, Ian Van Dahl, DJ Sammy, Alice Deejay, Fragma, Robert Miles, Tiësto, Armin Van Buuren, Paul Oakenfold, Paul Van Dyk, Darude

House artists:
Fatboy Slim, the Chemical Brothers, Groove Armada, Basement Jaxx, Massive Attack, Röyksopp, Orbital, Propellerheads, Underworld, David Guetta

Australia and New Zealand
Rock bands:
The Vines, Wolfmother, Powderfinger, The Vines, You Am I, Silverchair, The Living End, Eskimo Joe, The Feelers, Evermore

R&B acts:
Hollie Smith, J. Williams, Stan Walker

Pop acts:
Kylie Minogue, Delta Goodrem, Brooke Fraser, Aaradhna, Vince Harder, Anika Moa, Ladyhawke, Carly Binding

Alternative bands:
Evermore, Youth Group

Hip-hop acts:
Hilltop Hoods (the first successful Australian hip-hop group), Bliss n Eso, Scribe, Savage, Smashproof, David Dallas, Young Sid, Nesian Mystik, P-Money

Latin America
Pop acts:
Shakira, RBD

Reggaeton acts:
Aventura, Don Omar, Daddy Yankee, Pitbull, Wisin & Yandel, Calle 13

By the mid 2000s, Reggaeton had replaced salsa, merengue, and cumbia as the main dance genre in nightclubs for young people all over Latin America, reaching popularity in parts of Spain and Italy as well.

Salsa and merengue:
Although salsa and merengue began to decline in popularity, merengue would have new life injected into it thanks to the subgenre known as "merengue de calle" (street merengue).

   This subgenre, combining elements of merengue, rap, and reggaeton, would be popularized by Dominican acts such as Omega, Silvio Mora, El Sujeto, and Tito Swing.

Pop rock acts:
Camila, Kany García, Jesse & Joy, Belinda Peregrin, Ha*Ash, Maná, Juanes, Julieta Venegas

Also, more established pop acts such as Pepe Aguilar, Alejandro Fernández, Luis Fonsi, and ex-OV7 member Kalimba used pop rock in their repertoires.

Asia
The independent music industries of Asia have seen considerable growth because of the rapid development of Asian economies during the 1990s and 2000s. Asian countries such as Japan and India have the largest music markets in the world. Very few artists from the Western world manage to break into those markets.

Japan:
J-Pop is the most popular style of music in Japan. Japan also remains as the second most powerful musical industry in the world, and the second-largest music market, after the United States.

   R&B was popular at the beginning of the decade, with hip-hop also becoming more popular as it progressed. At the end of the decade, dance music and techno become the most popular genres. Bubblegum pop remains extremely popular during the entire decade.

Japanese artists:
Ayumi Hamasaki—The Empress of Japanese Pop
Ken Hirai—The most popular male solo artist
Namie Amuro, Misia, Hikaru Utada, Kumi Koda

- Vocal groups including Exile and Tohoshinki gain popularity.

- Pop rock bands such as Mr. Children, Tokio and Glay remain popular.

India:
Previously dominated by the film music of Bollywood for much of the late twentieth century, the 2000s saw an increase in the popularity of independent Indian pop music that competed with Bollywood film music. It is a fusion of Indian and non-Indian sounds, which later influenced Bollywood music itself. Due to being one of the largest music markets in the world, India suffers from high levels of piracy.

Its music is partly influenced by the Asian underground music scene that emerged in the UK among British Asian artists.

Indian artists:
Bally Sagoo, Apache Indian, Panjabi MC, Raghav, Rishi Rich Project

2000–2010 History of Recorded Music

With digital technology influencing the music industry and the space available on smaller hard drives and discs increases, the reduction of price of this technology increases its popularity. Computers and computer networks in the first decade of the twenty-first century are the primary means to play, record, and distribute music.

With this shift in technology it changes the relationship between the people involved in creating, promoting, and selling music for consumers. Because of this shift, album sales decline, as it becomes popular for consumers to buy single songs instead of downloading entire albums. And peer to peer (P2P) networks such as Napster and Kazaa illegally allow music files to be exchanged between consumers.

Avid's ProTools and other recording software renders multi-track recording on magnetic tape almost obsolete. Records are created using both methods simultaneously, if not completely digitally at times. Towards the end of this decade inexpensive recording hardware and software make recording high quality music at home possible. With the acceptance of broadband, individual artists can equally distribute their songs online.

As CD, vinyl, and cassette sales drop by almost $5 billion in sales from 1999 to 2008, box stores such as Wal-Mart and Best Buy replace record stores such as Tower Records, who had considerable influence on artists' careers. Eventually Tower Records goes bankrupt and closes all their stores. Music promoters such as Live Nation then promote live performance as a means for merchandizing and income for artists.

EXERCISES

2000–present   As Many Ingredients as Enrich Your Intention.
                   Find an image of the time period. Take the listener on a journey
                   that shows a rich, complex aural expression of the visual in order to
                   evoke an emotional response. Keep in mind the myriad genres and
                   subgenres of this time. Also, note the listener of each type of music.
                   Remembering that music evokes an emotional mood, focus on the
                   specifics of the themes you are presenting. The cue should be no
                   longer than thirty seconds.

Critical response
- Is there a story being told?
- Is it in the appropriate genre, time period, or style?
- What mood or emotion is evoked?
- Does it speak to the appropriate aural subgroup?
- Are the technological sound aspects represented?
- What tools in your DAW were effective to create the cue?
- What tools from your toolbox were used?
- What is your intention? Was it conveyed to the listeners?

PART THREE

THE COLLABORATIVE PROCESS

This section of the book will help you as the sound designer bring the evolutionary and associational responses into a production. When we use the knowledge of how we hear, and then purposefully use the intention of how we wish to affect an audience's emotional journey, it is best to understand how to implement the resulting designs collaboratively with our fellow theatre artists.

5

APPLYING TOOLS AND ARTISTIC COLLABORATION

Working with Text

You will undoubtedly develop your own style of how you approach a script or theatre piece. I will start with my own way as a suggestion, and you can then adapt it to fit how you work best. The first time I read any text, I read for understanding of the story and the characters. The more I read a script, the more I build an understanding of the intention of the playwright and the deeper meaning beyond the scripted lines.

When I begin reading a play, I make sure that I have no distractions and that I have enough time to get through the entire play in one sitting. I keep a pencil in my hand at all times. I'm not the fastest reader unless I read the play out loud, because my brain will try to figure out the myriad ways each line can be interpreted. So, I read out loud and quickly, picturing the most exciting, dynamic, aurally rich production in my head.

Whenever I feel moved or feel the need to support the script with sound, I make a dash on the right-hand side of the paper or annotate the digital file. Whenever the script specifically calls for some sort of sound event, I circle it and put a dash on the right. If there is knocking, voices off-stage, or anything that could be done live, I put a question mark on the right, knowing that I will have to ask a question about that moment. If there's anything written in the script that seems incongruous to what I feel would be a supported moment, I also put a question mark. This is how I approach finding the sound that encompasses the words.

I tend to think in a cinematic response. And this comes about for two reasons: most scripts are written in a cinematic style these days, and the cinematic language of sound design is what an audience has come to expect in entertainment because movies are easily accessible. When I feel sound should be present, I mark it down with no judgment. I take as many times as I need to read through and mark the script to get the fullest interpretation of the play and what I think would best serve it from a sound and music perspective.

This is how I do it. For you it may be different. Some people need to not think of sound and just read for meaning. Whatever way you need to approach a script will show itself the more you work in theatre. However is best for you, there are some conclusions you should reach in order to begin focusing on how your sound design will support the piece.

When reading a script, some of the points you want to focus on are as follows:

- Understanding the plot
- The intellectual message or massages
- Does it make logical sense?
- Does the piece pose a question?
- Where does it take place?
- When does it take place?
- How is the play structured?
- Is there exposition before the story?
- What is the climax of the play?
- Does it contain a denouement after the climax?
- What is the major point of conflict?
- Where are there moments of tension?
- What are the arcs of the characters' journeys?
- Who are the protagonist and antagonist?
- Is there a result to their action?
- From whose point of view is the story being told and is it more than one person?

These are just a few of the questions that arise. Because every script is different, it requires its own set of questions to get to the heart of why this story is being told right now and how it will be presented.

When looking for moments where sound can support these aspects, look for the following:

- Scene transitions—sound supports the in-between moments
- Repetition—sound can focus the repeated action, places, people, objects, or themes
- Different locations—sound gives the impression of spatial awareness for an audience

- Action or fights—sound makes what is choreographed feel more dangerous

- Special effects or video—sound plays a supporting role to the magic of the piece

- Discoveries—sound can aid in how the show is unfolding

- Recurring motifs—sound can use repetition to highlight and show change

- Counterpoint—sound can act as an antithesis in juxtaposition

- Foreshadowing—sound can help point out specific details to an audience

- Comedic moments—sound motifs or accents to action or language highlight humor

- Contrast—sound can add color to the comparison

All of these moments are meant to be explored depending on the style, genre, and emotional journey of the play.

Terminology in regards to analyzing the script is not consistent across the field of sound design in theatre; however, the ideas are essentially the same. It's the depth you are gleaning from the script and the interpretation of meaning, both intellectually and emotionally, that are important.

When you first read a script, you are the objective reader. The emotional response you have that first time is something of which to take note. Focus on how the play makes you feel as you work on it. This initial response is what you begin with when discussing how to approach the presentation of the play with the artistic team.

To me, the most important aspect to beginning the process of determining sound for a script is that it is always better to be prepared and have the ability to edit multiple options. You want to be prepared for every possible outcome. To me, there is no such thing as overdoing at the start of a process. It's much easier to take away than to add later.

Marks in the Script

While you are marking the right side of your script with dashes where you know a called "go" will happen, you may find it helpful to put an arrow along the page to determine how long that cue is going to last. Does the arrow continue until another "go," or does it need to fade out separately from a cue with its own "go"? I create a map in the right-hand margin that will eventually have numbered dashes marking cues and arrows between them demarking length. (See Figure 5.1 for example.)

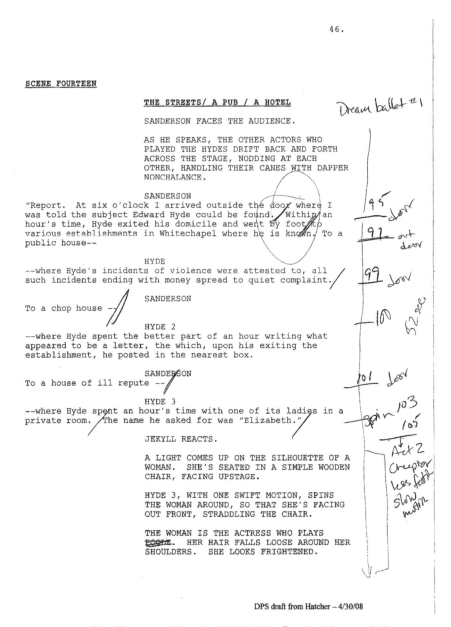

Figure 5.1 Act One, Scene 14 of *Dr. Jekyll & Mr. Hyde*. Reprinted by permission Paradigm Talent Agency on behalf of the Jeffrey Hatcher Copyright ©.

When you see a designer run, you can then add the timings of the arrowed sections of the script. If you have an arrow for seven pages, time it so that you know how long you need to make your cue. If you have five dashed cues in a row, with only the third dash continuing to the fourth, time the whole thing by using the lap function on a stopwatch. You can tap the stopwatch at the "go" and notate the time for each cue and the total.

What you are working towards is an efficient use of quiet time in the space by having already planned out approximate timings of design. It doesn't have to be pretty; my script is usually messy by the end of the process. You are the person who needs to understand the markings. Your script is your reference point.

Cue Numbers

Every designer will create their own style as to how they hand over their design to the stage manager to call. As you are still learning how you work best, make sure you leave enough room between numbers so that any additional cues added during tech can be inserted without using any decimal numbers (2.5, 3.1, 4.7, etc.). Eventually, with experience, you can separate your cues by two to five numbers, but while you are learning your own process, give yourself room between cues to accommodate the unforeseen.

Some designers like to check in with the lighting designer to see how they are numbering their cues, so as not to create moments where the stage manager is calling cues that are the same or similar numbers. This helps alleviate confusion for the operators during the show. Always think about your stage manager and the most efficient way to call your design when developing your cue list.

I know some designers who number according to scene, use point cues, and separate by large gaps, but it is my opinion that simplicity in function leads to efficiency in action. The reason we number cues is for the calling of a show. When the stage manager is rapidly calling a show, you want to give them what is best for them to perform their job to their fullest capacity. Decimal cues slow down the calling of a show. A good stage manager will be able to call whatever you give them, so don't worry if you have a few decimal cues because of a major change in tech. But if you hand over your initial cue sheet without any decimal cues in it, your stage manager will appreciate it.

Mark down in your script anything and everything that comes from your research and imagination, because your script is your roadmap to your design. It is the basis from which you will program your show control, and it will be right next to you in tech when you are working on specific moments, figuring out timing, and determining where exactly the cues will go. It remains a fluid document throughout the process, so make sure you use pencil.

Cue Sheets

Cue sheets are for stage managers, and should give them the information of context they need as they mark up their script before and during tech.

A cue sheet should contain the following in the header:

- The name of the show

- The producing theatre company

- Your name, phone number, and email address

- Union affiliation—if you have one

- Copyright symbol and date

In the body:

- Cue number

- Description (one to three words)

- Source (QLab, LIVE, microphone)

- Cue-line words or action that precede the "go"

- Speaker source or assignment (mains, sub, surrounds, stage, overhead, radio)

- Whether the cue plays out, continues, or fades

- Page number

A stage manager needs to know your intention of the structure of your cues in order to maintain your design throughout an entire run. The clearer you are to start, the more efficient the process. And your design will remain consistent and intact through the run of the production. In Figures 5.2 and 5.3, you will see arrows to show how long a cue is playing, the cue numbers, a brief description, SFX, and scene numbers for the digital console, cue line, assignment, fade properties, and page number.

For me, creating the cue sheet helps organize the structure my design will take, and I tend to do it during the rehearsal process. Between both the in-depth notes in the script and the outline of my cue sheets, I have a clear picture of how to approach the creation and delivery of the design. The cue sheets solidify further after the designer run, when most of the changes occur. And then I tend to not use them again and rely on the script during technical rehearsals.

I will never withhold cue sheets if asked for them. This varies for every collaborative process, but for me, it is my personal preference to not give the director the technical outline of the sound cue sheets. I want the actors and the director to focus on the feeling of when a cue starts and ends. I prefer to not give the details of when the cue technically begins or ends, because I want an objective response of whether I've achieved the appropriate support.

As sound designers, who have built our cues, we may be the only ones who know that the cue needs to begin three seconds before it is audible in the room

cue	description	source	cue line	assignment	fade	p.
PRE	Preshow	SFX	With House Open			
.9	Announcement		-		Fade Preshow	
1 Mies	Prologue	SFX	With lights	Mains Subs Ring -		4
3	Blackout Reverb	SFX Sc. 2	"have not witnessed"	Mains Subs	- Q1 out	4
5	Whistles	SFX	After scream	Blackstage L/R mains	Plays out	4
7	Door crashing Drone Reverb out	SFX Sc.3	With actors entrance	backstage L/R Subs	- Q3 out	5
9	Scene 1	SFX	"let me begin"	Mains Subs	Plays out	5

cue	description	source	cue line	assignment	fade	p.
149 Mics	Act 2 Scene 1 Gurney	SFX Sc. 8	With lights	Mains Subs	-	65
151	Switch	SFX	"And a note"	Mains Subs	Plays out	65
153	Reality	SFX	"Signed Carew"	Mains Subs	Plays out Q149 out	65
155	Scene 2	SFX	"Who?"	Mains Subs	Plays out	66
157	Hyde Event	SFX	"I should think"	Mains Subs	-	68
159	Hyde Switch	SFX	"A moment, please"	Mains Subs	Plays out	70
161	Hyde Switch	SFX	"poor old Jekyll"	Mains Subs	Plays out	70
163	Hyde Switch	SFX	"Oh God … "	Mains Subs	Plays out	70
165	Hyde Switch	SFX	"But not to you"	Mains Subs	Plays out	71

Figure 5.2 and 5.3 Excerpts of cue sheets for *Dr. Jekyll & Mr. Hyde*.

to fade in gracefully. The only people that need to know that amount of specificity to the intention of the cue are the stage manager for calling purposes, and the lighting and projection designers, who are also building their cues in cohesive timing to our work. When in tech, you will always come back to the intention of emotional response, and it has to be timed and in sync with the other elements.

Transitions

Mark down every transition, but realize that the scope of how transitions will be completed and what needs to happen during transitions will be determined by many different factors. Scenery may need to change or actors may need to quickly change their costumes, and a great deal of the work of how the actors will transition emotionally and physically from one scene to another takes place in rehearsal. Towards the ond of the rehearsal process, ensure that you understand what the goals are by visiting the rehearsals or talking through transitions with the director and lighting designer.

What can be difficult for a production is when you have a script that is written in a cinematic style quickly jumping as "cuts" to new locations, when you need time to emotionally and physically get to the new place in a live performance. Whether a transition is short or long, what is important is the focus on the emotional journey that happens in the in-between.

In a transition, again you want to think about your intention. Note where you are coming from, what emotion has just transpired, where you are going to, and what feeling, pace, and expectation the journey impresses upon the audience. More times than not, you are propelling the story forward and should focus on what's coming up next, but there are times when the story is best served by the audience taking the time to reflect on what has just transpired before you whisk them off to the next scene.

It's up to you to determine if you are attaching ideas to previous gestures, or whether this transition is a palate cleanser in mood or style. Is the gesture purposefully interruptive or conclusive? Does it resolve on its own, or give the impression of leading to something else? There are multiple possibilities to the approach of these short, emotionally telling, pace-setting moments, and you can aid in the interpretation by whether or not your music and sound resolves.

Another aspect you should look for in a transition is passage of time, and how you would support the feeling of time passing either slowly or quickly. This is accomplished through the relative pacing of your cues. If you are returning to a setting you've been to before, or you are following an object or theme, you may want to remind an audience through the use of repetition how you arrived there the last time, or what has changed with this theme along its story's arc.

If a playwright has written in previously published songs for transitions in the script, there is a conversation to be had about the familiarity of the audience's association with those songs. We know that association factors heavily into our emotional response, especially with music. The conversation can be about the specific associations of a particular song, and whether it is possible to achieve the same effect using a piece of music with which the audience is not familiar.

If you are able to speak to the playwright about the music choices, you can discuss how familiarity creates the possibility of association to something specific in the audience's lives. You want an audience to be free to feel an emotional immersive transition that will not draw them out of the story with their own historical association. You are the collaborator in the room that understands musical association, and you want to ensure that you understand the intention of the playwright when specific music is written into the script.

Transitions speak to the aural temperament of the moment and the reason why you are making a shift. These can be based on time, place, themes, characters, emotions, etc.

Sound Effects

Mark every place in the script where a sound effect is listed, but also pay attention to when it is not. The playwright does not always write that a train is still traveling throughout the scene, or the specificity of how and when sound stops. It may not say that birds are chirping in the park, or that crickets are singing at night during the entire scene. It's up to you to hear your surroundings and support what is needed to generate the correct place, mood, and aural landscape for each scene. When inside the building of a theater, you need an ambience to show that a scene is outdoors. You are creating the spatial reality of the moment.

Ambience is around us constantly; it is up to the sound designer to choose when the audience selectively hears it. Remember that you are supplying the correct amount of sound to support the story. It may be best to begin a scene with ambience and then slowly fade it to silence so that the audience "selectively hears" and focuses in on the important dialogue that is presented. Conventions are set throughout the tech process based on what works best for how the story is told. If you are fading out towards selective hearing, take note of when you use the convention and when you break it. A broken convention marks something different that an audience will subconsciously notice.

With all sound effects, be true to time period, style, and genre. For example, when there is a phone ring, make sure you represent the correct time period by using a bell or electronic ring. Be specific to the story you are telling, so that nothing you do distracts the audience from suspending their disbelief and following the story.

Silence

Often, a playwright will write in a silence or pause they wish to heighten in a script. When this happens, pay special attention to how this changes the pacing and rhythm of the play. These are very clear instances of style of presentation and the overall cadence of the piece. It can help you determine when you feel additional silence is appropriate.

I've shown how amplifying volume and creating more atmospheric pressure can affect an audience. On the contrary, in a show such as *Dr. Jekyll & Mr. Hyde* that is rich with music and soundscape, silence is a very powerful tool. It can pinpoint the focus of an audience on what is live and present before them. When there is silence, there is no aural support of the action, language, or event, and thus it can create a feeling of vulnerability.

One specific moment where this can occur in *Dr. Jekyll & Mr. Hyde* is at the end of Act Two, Scene 7. Dr. Jekyll goes to Lanyon's surgery already transformed as Mr. Hyde, and allows Lanyon to observe the transformation back to Jekyll. At the end of the scene it is obvious to Jekyll that he must kill his colleague. He does so by strangulation.

If you were to heighten the moment of strangulation by underscoring it, you would dramatize it by expressing it theatrically. The audience would be able to sit back and observe the strangulation. But the important part of killing by strangulation is hearing the gasping for breath and, more specifically, when the murdered takes their last breath.

Choosing silence and creating vulnerability for Dr. Jekyll makes the moment more real for the audience. They have nothing else to rely on other than one man strangling his friend right in front of them, live. They hear every awkward and repulsive sound of death alone in silence. This can be more powerful than giving the moment something that makes it easier emotionally on both the actors and audience.

This is not delineated in the script; typically, little or nothing of the aural mood-inducing sound design is notated. It is up to you as the sound designer to recognize when to use your dynamic control over the aural environment. One way is to think of your design as a symphony. The rises, falls, pacing, movements, pauses, rhythm, and syncopation, etc., all lend themselves to the same dramatic intent of storytelling.

In Table 5.1, I have borrowed a breakdown from David Sonnenschein's book, *Sound Design: The Expressive Power of Music, Voice, and Sound Effects in Cinema*. This gives a clear picture of how you can look at a play in a metaphoric way that equates to a musical sensibility.

Thinking of a play in this manner can help you to equate musical properties to the elements of a story. And if you have a clear definition of what you are hearing in the sonic aspects of your design, this can help you to compartmentalize the relationship between your design and the story.

Emotional Support

When looking through a script, emotional support is not always apparent. It may not become apparent until after the actors begin their work in rehearsal.

Table 5.1 *Design as a symphony.*

Music	Story
melody	character
harmony	setting/production design
dissonance	conflict
rhythm	pace
phrase	beat/scene/sequence
score/composer	playwright
musicians	actors
conductor	director

You can get a feel for the tone and intention after you hear the actors read the play at the first rehearsal, but when you are working on the script alone, it's up to you to imagine the optimal interpretation of the text and support it accordingly. In a way, you are thinking as the director and the actors, who interpret the emotional aspect in the appropriate manner to bring the script to life.

Underscoring dialogue works with certain styles of plays because when you bring music or sound underneath an actor speaking, you elevate it into a moment of theatricality. In our day-to-day lives, music does not automatically start when we think or feel foreboding or exaltation. This is reserved for a specific form of storytelling in theatre. If you are working on a contemporary sparse piece, underscoring may not seem appropriate and feel too melodramatic. Choose your emotional support with intention and style.

However, action (with or without dialogue) may need the support of sound. Adding music or sound to action can help clarify emotional intention, keep the intensity of storytelling impactful, make fights that are purposefully safe feel dangerous, and drive the pacing of the moment. This is something that is felt more than scripted.

Take note during rehearsals if any action creates the feeling of a dip in energy within the silence of the rehearsal room. Unless that dip in energy is specific to the arc of the story, these are the action moments that may require support.

When there is a violence designer for your fights, this is yet another collaborator with whom you can work closely to determine the emotional intention of the fights and the timing of the gear changes within. I don't like to prescribe the support before the fight is choreographed; I like to score what has been designed.

Themes

The exercise section of this book defines the concept of themes; however, it is important to address it here because how you approach a play is dependent on the themes the playwright or team is trying to convey. Throughout a theatre piece you can follow and support many different aspects of themes. These include the arc of the characters' journeys; objects that need to be followed because of their importance; different time and place settings that the audience will travel to and through; the mood and emotions, not only of the expression of what is on stage, but also the impression upon the audience; the style in which action occurs; and from whose point of view we are hearing the story.

When working on a script or text, keep in mind what the playwright has intended for the audience to walk away with in their hearts and minds, and then add in what the team wants to bring to the production. It's in your best interest to refer back to the script at any time there is a question. And with every suggestion made by the director or team, always think of how the script can be supported from a sound design perspective. You should also respond to how the script impacts your thinking and feeling with your personal contribution, both artistically and technically.

To track the journey of a theme, we have already outlined the simple graph with the theme on the vertical axis and the scenes on the horizontal axis. Determine what changes as you travel through the story through setting, time period, emotion, and aural temperament. This can allow you to define more closely how the theme begins, changes and ends. You can do this for as many of the themes in the play as necessary to help you to structure your ideas and process. You can then also compare different themes and how they interact with each other (see Figures 5.4 and 5.5).

When following themes, use the tools that are in this book: punctuation, repetition, dynamics, time, ambience, tension, and concrete vs. abstract. I make specific notes in the margin of my script regarding which tools would be best to use for each marked cue. Write down anything that helps you bring the themes forward in the way the playwright and team intend.

By now, with your research, you will have chosen the instrumentation and have an idea of complexity for the aural landscape you are creating. I tend to have a sound folder on my computer within the main show folder. Within it, I place a music folder, an FX folder, an mp3 folder (for the files not used in the show that are sent over the internet), and a show control QLab folder. I then throw all of my research into it as I gather together the sounds I think will work. I will also organize the folders themselves into more specific descriptions such as drones, storm, punctuation, etc. Do whatever you need to keep a clear picture on the files you are gathering.

JEKYLL & HYDE

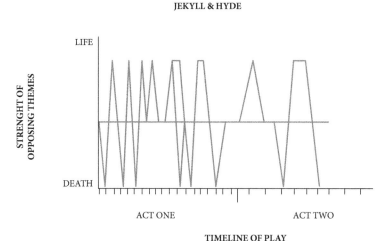

Figure 5.4 Thematic outline of life and death for *Dr. Jekyll & Mr. Hyde*.

JEKYLL & HYDE

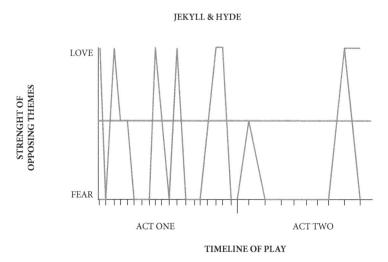

Figure 5.5 Thematic outline of love and fear for *Dr. Jekyll & Mr. Hyde*.

Storytelling Structure

It is important to understand the structure of how a play is written so that you are able to support how the playwright wants the story to be told. The creative team determines style and approach, but the structure is usually determined by the writing.

I'm going to use *Dr. Jekyll & Mr. Hyde* as an example of how to break down the storytelling structure in a script. In this play there are three distinct modes of storytelling: narration, heightened realism, and the story (which is actually in the past). How the sound designer approaches the differences between these three distinct conditions will benefit the comprehension of the text. A sound designer chooses specific music and sound to support how to deliver these differences.

Differences in how information is delivered in the play

Narration—single actor speaking directly to the audience in present time bridging transition into scene

Heightened realism—the ensemble acts out events while characters describe them as a flashback

Past story—dialogue and monologue showing the moment-to-moment reality of the story unfolding

These stylistic approaches should be delineated from each other so that the audience knows without thinking how the story is being told. You can approach it in the following way.

- Narration—underscore music or soundscape only to illuminate what was before or what will follow; otherwise, silence marked by punctuation in and out of the narrative moments, highlighting the intimacy of an actor alone on stage telling a story to the audience.

- Heightened realism—underscore with fully realized diegetic sound, with tonal music and sound, raising the moment's theatricality into the storyteller's point of view, with use of reverb to add fullness and signify flashback.

- Past story—realism, music or sound for transitions, and anything that is required to support the reality of the story.

All of your sound should create cohesion in style and genre. While you research the music and sound for the transitions of the past story, you can compile what you feel can underscore both the narration and the heightened realism. Keep in mind that the difference between narration, heightened realism, and past story will mean each has a different dynamic impact for your audience. Once you have all three structures clearly defined, determine how each one affects the audience by what is being told in those moments.

- The narrators feel removed; they are from the present, and less emotional about the story.

- The heightened realism feels the most dramatic, theatrical, and emotional.

- The past story is the journey of the how and the why the characters interplay, and the emotional response of the audience is dependent on the point of view.

After you determine the way the story is being told, you can go back to the script and mark where you, as the sound designer, feel you can support the shifts into each mode of storytelling.

Looking at the first few scenes of *Dr. Jekyll & Mr. Hyde*

Prologue—Narration, heightened realism, narration
Scene 1—Narration, heightened realism, past story
Scene 2—Past story, narration
Scene 3—Narration, past story
Scene 4—Narration, past story
Scene 5—Heightened realism

Once you have outlined the structure and how you wish to approach each mode of storytelling, bridging between them in a smooth and seemingly effortless manner lends cohesiveness to your design. This is where repetition of punctuation will help you.

Your punctuations should live within the aural world you are building. They can be a final chord of a piece of music you are using, a manipulated sound effect from your soundscape, or something that is foreign to the rest of your design that juxtaposes it for effect. Again, the choice is about your intention.

Because not all transitions are the same, look for and create punctuations with a range of dynamics in volume, pitch, time, and complexity. You want the punctuations to reflect the mood and feeling of the moment, so finding a range among them will help you understand the emotional range of movement from one storytelling mode to another.

Also, assign different punctuations depending on how they live within each mode of storytelling, based on the following: the pacing of the show—driving through to the next moment or allowing the audience to reflect; the characters' journey—the arc of conflict or resolution and emotion; and the themes represented—intellectual and emotional ideas and overall impact.

Narration

Take into account which character is the narrator and their style and emotional basis for telling the story—Utterson, as Dr. Jekyll's colleague, will tell a story differently from the maid who witnesses a murder at the end of Act One. Note what has come before the narration, and match the pacing you need to the reason for interrupting the story. What is the information that is being told? At what pace do you need to get into the next moment?

Heightened realism

Take into account what is happening: how it is told, and how it is acted out—when the story is told of Hyde etching into the back of a prostitute, it has a different impact upon the audience than when they are told of the killing of Sir

Danvers Carew. Who is telling the story, and to whom? The point of view of what is being acted out will add to how the audience views the main characters.

Past story

Take into account how the story is changing—the arc of the characters involved will determine the pacing and dynamics. Dr. Jekyll is much more measured at the start of the play. Towards the end he has lost control of his faculties and is emotionally reacting to his perdition.

You are supporting the story through the exploration of the themes presented, following the arcs of those themes and the characters' journeys, and the way the story is being told. The clearer you are in determining how you support the shifts in storytelling, the richer the aural quality of your design will seem because of its appropriateness.

The Opening Sound Cue

The opening cue is an opportunity to create a short overture that implants an audience with an aural narrative. It can be the embodiment of the entirety of the production, which plays upon the audience's expectation of the experience and the excitement they have about what is going to unfold before their eyes. If it is a well-known story that is part of a common collective knowledge base, you have a choice to go either with what is expected or deviate from the norm, depending on what you want the first impression to be for the audience. The opening sound cue can be a way to misdirect an audience.

It is up to you to determine whether it is empathetic, sympathetic or contrasting based on your intention. The opening of the show can be all about sound. There is usually little visual to accompany lights going to black or transitioning into scene. It is often up to the sound designer to set the first emotional impression of the play, even if that impression requires silence.

Opening cues, for me, tend to be among or reminiscent of the inspiration pieces that were part of my sound design research. It's the music that seems to encapsulate the very essence of the emotional journey and what you think the play is about. It's the music that, when you first hear it, speaks to exactly what you wanted to achieve in your design.

The opening cue can convey a wide variety of intention based on the style and genre as well as emotional expectation. And it's very important that it represents how the team wishes the experience of this story to begin. Keep in line with whether the start is boldly telling all, or hinting with subtlety at what's to come. As in cinematic sound design, the beginnings can vary from epic, adventurous music to absolute silence. You are supporting whatever choice is correct for the story.

If we back up to when the audience is entering the space, the first choice is whether there is preshow sound or music. This is solely up to the impression of how you want the room to feel when people enter. A preshow is a gesture that can create a sense of magic or expectation; it can be energizing, and it can be a specific place or time that pinpoints an environment immediately. Keep in mind how human beings react in a space that is public. Do you wish for it to feel lively or contemplative?

Even if the choice is silence, it is up to you to speak to your concept of how you would like the experience to start for the audience. I am personally not a fan of the preshow announcements, but that decision usually comes from the needs of the administrative staff of the venue. Whatever they need to do for their audience is what you will implement.

Theatrical Application

The opening cue of *Dr. Jekyll & Mr. Hyde* is a prologue that shows the end of the play as a means to set the story into a flashback. It is only two pages long with very little dialogue, but there is a lot of information that is told in a unique, truncated theatrical style (see Figures 5.6 and 5.7).

Audience Expectation

At the start of the play there is an expectation of what the audience believes the production to be before it begins. This is based on what they know of the story before coming to the theater, and what they have read of other people's opinions in critical response to the production. This expectation can change throughout a run of a show, when more information is released about the production through reviews and word of mouth.

It is up to the team how best to treat this, but a stage picture, sound, and lights will typically be the first experience the audience will have in the theater at the start of a production. And again, if there is preshow, that adds another element to the setting-up of an aural world before the production begins, and you can play with either feeding into expectation or playing against it.

The audience enters the space in present time, concerned about the world of how they arrived to the venue, received their programs, found their seats in the theater, and are now possibly socializing with others. You, as the sound designer, are transitioning them from their public communal experience into the world of the imagination of the production when the sound begins. Throughout the experience, they remain in a public environment and behave as such; however, there is now the added element of creating worlds in which they are either immersed to experience, or removed from to observe, the story about to unfold.

The Setting

Assuming the production's presentation is based in the original setting of 1883, sound allows the immersion of the audience at the start, to guide them back in time. The story is one that explores right and wrong, external perception juxtaposing internal wants and needs, the duality of human existence, and a split in society, all within a very dark story of love, fear, death, and suspense.

Although it uses the devices of shocking an audience and foreshadowing tension, it is not strictly a story that lives solely in horror. It is the environment of the time and place that creates the balance, or imbalance, between the opposing themes in the play. The audience may find meaning in their contemporary life through journeying into the past to see that things have either changed or remain the same through time. The sound designer aids in bringing the audience to the specific time and place in the very first moments sound is heard.

The prologue begins with narration of characters from the 1800s telling the audience that this is a story that has happened already and even they as characters may not have all the facts. This is the moment that sets up the characters to act as observers to the events in the story. And as the observing world of this society is integral to the storytelling because of their judgment, they represent a different aural quality than the other characters that tell their personal version of the events that are about to occur.

The Visual Aspects

For illustration purposes, let's begin with what the play's action looks like visually, so that we have a basis of understanding of what we are supporting.

It begins visually with an environmental setting that acclimates the audience to the style, state of mind, and emotional feeling of what to expect, as the lights go down slowly. Lights go down to black, the actors enter in the dark, and footlights bump up in a zero count for the opening lines of dialogue. After these lines, the lights black out on a zero count with a woman's scream. We remain in the dark, while the actors shout their subsequent lines while breaking down a door to reveal Dr. Jekyll lying on the floor in Elizabeth's arms for two lines, "Is it him? Is it?!" Lights change to begin narration with one line, "Let me begin." And we then transition to Scene 2. This all happens in approximately thirty-five to forty seconds.

Because this is a prologue, and the transitions within it are brief, I consider this a single, fully realized sonic event. We want to support the prologue being set apart from the rest of the telling of the story, as its own entity, because it will then live in the future once our story goes back in time.

4.

PROLOGUE

FIVE ACTORS -- TWO WOMEN AND THREE MEN -
- STAND AT THE STAGE APRON, IN LATE
VICTORIAN CLOTHING, CIRCA 1883.

THEY STAND IN FRONT OF A RED DOOR, USC.
THE DOOR SEEMS TO FLOAT IN DARKNESS.

THE FIVE ACTORS LOOK OUT FRONT,
FOOTLIGHTS BEAMING UP AT THEM.

                    WOMAN 1
This is what I know.

                    MAN 1
I'll tell you what I know.

                    MAN 2
What I saw, what I heard.

                    MAN 3
The events as I would recall them.

                    WOMAN 2
I cannot speak for what I have not witnessed.

                    BLACKOUT.

                    IMMEDIATELY WE HEAR --

                    A WOMAN'S SCREAM.

                    WOMAN 2
AIIIEEEE!!

                    WE HEAR A VERY LOUD LONDON POLICE
                    WHISTLE, AT LEAST THREE BLASTS.
                    OVERLAPPING THE WHISTLE, WE HEAR VOICES
                    SHOUTING IN THE DARK:

                    MAN 1 (O.S.)
Jekyll!

                    MAN 3 (O.S.)
Break it down!

                    WOMAN 1 (O.S.)
He's in there with him!

                    MAN 1 (O.S.)
Stand back!

Figure 5.6 and 5.7 The prologue of *Dr. Jekyll & Mr. Hyde*. Reprinted by permission
Paradigm Talent Agency on behalf of the Jeffrey Hatcher Copyright ©.

5.

```
                         LIGHTS ON THE RED DOOR.

                         THE RED DOOR BURSTS OPEN, OPENING D.S.
                         TOWARDS US. THE DOOR HANGS BY A HINGE.

                         FIVE PEOPLE, BACKLIT, COME THROUGH AND
                         COME DOWNSTAGE.  THEY STOP IN THEIR
                         TRACKS.  GASPS.

                         NOW WE SEE A BODY ON THE FLOOR,
                         DOWNSTAGE OF THE DOOR.  IT MIGHT EVEN
                         BY TWO BODIES.  ALL WE CAN SEE IS A
                         SWIRL OF DARK CLOTHING.

                         MAN 2 BECOMES "THE POLICE INSPECTOR."

                         INSPECTOR
Is it him?  IS IT?!

                         PAUSE AS THEY STARE. THEN --

                         LIGHTS CHANGE.

                         MAN 1 BECOMES "UTTERSON."

                         UTTERSON COMES DOWNSTAGE AND SPEAKS TO
                         THE AUDIENCE.

                         UTTERSON
Let me begin.

                         LIGHTS CHANGE.

                         THE RED DOOR IS WHEELED DOWNSTAGE IN
                         FRONT OF THE "BODY(IES)."

                         THE ACTORS GO O.S. AS UTTERSON SPEAKS.
```

In the first two pages of the show, there are many examples where you can use punctuation. Punctuation aids in telling when fast shifts are occurring. This is the first chance to set up the structure of the storytelling for the audience. We then follow the rules of convention as we seamlessly travel along the story, because the audience has learned the structure and how we are conveying it.

A lot has to be expressed in this moment, as it is a shortened telling of the ending of the play that the audience does not know. What is important for sound is that we mimic what we are choosing to do at the end of the play, and then truncate, as the script has done, for the opening moment. These gear changes, or shifts, are aided by punctuations.

Structural Shifts in the Prologue

Because the timing of the entire prologue is short, these can be noted as interior punctuations to the overall event. In order to remain cohesive and support this is as one aural event, they should complement the switches of mood, feeling, and pacing and live within the world of your design.

As lights are going down to black from preshow, sound sets up the aural landscape of what is to come in the evening. This can be shown through the style and pace of music and sound, the amount of consonance or dissonance, thematic elements, how the sound is distributed in the space, and how many layers add to the complexity of the design.

When the lights bump up to only footlights to reveal the actors, that is a very strong visual gear change and the actors are now speaking. This is an excellent place for a punctuation that will change the sound from the grandness of the all-encompassing world of your design to the underscoring of the narration for the society at large.

As the woman screams the lights black out to accentuate it. The sound of a woman screaming is within itself an aural punctuation. It can be live, amplified, or recorded; it is up to you how large to make the moment through the use of the sound designer's tools. This shifts the stage picture into the dark for solely an auditory experience. The punctuation should signify an aural change into actors shouting over the sonic elements, supporting the energy and emotion of breaking down a door.

Lights come up on a red door and there is a reveal of a different stage picture, one with a different mood and expectation for the characters and the story. Following the timing of the lights on the door with punctuation is central to creating a cohesive moment with the pacing and action of the visual. This change of music matches the emotion that underscores the two spoken lines.

Then there is yet another shift from the past to the present, to transition to narration of Dr. Jekyll's colleague Utterson. After his one line, the story then takes flight and the prologue is complete.

Dynamics in the Prologue

To understand now how to support these ideas of punctuation as gearshifts in mood and feeling, it helps to look at the dynamic structure of the impression upon the audience. The highs and lows of just these two pages will set up the audience's expectation for the rest of the play.

Dynamics accompanying the structure

Opening—High: encompassing of design ideas, large in scale, complex, full, loud in volume

Underscore of actors—Low: emotion of the characters, sparse, low in volume

Blind event—High: (scream of a woman, actors shouting, police whistles, breaking down a door in the dark), past time period, descriptive, large in scale, complex, full, loud in volume

Reveal of Jekyll—Medium: emotion of seeing a friend dead in the arms of a woman, suspenseful, low in volume

Narration—Low: solo presence, present time period, diminished from past event, sparse, low in volume

With the structure and its dynamics outlined, let's shift our focus towards the emotional expectation of, and the intended response from, the audience. Let's look at the "why" behind each of these moments. This will help us to design the mood, feeling, and pacing to support each gear change in the prologue.

Musical Elements of the Prologue

As we know, music association and its link to the limbic system's control over body function and emotional reaction is the most effective tool in creating an emotional mood for an audience. If we assign adjectives for each moment of the structured prologue, we can come closer to finding or creating the music that speaks to certain emotions.

Emotional adjectives accompanying prologue

Opening—dramatic, dark, suspenseful, energetic, duality
Underscore of actors—seedy, questionable, other, accusing, dirty
Blind event—exciting, frightening, anxious, forceful, bold
Reveal of Jekyll—shocking, questioning, love, sadness, revelation
Narration—narrative, cold, singular, observant, present

The next step is to define the adjectives in a musical vocabulary that you, the director, and the team feel supports each of these moments. It's best to start in the time period and location that is determined by the script.

Because of the grand scope of the production's style, it is appropriate to look at classical orchestrated music of the time. In this play's case, should the production wish to create an abstraction by updating the music or style then you would search accordingly. For our usage, we will follow what is written for the time period.

If your search exhausts the country the play is set in, try seeking other composers of the time from other countries. What you are trying to find at first is a common language of what the audience is accustomed to for this type of story. It is after you know the familiar that you can focus on making it unique to this production.

Another tool you could use is to listen to movie soundtracks that are set in the same time period. This is because the audience that goes to the theater also goes to the cinema, and they will have a collective knowledge of that style. Let the rabbit hole of the internet and everyone's suggestions guide you. When you find the piece that speaks to what you are hearing in your head, you will know.

For me, it all began with Khachaturian's *Suite Masquerade Waltz*; this was a suggestion from the actor playing Dr. Jekyll. I then moved on to Patrick Kirst's *PK Says Hello*, and then on to Warren Furman, Michael Pillitiere, Brahms, and even to the *Ravenous* soundtrack.

I want to remind you that you want to use familiar music only when you are referencing a specific association. To ensure that an audience is not removed from a production into their own association to the music, try to create a design unique to this specific version of the story. I find it most exciting when the music is obscure, and has introduced new music to a genre of storytelling. If you are composing and wish to use association as a tool, compile what you like and compose similarly in that style.

Music styles and gestures for the prologue

Opening—fully orchestrated, sweeping and dramatic, brass and string heavy

Underscore of actors—alternating staccato tonal rhythm with strings, short phrases of melody ending in staccato notes

Blind event—fully orchestrated, adventure, brass, string, timpani and percussion

Reveal of Jekyll—strings only, slowly arpeggiating upward

Narration—slow and long single notes on strings, dissonant

The Why behind the Music

Opening—When I hear a piece of music that is fully orchestrated, it feels complete to me. Every instrument is cooperating together to bring forth the feeling the composer wishes. When a piece of music highlights the brass instruments, it gives me the feeling of strength, power, forcefulness, and largeness due to volume and tone. When strings work in conjunction to the forward-sounding brass, it gives the emotional support and continuity of phrasing. When the music moves in sweeping gestures of dynamics and range, it reminds me of the stories that are larger than life.

Punctuated gear shift—Orchestrated to give a feeling of finish to the opening.

Underscore of the actors—Choosing an alternating staccato rhythm in the strings, mostly in the cello and bass to provoke a gut reaction from the audience, maintains the pulse of timing and pace from the previous piece of music. It also brings the dynamics down to the singularity of strings from the orchestrated, thereby taking the music from complex to sparse, to feel like a reveal. The short phrases of melody lend themselves to not feeling full, so that it seems the perspective is from only one side. Ending with staccato notes creates a questioning feeling. It's not a note that is held out and felt through time. It happens and is gone. It's more of a surprise ending to a phrase.

Punctuated gear shift—Scream—recorded to avoid relying on actors getting into place in the dark, and with added reverb and delay to appear as though it was heard throughout all of London.

Blind event—Returning to full orchestration for a moment, where we are completely in the dark with specific sound effects telling the story that is happening, creates a sense of adventure. Since the sound effects can be dramatized through higher volume, the underscore does not need to get out of the way of the recorded diegetic sound. The woman screams, the police officers whistle, there are sirens, actors screaming, and the breaking down of a door to get inside. The action of this moment sounds very bold and dangerous to me. Hearing this all in the dark is supported by a very dynamic choice in music. The addition of focusing on timpani and percussion not only aids to fast-pace time, but also by mimicking the sound of the physical act of breaking down a door with an ax.

Punctuated gear shift—Orchestrated, same as the first one, to put a finish to the blind event, and identical or very similar in nature to the first shift to maintain continuity.

Reveal of Dr. Jekyll—This is the moment of suspense in the prologue, and it is a stark contrast to bring the dynamics down to strings only, on sustained notes, after the largest and loudest moment. This contrast shocks the audience and helps in the reveal due to the range of dynamics. Strings moving up the scale in pitch aids in the feeling of questioning whether the body is dead or alive. And violins always make me feel more in my heart and chest region, which helps to guide the audience towards the feelings of love and sadness.

Punctuated gear shift—Lighter to remain in the same dynamic range we are in, and setting up what will be used for Utterson's asides throughout the play.

Narration—Slightly differing single notes on strings, with brief dissonant punctuation, help transition from the suspenseful reveal by remaining in the same instrumentation. It also aids the continuity in moving from the past event into the present time because it has a different attitude—one from the narrating character's perspective. The single note matches the visual of a single-actor narration and the dissonance in the long, steady notes shows that there is conflict within this person's telling of the story.

In summary
Understanding the text and all the analysis it needs, your audience's expectation, the setting of the story, the visual aspects designed by your collaborators, the structural shifts, the emotional dynamics, and the why behind your choice of musical and sound elements all lead to a distinct perspective only you as an artist can bring to a piece. No one else will interpret and hear the way you do. Other sound designers may understand how sound affects a human body, how to support a story, and how to create an emotional journey. But what each artist brings to a collaboration is unique because of their approach, detail, and quality of work.

6

COLLABORATIVE PROCESS OF A SOUND DESIGNER

Using refined communication skills, the goal of good collaboration is a free-flowing, respectful exchange of ideas without ego. Every person's goal is to enhance the production, and by the acceptance of each idea into the whole concept, the ownership of design interpretation is no longer the individual's, but the group's. When everyone's input is valued and respected, genuine artistic discovery can occur, because you have created cohesiveness of the ideas implemented within a safe space.

How sound designers discuss and add to the process, when what we do can seem so intangible to others, can be tricky and at times misunderstood. It is up to the designer not only to do their division of the work, but also at times to remind and teach others how and why his or her work is supporting the production.

To be an effective sound designer, you must know and understand how every decision in the scenography was developed. With every decision that is made, immediately think how it pertains to your field and how it impacts your work. We assimilate all the information about what the production looks like into how we are to approach our work as the other design elements begin to take shape around us.

Because of the timing of theatre and the need to build from scratch, most of us know that scenic, props, and costume elements are decided upon earlier than sound, lights, and projection. This does not mean that we are not working, researching, or finding pieces of music and sound effects to help us narrow our approach. We are creating the world alongside our fellow designers so that when our element is introduced to the process, it is in harmony with the rest.

Intellectual Interpretation

As with all theatre designers, sound designers begin with the script, as outlined previously. The conclusions we come to from working with the script create the basis of the intellectual interpretation that conveys feelings to the audience. The next step is to see if your initial ideas coincide with the director's vision.

What is rewarding about this early stage in the process is how we influence the entirety of the production's design in its early stages, because as sound designers we tend to look beyond the conventional where music and sound are concerned. Most of us have a love of music and technology that can at times stretch into the realm of the fanatical.

It's satisfying for us to find something absolute in displaying feeling and intention, especially if it is unknown to others. And if we can create wonderment within the team, we will definitely bring something new to an audience. Unless specifically needed for the production, conventional choices are not as exciting, because we've all heard those choices before. Sound designers strive to create amazement in finding new, interesting, and unique ways to convey feelings and emotions.

The other aspect to the joy of contributing at the early stages of the design process is that, as sound designers, we are focused from the start on the impression upon the audience and their emotional journey. We are already thinking ahead to an audience's involvement, interpretation, and reaction. Our perspective can be a rich element of collaboration that informs the choices the team makes early on.

Design and Production Meetings

In your design and production meetings, maintain the perspective of your design element with every discussion that comes up and comment on how it affects your work. Also, more importantly, do not feel shy about expressing your feelings and reactions to the other designers' concepts. They want response to their work as much as you do, to create a group consensus.

If you are composing, designing, or both for a production, the inspiration pieces you create or find in the early part of the process serve as your sketches to represent the final product. Your inspiration pieces are parallel to a scenic or a costume sketch, or a lighting designer's renderings. These pieces are there for comment and delineation of style, meaning, and feeling. They are approximations and not the final work.

This can be tricky at times because fellow collaborators may settle on, or get used to, what you present initially. There is always the possibility that once a production goes into rehearsal, the initial impulses may no longer be valid. You must find a way to establish a means for transformation within the process.

If your sound design is allowed to grow with the rehearsal process, your choices of support will be more accurate in the final product. Stay close to the conversation and discussion shaping the production, because ideas can come quickly and change can at times be drastic and swift.

Rehearsals

If possible, attend rehearsals as they grow, to see how the director is working with the actors. This is where you discover the pacing, style, and interpretation of the initial intellectual ideas. Once you hear the actors' speech patterns, the timbre of their voice, and see how they move around the space, you start to put together a fuller sonic scope of what you are to support. Rehearsals are also where the discoveries of intention lie. If you are to support the intentions of the piece, it's helpful if you know how they came about. If you cannot attend rehearsals, these discussions can be relayed through rehearsal reports and then in more detail through your conversations with the director.

Previously, I outlined what we as sound designers find in a script to support. But now, in rehearsal is where we learn about the instances of support that are not evident in the script. With more sound design experience, the moments of support will show themselves clearly in rehearsal; you will learn how to spot them more quickly as you continue in your career.

As sound design for theatre has advanced, it has taken on properties from the movie industry because cinematic sound is a common denominator for a twenty-first-century audience. It is up to the team to decide the correct style for each production. However, while a cinematic approach can be a tactic to control an audience's emotional journey, sound in theatre is paramount to support theatricality.

This can be shown in myriad instances from underscoring choreography and supporting violence design to transitional support. In rehearsal, try to spot the areas that feel extra silent or dry theatrically. As you discern these moments, determine if you can support the actors' emotions and intentions or change the feeling of the pace to be faster or slower when you get to the stage. Then it's up to you to discuss these ideas with the director and team. The further into the rehearsal process you go, the closer the timing and emotional expression will be to the final product.

There are many different processes to how a rehearsal room will function. Every director has their own style moving the play towards its final goals. And stage managers have their own style of managing the room and all of the communication. It's up to you to navigate the group dynamic respectfully to ensure that your design is supporting what is happening in rehearsal, as well as feeling valued and respected by the others in the room.

If you are ever unsure of anything, ask a question. When you suggest your ideas of support to the group during the process, it invigorates your collaborators to join in on that discussion.

After the designer run or the final runs in the rehearsal room, our next important moment is quiet time and level set.

Quiet Time and Level Set

There are two aspects to quiet time and level set. One is the electromechanical aspect of making sure the system is behaving in the manner you wish for the production. This is about a system balance and generalized consideration of sound. The other aspect is how the aural architecture envelops the audience's spatial awareness with dynamics from subtlety to loud sound. You determine what the details are for actors hearing on stage as well as what the audience hears, and how the sound waves are going to travel based on how you have set up your system of speakers and fills. The sound delivery system is an extension of your imagination.

Quiet time is the most precious moment you have in the theatre. It is the moment of actualization of your ideas into a form where you create exactly how you want the audience to hear your work. This is when you have the space in silence to perfect what you want with no judgment from external listeners. When you play through your cues and set the source placement and levels in the theater, relive in your mind, to the best of your ability, what the actors were doing in the rehearsal room. This will help with volume and timing.

For example, if you remember an actor whispering the lines that you are underscoring, you will have to err towards a quieter delivery. Or if an actor runs off stage before a transition, then you know that it will be a two-second fade-up rather than a five-second fade-up of your transition music. It's important that in quiet time you get as close to ideal as you can achieve in regards to timing and volume. It's not an uncommon occurrence that a cue that could have possibly worked at a lower volume level is cut because it was played too loudly the first time, because contextually it seemed too obvious for the moment you were supporting.

When you're alone in the theater, pay attention to the aural awareness you give to volume. A well-framed sound design is sensitive to this. What sounds loud to you alone in the theater is not going to be as loud when an audience occupies the space, because bodies absorb sound waves. When setting levels, the quiet cues will always need adjustment when you get action or dialogue over them.

I tend to aim louder on the loud, and quieter on the quiet when I first set levels and then adjust once tech begins. We know that volume awareness is relative and that bodies will absorb sound. So, when you're alone in the theater, the sound can bounce and appear to be louder because of the relativity of space. If you aim higher on the loud cues it will adjust to the volume you want once people are occupying the space.

And as far as aiming for the quieter edge of discernment, when alone in the theatre you don't have the relativity of the actor's voice or movement to fully judge volume. Aiming lower will help the subtlety of support and the theatricality of underscoring not to seem too bold. In tech, you can adjust higher. If you come in too strong, you risk it feeling placed upon the work and not in support of what is happening on stage.

In time, you will learn through experience the qualities between the extremes when alone and with others in a theatre space, and how to set your levels accordingly.

In quiet time, start by making sure that your opening cue is completely to your liking. Because typically sound is the prominent design element to the opening of a production, you don't need the other elements to create it exactly as you like. On the first day of tech, you want it to sound the way you intend it to be heard when you play it in front of the entire cast, crew, and team. They are your first objective listeners in the space.

Once the opening cue is set, work diligently through the show to set your levels. Fade times will depend on action, so approximate according to the timings you took in the designer run and by remembering the pacing of the actors involved in that moment.

And know that after that first quiet time in the theatre, it is not an easy task to get the theatre all to yourself again during the technical rehearsal process, so make the most of your time when you have it, completing as much as you can in the time allotted.

The First Moment Sound is Heard

Part of the reason for having it sound as close as possible to what you want is to garner advocacy for your contribution to the process. That initial moment in tech of pressing the first "go" is nerve-wracking for every sound designer. It's the moment that screams to all in the room that your design either works or doesn't work. Sometimes others forget that this may be the first moment we bring our work into the process.

Actors play a strong role in sound's acceptance, because they have not heard your work in context yet and may rightfully have particular expectations for the production they have been working on for a month or more. You will always attain a graceful acceptance of your intention if the actors react positively to it. They are the objective ears in the room at that moment and it is important that you assure them that you are supporting them with the appropriate style and theatricality. If they react positively at the start, their trust that you have served the intention of the piece will likely be maintained throughout the process.

Tech

The best way to secure the inclusion of your design ideas is to try them in the context of tech. Before tech you can determine style and feeling, and in rehearsal you can even work out timing. But until your ideas are heard within the pacing of the live element, using the speakers that will produce the sound, how it affects the emotional journey of the audience cannot be experienced fully.

Most directors now understand that sound can be manipulated very quickly in a tech rehearsal and therefore changing sound is not something that will greatly stall the process once you are in the theater. When you have a director who may not understand what you are trying to achieve, ask to "try it" in tech. Do not fear asking this; it's part of the process and the joy of tech, especially if you are prepared with options for sound and music. The only way to know if your sound design ideas work is to hear them in context.

When you are in a tech process and you wish to discuss any element, including your own, try to phrase your concern as a question. The best way to achieve what you wish to occur is to tie it back to what was discussed previously by the team. If the team wishes to detour from what was agreed earlier, that's perfectly fine, but you won't know if you don't ask the question.

However, asking too many questions should be avoided. It may appear as if you don't know what you're doing, or that you will accommodate any whim that is suggested. Find a balance between when it is appropriate to explain with statements or ask with questions.

During tech there is a fine line of balance between being a designer and a facilitator. This goes back to the concept that everyone in the room has a valid opinion and sometimes someone else may have a better suggestion. And sometimes they may not. Your confidence and the style in which you communicate is how you navigate your way through tech. You don't want to have the feeling of facilitating others' ideas; you want to come to a consensus of intention through collaboration.

With directors and designers that you've worked with many times, it is not so challenging to maintain cohesion in your design and receive suggestions at the same time. It's when you don't know each other very well, or if you strongly disagree, that the moments can become stressful. Remember that it's not a personal attack against you or your art. Everyone is focused on the best way to tell the story and how to represent the goals of the production. And sometimes you have to show yourself, or someone else, that the idea will or won't work before you can move on.

Tech is for trying things, but make sure that it's not your indecision that is causing the room to offer up solutions to any issue that arises. Your best tactic to keep things on track is to ask questions of intention that bring the team back to the initial decisions of goals in your design and production meetings. If someone can distinguish how his or her idea is rationalized within the scope of the production, it's worth trying. Remember that you are the expert in your field, and you have a collaborative voice in achieving intention and goals.

When posed with questions of large change decisions, make sure to look at what you gain and lose with each choice. You can solidify what choice is best to support the storytelling if you understand the pros and cons of each decision the team makes. Always refer back to the script and design meetings to support your case. When a change is discussed, a typical response of mine is, "Yes, we can absolutely do that. Do you feel we will then miss (whatever is changed)?" You are showing that you are open to changing the idea, and you are also highlighting what you liked about what you had already. Usually, what happens is you try it and discuss the response that arises from the change.

I have found that the most successful start to tech is when the lighting designer and sound designer have discussed and played through the opening of the show, before involving the actors. It helps tech begin on a solid foundation. If you can find the few minutes to do this before tech begins, you will be rewarded with a strong start to the process.

The goal of tech is to set the cues of every technical element that is needed to run a show. As a sound designer, if you get bogged down in the minutiae of individual moments without seeing the bigger picture, you can lose the understanding of the elasticity of dynamics within the scale and scope of the production.

If you do not need actors to be present to fine-tune your work notes, take a note and move on. But, if you need time to work, because you know you will never return to this moment with such precise detail, take that time.

Time is of the essence and you should work constantly, especially when others are taking time for their elements. It's best if you can work ahead of the curve, time-wise. Once you get the cues set and you are running the show, you can fine-tune and work on the timing, volume, flow, pacing, and emotional journey of the story, because you will be experiencing the entirety of the work.

Objective and Subjective Listening

You will vacillate between being an objective and a subjective listener throughout the process of creating your work. Being subjective comes from the mind of the designer or composer, and being objective comes from the mind of the audience. This is important because you want to think of the expression of your art as the designer, and the impression of your art upon the audience, at the same time.

Table 6.1 *Objective and Subjective Listening*

Stage of process	Point of view	Role	Design effect
First reading of script	Objective	Audience	Impression
Research	Subjective	Designer/Composer	Expression
First read-through with actors	Objective	Audience	Impression
Working on your cues	Subjective	Designer/Composer	Expression
Designer run	Objective	Audience	Impression
Quiet time and tech	Subjective	Designer	Expression
Previews	Objective	Audience	Impression
Tech during previews	Subjective	Designer	Expression
Opening	Objective	Audience	Impression

Previews

You may not always have the preview stage before you open a show, and its length may vary from one production company to the next. If you do have a chance to be able to witness the objective view of an audience before opening, you can determine whether they are emotionally reacting the way you intended. The benefit to having a preview process is that change can be made the following day in tech rehearsal according to the audience reaction the night before.

This is a valuable tool at this stage of the process, especially for new works, because everyone on the team has now been involved deeply to the point of not having a clear objective view. Use the audience's reaction to enlighten you as to whether you have achieved your intentions and goals. You will know immediately if your design works, and usually you will know exactly how to fix it if it doesn't.

If you don't know how to fix it, ask the team for their impression as they too have been experiencing it with the audience to see if their work is doing what they wish it to do. The rehearsals between previews can sometimes involve huge changes. Scenes can get rearranged and design choices can change drastically. Remember that the goal is always to support the production and that nothing is personal. Keep an open mind throughout the entire process and support the story.

You rely wholly on the stage manager to keep the integrity of your design throughout a run. If you have been clear with the communication of your design intention throughout the process, an excellent stage manager will ensure that your work lives and breathes with the live aspect of the run of a show.

Ownership

The best collaborations are when all parties have contributed to the process with their own individual artistic additions by adding to each other's ideas through respect and generosity. We all want to be able to say we own a piece of our productions. Theatre is a fleeting art form; it has an opening and a closing night. And if you didn't get a chance to see a production while it was running, you missed what all of those theatre artists produced. Luckily for the visual aspects of theatre design, there are photos and videos; however, for sound there is no way to place anyone in the exact place and time to experience our work within the context of which it was intended.

As a sound designer, you will become accustomed to an audience not knowing your contribution or understanding how you supported the production. If sound is well integrated into a production it becomes another character in the piece. And then, after the show has closed, there is no way to recreate the full experience of your work. It's not a job with a lot of accolades, and the continual need to explain what you do can be tiresome at times. But if you are okay as a supporting character, and secure in your art to understand the depth of your work, you will have many rewarding experiences in theatre.

7

COHESION, CONVENTION, AND IMPLEMENTATION IN TECH

Cohesion

Once you have determined the style, feel, and effect you are going for in your design, remain purposefully committed to the intention of your design even if the style is meant to be eclectic. You want to ensure that the audience is not thinking about anything else during the performance other than what the team wants them to think. If an audience member starts to question when you didn't want them to, they will be pulled out of the story. If you keep your design cohesive in its intention with regards to feel and style, it will appear more polished in the end as a complete package. You are expressing an intention that you hope is recognizable and interpreted the way you intended.

With specific intention, your music should live in the appropriate genre and style, your punctuations should live in the same world as your play, your abstractions should break the rules of the standard that is set, when following a point of view you should remain consistent to who is telling the story, and when following a theme or character you should maintain meaning and communicate change according to how the theme or character changes.

You are creating worlds within the realm of the theater. The audience has come to the theater expecting an experience. Sometimes that can be one where they feel safely guided through the story. And sometimes, the intention may be that they do not feel safe within the world you are creating. If you remain consistent with your intentions, and how you convey them through convention, you will achieve a more believable world in which the audience can safely lose themselves even if it feels dangerous to do so.

Convention

We use the word convention to mean the way something is repeated specifically in a technical process of a production. In order to create believable conventions, we maintain consistency between the way the set moves or changes, how the lights create mood, place and style, and the dynamics of sound. These should remain logical and meaningful to the intention and style of the overall production.

As the sound designer, you set the dynamics of your transitions outside of the tech process when you are building your cues. You choose if the music fades in or out, or bumps in or out, prior to working with other designers. This is your initial choice as to how you feel the pacing of your work should be experienced. Once you bring your work into the theatre to implement it with the rest of the technical elements, you will either govern the pacing or have to change it on the spot. The more you can glean from rehearsals, the designer run, and conversations with the artistic team, the better chance you have of getting the intention of your design correct the first time through.

Sound, lights, and projection work most closely together to create conventions of how cues are timed and called. Scenery moves in the most efficient way, given what the physics of the structural pieces allow. There's not much change to how scenery moves unless it is to become more efficient throughout the technical rehearsal process. Therefore, sound, lights, and projection work with the timings of scenery and then in close tandem with each other.

In more cases than not, technical elements work best when they start at the same time, last for the same duration, and end in the same manner. If lights are fading, then we fade for the same time. If we are bumping out, lights most probably will join us in that process.

Whatever the choices are, as the technical process continues, the conventions start to take shape. You might see that going into one particular setting the convention remains the same, which might then dictate how you go into the next setting, and so on. As the conventions start to take shape, take note of them, and then begin to make the conscious choice to adhere to them, or not, in order to support storytelling through the style of the production.

There are many times in tech when the question, "Is this the first time we are doing this?" or the statement, "This is how we got here the last time," is heard. Consistency, for meaning and style, will not only make your show look skillful and appropriate, it will aid in the storytelling and impression upon the audience.

Cohesion in the Tech Process

When in tech, and needing to make a change that involves cohesion with others, try to have a possible solution to the issue before you bring it to the attention of everyone else in the room. If it's complex or you're uncomfortable with voicing the solution as your own, you can steer the conversation in that direction by using questions that help define what the issue is and the best way to fix it.

For example, if it's something as simple as needing the actor to enter on a certain note in order to ensure the perfect ending to that entrance, know your intention and convey it to the director when talking about the change of blocking.

For me, tech is a rehearsal that is driven by the stage manager's discretion. When raising concerns in tech, the director will always be the person who is steering the intention of the production. Speak to the person who needs or wants the information you have, but always include the director and as many as possible of the other people involved. This avoids confusion and possible double work later caused by two people solving an issue independently.

If your question is directorial or concept-driven, speak to the director. If your question is about the calling of cues and understanding of placement, or overall information regarding the tech process, speak to the stage manager. If you need to discuss timings between lights and sound, speak to the lighting designer. Regarding actors, I prefer to speak through the director at first because they have a shorthand of conversation from the rehearsal process. But with having spent time in the room, and the fact that you may know the clearest way to communicate how the sound is supporting the actors, it's best to talk directly to them to aid in comprehension. This of course varies for every production, based on how well you know the other artists with whom you are working. Know how to direct your questions and concerns to the appropriate people.

Learn to work quickly in tech and utilize the time you have right then and there. Your worst enemy is a cue played incorrectly more than once. You don't want the actors and the artistic team to get used to a cue that is not delivered how you intended. If it's not the intention you want, changing it may cause timing, cueing, and motivation issues for the actors. It could even get cut. Challenge yourself to work quickly in the moment and I guarantee that you will speed up with more practice and experience.

Work whenever possible during tech. When a cue is running and you have time within it, you can adjust its levels and placement so that you get a greater depth of context. And if you are content with the changes as it's running, you will not have to waste time by going back and doing it again.

When sound is constant for multiple cues and yet worked on in segments, it's difficult to understand if the flow of what you're trying to achieve is correctly supporting the story. In order to save time in tech, sometimes you need to hear a long segment of cues in its entirety before a hold is called. Make sure you communicate this to the stage manager. This will avoid the need to back up to repeat the beginning of a large section of tech. You can also ask to run a large section before adding sound, to get approximate timings.

The beginning of tech is about getting the cues booked and conventions set. When you get to the point of running the show, this is where sound designers understand the pacing and flow of their work. Your goal is to get to the running stage efficiently so that you have time to perfect timings and intention when running.

While in tech, think about the shape of the sound waves and from where they are emanating. Use your skills of spatial awareness to direct an audience's attention, and give a sense of reality to the moment. A river sound would not feel right if it came out of speakers above your head. Think about whether the sound originates from the stage and emanates out, or is a surround-sound immersion moment, and shape the design with all the tools you have in the room.

To refer back to a symphony again, a production is filled with movements, solos, and changes in dynamics and range. What you are looking for in tech is the emotional and physical gear changes of these movements. Whether the play is natural, abstract, or anywhere in between, what remains constant is that there will be emotional shifts and physical movement. While working in tech, note whether tech is driving the actors in a specific movement of your symphony, or if the actors' change is what is driving the aural narrative. If sound supports the movement, lasts as long as the shift does, and emotionally supports the gear change, it will feel right for the moment.

Most importantly, be mindful to not qualify whether you are successful during the technical process. Remember you are continually working towards refinement, and that your approach could change at any moment.

Cohesion with Voice and Movement

Because a truly supportive sound design is one that is felt as well as heard, whenever possible try to mask the starting and ending of cues with the actors' voices or movement of the piece. A new idea can be introduced when a character enters or exits the stage. These can be done in multiple layers as well.

Take, for example, coming out of a transition and going into a restaurant scene where two characters meet a third. One of the characters leaves, and the two that remain have a casual conversation that becomes more intimate. You can start with your transition into the scene; perhaps there's music playing with a restaurant ambience. When the one character leaves you can fade down the music slowly (matching that actor's exit) to make it a little quieter for the scene. Then, when the conversation becomes intimate, the restaurant ambience and music can slowly fade away to highlight an intimacy of selective hearing. Now the audience can tune into the intimate conversation without distraction. You mask these changes with the action on stage or when actors are speaking, so it feels timed and specific to the intent and motion of the play.

If your convention is to begin ambience at the start of a scene and then slowly fade it out, you can choose a moment in the scene where you want to pull into the conversation as if you are zooming in with a camera. Then gracefully take your time to fade out to infinity so as not to draw attention to the sound going away. Make it seem as though the audience has selectively concentrated on the conversation or action and omitted the background noise. Remember that the neural pathways are established between five and seven seconds, so after that amount of time you can "selectively hear" the sound dissipating.

The same tool can be used for the starting and ending of a drone. The way to draw attention to sound that the audience has selectively tuned out is to change its attenuation or frequency. You can bring in a drone strongly if you want people to notice it. But if you do not want the audience to take notice, you can mask the start of it under dialogue or action and be very considerate to the same as you take it out. What is left in the silence after a drone will feel like important dialogue to hear, or important action to observe. This is one way you can accentuate your most significant choice of silence.

When creating the moments you wish to highlight during the technical rehearsal, be specific about the placement of the beginnings and ends of cues to ensure that you have supported the moment and left the way clear for the expression on stage.

For example, when highlighting a moment of revelation that is then followed by dialogue, you can support the exact moment of recognition of the audience's understanding with punctuation, and then get out of the way of the actor's work. You want to match the moment by either fading down sound yet remaining a part of the actor's discovery phase, or fading away entirely if you need to focus on what the actor is saying directly after the discovery.

Masking is for the beginning and ending of gestures within the movements of a story. And it is not a rule; it is a tool.

Cohesion with Your Collaborators

Just as we stay close to the conversations and discussions in the process of designing the production, the same is true of the tech process. Change can be drastic and swift, and you want to make sure you are a part of the conversation. At times you will have to maintain a multi-split focus between all the other people in the room's intentions. You should be aware of what is changing in the room so that you are not behind the work, but possibly ahead of it.

Stay figuratively close to the director at all times. Sound's primary function is to understand the intention of the director's vision and to impress that upon the audience. If the director is changing something in tech, pay attention. Most probably it will affect the sound, because we are most closely linked to the emotional journey and timing of action and dialogue.

Watch the actors and how they change what they are doing now they are on stage. Timings and intentions vary due to many circumstances and the best interpretation for them may shift at any time. Sound supports their emotional journey and intention, and you need to be aware if and when it changes.

Be in contact with the stage manager at all times. They are the keeper of communication and if you've missed something or need to communicate anything, your stage manager is going to be your best advocate. Since they have been in the room with the director from the start, they will understand the quickest way to communicate when something is changing and whether it will need amendment from the designers.

Stay close to all the other designers, especially the lighting designer and the projection designer. Sound, lights, and projection are intrinsically linked; if you are not in sync with your lighting or projection designer, the production will feel bumpy and it will look as though mistakes are being made. When sound, lighting, and projection design are perfectly in sync through intention, moments in theatre can feel magical. Know what all the other designers are doing throughout the process and match them accordingly.

There are many communication dynamics that unfold during a tech process. If you find you are unable to communicate effectively to the director or other designers, make sure you that you are in direct contact with the stage manager to understand what is happening at every moment. This is not the ideal way to work collaboratively, but you need to be prepared for anything that may happen in tech once emotions and vulnerability are at a high level. Your stage manager will always be there for clarification.

If the production is successful, and it looks and feels in perfect sync with the expression the team wishes to impress upon an audience, then all the drama that can happen in tech will be forgiven. Trust that this job is fleeting, that the show will open, and it will all work out in the end if you've respectfully done your job with artistic intent.

We all put our work out there; we fear judgment, and we wish for praise. Even if failure can feel singular and your own, success is based on how well your work supports the whole through your collaboration with others. Know that every artist in the room is feeling vulnerable and when you communicate effectively and respectfully in tech, great work can be accomplished.

8
COMMUNICATION FOR THE ARTISTIC PROCESS

As an artist, you want to learn how to communicate effectively—especially if you contribute your art to a group dynamic, as we do in theatre. It's very important that complete understanding of ideas and beliefs occurs so that you are able to work together to achieve a common goal. Collaboration in theatre is a learned behavior and it involves the ability to work well with others, relying on your own leadership skills to bring your design medium to the team.

A successful production gives each artist his or her own success; it is not the other way around. It is the sum of the parts that make up the whole. Every member of the team shares the workload within the specialization of which they are hired. It is not about getting along, making friends, or not speaking your mind. It's about working together and bringing your own expertise to the team. If you get along and make friends, that's definitely a better situation, but you should be prepared for all scenarios—positive and negative.

I want to start with how a person is perceived by others. The moment you walk into a room at the start of a production can make anyone feel insecure, especially if you're young and don't know anyone in the room. It's a moment of vulnerability and first impressions matter. We want to have the ability to appear confident, and the way to do this is to look at how people interact when brought together for the first time.

Any first interaction is visual and non-verbal, and sensory data, if mindfully processed, can offer a lot of information from the observations that you make. Also realize that others are observing you as well, and drawing their own conclusions about you before you even utter a word. All of this is done subconsciously, and we do it all the time. Sensory perception never stops. Learning how you currently see others is a way that you can then control how you are perceived in the future. Start paying attention to yourself and your behavior, and why you are drawing conclusions.

You can tell a great deal from the following:

- Body posture
- Arm positions

- Leg positions
- Hand movements
- Foot movements
- Eye expressions
- Mouth position
- Facial complexion
- Tone of voice
- Loudness of voice

For example, a person who covers their mouth when speaking is not going to effectively communicate their ideas. Someone who has crossed arms and legs gives the perception of being closed off to ideas. Someone who doesn't look you in the eye when talking to you seems less confident of what they are saying. You want to be able to train yourself to be perceived as confident, open, intelligent, and all of the best attributes that help you to accomplish your art.

EXERCISES—OBSERVATION OF BEHAVIOR

Pair up and take turns telling your partner a positive experience for five minutes. While one person is speaking, the other is marking down the observations they perceive. Do they cover their mouth when they speak? Do they look up or down? Do they make eye contact? Are they smiling? Do they speak loudly or softly? Do they end their statements as questions? Anything that is seen and heard is written down.

Then have the same person speak of a negative experience for five minutes while the other writes down their observations. Switch who is communicating and who is observing, and then discuss with each other the impression those observations made about how you perceived your partner.

Most of us know our own behavioral patterns, but it is helpful to know specifics if you are not aware of how you are perceived. This exercise is the start of the process of being mindful of how you personally come across to others. Changing behavior is not easy and restructuring how we speak and communicate to be more effective in our collaboration with others can change the overall experience of any situation.

Group Dynamics

Once you begin to focus on yourself and amending how you communicate non-verbally, then you can turn the observation towards how you are in a group setting. There are many stages and levels to small and large group dynamics, especially in groups who don't know each other well before they mature as a group.

Working in theatre, you encounter new artists regularly, with whom you will have an intimate, artistic sharing of ideas. If you, as an individual, have barriers to your expression of thoughts and ideas, it's good to understand them in the safe environment of a controlled group instead of the workplace. Here an individual can work on why they may be reticent or shy, or if they come across as autocratic. The goal remains that we all wish to be better communicators so that our collaboration with others is efficient and effective.

Some of the initial questions that can arise in a group setting are as follows:

- Who are these people?
- What do they know of me?
- Is there prior experience of relationship?
- What has brought them to this moment with me?
- Will I be accepted into this group?
- How involved do I see myself becoming with them?
- Will I feel as though I belong if I am accepted?
- Do I like these people? Do they like me?
- How much am I willing to boldly risk with them?
- Can I be vulnerable with this group?
- How much can I trust these people?
- What is the dynamic of this group?
- What do they believe? Do I share their beliefs?
- What do they expect of me?
- Will I be able to speak my mind without judgment?
- Will this group be respectful?

Once a group starts sharing and talking, the trust level within the group increases and you can be more vulnerable when expressing yourself. In order to build fundamental communication skills, you must have self-awareness of how you communicate.

DISCUSSION—PERSONAL RESPONSE TO GROUP

Go around the room and have everyone recount what it was like the first time they came into this group with those they did not know. What specific judgments did they make of others, what fears did they personally have, and how long was it until they felt able to be vulnerable and share within the group dynamic? Then have the group respond to the individual, revealing which of the assumptions about the individual and the group were correct and which incorrect.

This discussion is to open up the awareness of how each member felt when they first entered into the group, but also to hear what others thought of them. If there is already an established trust in the room, you can speak more about how those initial fears shaped the group, and if they have changed since the group's inception. You can also revisit this later in time.

Behavior and Attitude

There are two defining characteristics to communication: behavior and attitude. Behavior is the observable words and actions you exhibit, and attitude is based on your underlying beliefs, feelings, and intentions.

To break it down further, there are two basic attitudes you can hold toward yourself or others. The first is "I care" and the second is "I don't care." In every communication you have with another person, you communicate whether or not you value and respect them, and whether or not you value and respect yourself. And that choice is up to us every single time we communicate.

Behavior is something we can remark upon and even change. Attitude is a perception that behavior creates. If someone says that a person has a bad attitude, it is because his or her behavior is exhibiting something that creates that opinion. We want to ensure that others do not have bad opinions of us, and the only way to keep that in check is to observe our own behavior and modify it to reflect a different attitude.

In a verbal conversation there are eight possible kinds of communication:

1 What I'm meaning to say
2 The words I actually say
3 The words the other person hears
4 The other person's interpretation
5 What the other person is meaning to say

6 The words the other person actually says
7 The words I hear the other person say
8 My interpretation

It's important when communicating for artistic purposes that you are very clear and make sure that your meaning is what the other members of the team hear. Do not leave a conversation if you still have questions to ask. I cannot stress this enough.

In theatre, we have to act upon what others have conveyed. If you think you understood and still have questions, there is no way that you will achieve what is expected from you. And beyond the idea of ensuring that you have all the information you need to continue in your work, do not proceed on your own unless you are in agreement.

EXERCISES—OPPOSITE POETRY

Sit in a circle and have one person write at the top of a piece of paper a sentence—a question or statement—and pass it to the next person. The next person writes down the absolute opposite of this sentence, phrase-by-phrase, with any idea acceptable regarding what they feel is "opposite." The second person folds the paper so that the first sentence is concealed and passes it to the next person for them to add an opposite sentence. By covering the first sentence, it turns the negative statement into an affirmation that now must be negated. The third person creates the opposite sentence and then folds over the top sentence and passes it on. Continue this until you go around the circle. When you complete the circle read the opposite poem aloud. Discuss how the meaning changes statement by statement, and how opposition can create something different and unintended.

This exercise is to show that if your sentence structure is not specific, the meaning may not come across as intended when trying to find its opposite. It also shows how a negative idea can become a positive one, and how every addition can lead to something greater than its parts.

Motivation and Self-Empowerment = Assertiveness

Motivation is the incentive to act toward our objective. The mind creates a target, goals, objectives, and perceived ideals of the expected outcome. A motivated communicator is someone who can see the final outcome, and who knows where to go, while having the will to achieve it. Unless we use purposeful action, the possibility of hindering our goals comes from fear and stress. One must feel self-empowered in order to apply effective communication skills. You want to get the most you can out of your own work as well as your work with others.

It's easy to confuse assertiveness within the extremes of passivity and aggressiveness. To be assertive means to not be passive. Passivity is a silent acceptance or approval of a situation or task. When passive, emotion and energy remain internal and you are not communicating with complete honesty with the people around you. On the other end, more importantly, to be assertive does not mean to be aggressive. One easy way to know if you've been aggressive in your communication is if you regret what you've said. Aggressiveness shows no consideration or respect for the other person.

When you are assertive you approach a situation like so: I have an issue, this is what's happening, this is how the issue is affecting me, and this is what could be done to solve the issue. And therefore, this is what I want.

I use this approach very often when troubleshooting issues in theatre. It starts with an observable behavior, a comment or opinion on how that behavior or issue affects my work, and then a solution posed to help further the process.

There is a perceived difference between the masculine and feminine dynamic with regards to assertiveness. You want to approach this cautiously so that you are not labeled as a byproduct of speaking assertively. Women can relate to being given certain labels when they act as assertively as their male counterparts. This does not mean that it doesn't occur with men as well—it does. This is because there are some people who feel challenged when someone is assertive towards them and it is misinterpreted as aggressive. You want to ensure that you are not perceived as aggressive.

Assertive thinking and response will make you a more honest person and will be better for your own mental health. It does not solve all problems, and other people will make their own choices about how to react to what you say. But if you tell the truth tactfully and appropriately, it will help you feel calm and in control when communicating with other people.

In theatre, the ideal situation is being able to respect another artist's vulnerable contribution to the team, while still being able to contribute what you need to the overall artistry. We all have personal opinions about art: it is meant to evoke a reaction, and not every member of the team will agree all of the time.

To be an effective collaborator, you must learn how to add your idea to another's idea without diminishing them. You may not always get what you want, but by applying an assertive approach, you effectively speak more honestly and you will be heard completely, since you did not dishonor another's contribution. It's about how you use your confidence constructively.

Confidence is what helps when navigating secure or insecure people. As David Budries, Head of the MFA Sound Design department at Yale School of Drama once said to me, "Subtle quiet confidence is the sexiest quality of a good designer."

Self-Awareness Skills

So let's look at how we are constantly judging. This will help us determine our own thought process, and in turn, give us the possibility to amend it. As theatre artists, we are always judging, for better and worse. We need to be able to critique without being critical.

The human brain will start by making a judgment about a specific situation; it then looks for evidence to support and prove its conclusion by interpreting relevant and irrelevant observations into what it has determined is correct. It's hard to regulate what the brain is thinking as it happens so quickly and becomes innate to how we as human beings are able to process the constant contemplation that is occurring.

One way to identify what the brain is thinking is by focusing on your self-talk. Self-talk is the dialogue you have with yourself in your head. It is very powerful because we believe the voice in our head to be the truth. That is not always so. For purposes of becoming better collaborators, I want to focus on the destructive self-talk that can get in the way of how you communicate. And by changing destructive self-talk to constructive self-talk you will find solutions more easily.

Self-Talk

According to John Nielsen in his book *Effective Communication Skills*, there are nine types of destructive self-talk:

1 **"I can't help it"**
   Even in the worst of circumstances, there is always something you can do to better a situation. It's possible that there are things you cannot change, but if you say you "can't help it" to yourself, you are throwing away all of your power to affect change. Example: throughout the entire design and tech process there are moments where the team does not achieve the correct balance of what is needed to support the piece. Always think from your perspective, use your experience, and search for a solution from your own point of view and share it with the team. One of you is bound to land on something that works to resolve the issue that the rest will want to try. You are a part of the team for the sole purpose of helping in the situations that feel impossible.

2   **Focusing on negative only**

In every terrible situation there can be something positive, and in every positive situation there can be something negative. If you focus on the negative only, you will cloud your judgment and not have the ability to find the positive about any part of your work with others. Example: You're in tech and the director turns around and says, "I don't like this cue." Do not focus on failure or how you must be bad at what you do because he or she didn't like it. Turn that around to focus on the details of what exactly is incorrect about the storytelling aspect of the cue, e.g. mood, pacing, timing. And work towards achieving a collaborative moment of making it better together.

3   **Obligation words**

If you claim you "have to" do something, your brain will think there is no alternative. The brain will interpret word-meaning literally. It will not give you the ability to change something you don't like or express the wish for something you do not have. It forces the situation into the area of fate, meaning there are no options. Word usage is very important to get across clear meaning. You want to change the obligatory words you are thinking into words that help you achieve a more assertive, respectful dialogue. Theatre is about changing things constantly; it is often a trial-and-error situation. Using finite words can halt collaboration.

Example:

This should …	*changes to*	This could …
This must …	*changes to*	This wants to …
I have to …	*changes to*	I choose to …
I need to …	*changes to*	It would fit my goals if …
I've got to …	*changes to*	It is in my best interest to …
I ought to …	*changes to*	It would help the situation if …

4   **Reading minds**

It is hard to notice when you read minds, but anytime you claim to know what another person is thinking, feeling, or wanting, check and see if you are telling yourself this or if they have actually communicated it to you. If they haven't, you are interpreting what you have assumed is their opinion. If the other person has not specifically said their opinion to you, you are therefore guessing at their thoughts through what you are thinking of them, and that will either be wrong or incomplete.

Example: while in a production meeting a member of the team makes a face while you are discussing your artistry. Do not assume that the face is meant for what you've just communicated. Give that person the benefit of the doubt that perhaps their own self-talk is telling them something that is causing their facial expression. For all you know, you just reminded them of something important that they have forgotten to do and they are upset with themselves. You can never be sure that others are living in the moment, so do not insert meaning where words are not spoken.

5   **Generalizing people**

It is okay to have an opinion about a behavior that you have observed someone else do, but as soon as you label someone with a generalization you lose the ability to see that person clearly. If you call someone an egotist, misogynist, irresponsible, etc., your brain will believe those words as fact and then use the observances of that person's behavior to prove itself right. You also preclude the ability for that person to change your opinion of them, which is unfair as we are all hopefully learning and growing throughout our lives.

Example: you witness how a stagehand repeatedly drops his or her props and is late for their cues. You label them as clumsy and unprofessional. Now every time they mess up, you will have more evidence supporting your opinion and the label you placed on them. But it's possible that he or she is not feeling well and is trying their best to get through the day on cold medication that is affecting their motor and memory skills. The label you placed upon their behavior may not be the reality of the situation.

6   **Always/never**

Try not using the words always and never, when it's not applicable to the situation. There are variances to everything we come across; remember this and you will be able to find solutions. Choose more descriptive vocabulary words to truly convey your meaning, even it it's just to yourself. Once you notice yourself using these words, they will stick out prominently. It will force you to recognize when it's best to actually use the words always and never.

Example: "The cue into the outdoor scenes should always be a fade." This is the simplest version of the use of the word. It gets more complicated when the statement reveals something about your collaborative skills. "I never like starting a show with preshow music." You want to remain open to any possibilities that will support the production.

7   **Prediction of the future—fear and worry**

This is not about looking forward towards what may happen in order to be prepared; you should consider different outcomes and make plans to prevent any issues that may arise. What is damaging about predicting the future, however, is to be controlled by self-talk that is full of fear and worry about what is to come. It demonstrates that you are not living in the present, and you will not acknowledge and act in this moment if you are stressed about the future. Additionally, when you imagine a worst-case scenario, the body produces the same chemicals that are produced in an actual stress-induced situation. It feels as if it is really happening right now, and the damage can be as great to your mental or physical health as from the real-life trauma.

Example: it is debilitating to the creative process to worry with fear and stress over the effect of your design upon the production. You will be unable to create if you feel those emotions at the early stages of development. Live in the moment and create your artistry with confidence. When you get to the later stages, you will be in that moment and can amend what you've done previously.

8 **Focusing only on yourself**

Our brains tend to take things personally and will interpret behavior to have personal meaning, when in reality the situation may have nothing to do with us. We are the stars of our own daily movie. If you learn to not take a situation personally, you will be more effective in finding a solution instead of becoming stuck in an emotional reaction.

Example: if someone did not acknowledge you today, it may not mean that they are mad at you or that you've done anything wrong to them. Life is full of coincidence that has no personal meaning. It is unlikely that everything should be a sign about what you have done or what you could do.

9 **Believing emotions**

We have feelings for a purpose. They are signals to tell us that we are reacting for a reason. It's best to not believe everything you feel, but to use these feelings as a flag to notice what they are telling you. Once you stop believing your feelings to get a more objective view, see if there is any evidence to support what you believe to be true.

Example: no one asks you for your help, and you react with the feeling that they do not trust you. Step back and look at the situation and see if you generated the feeling first. Maybe they didn't ask you because they think they need to solve it on their own. Or maybe they've got it covered. You made the inference that it was personal because you had an emotional reaction. If you step back, you will realize that there is no evidence to support your conclusion.

When you are stuck in destructive self-talk and you are unable to take action: In the process of looking at self-talk, which is not easy, you want to be clearer about your reactions and what you tell yourself. You want to look for the reality of situations, be open to change and compromise, and be effective doing your part of the work. Your internal communication with yourself will inevitably influence how you communicate with others.

- Seek more sensory data

- Reframe your thinking

- Revise your expectations

- Work through your fear and worry

- Reorder your priorities

- Expand your comfort zone

- Release irrational beliefs or wants

Taking Self-Responsibility

When you use "I" statements, you are taking responsibility in a group environment. This supports the safety and respect of others while being direct, which allows you to reach the point of your communication more quickly. Responsible people speak for themselves because they are self-aware; they are aware that their observations are their own and can identify them with skill. They leave space for others to communicate things differently by letting them speak for themselves.

The "I" statement is the foundation of using assertive communication. You don't need to make someone think the way you do; you show respect by telling your truth and leaving room for others to tell theirs. It shows that you are worthy of your own opinion and that you care about what other people think as well.

The common statistic of perception is that comprehension comes from 7 percent verbal communication, 38 percent non-verbal communication, and 55 percent interpretation. You could see how if you are not clear with your words and how you present yourself physically, and do not ensure correct interpretation, your meaning may never be truly understood. This can also lend itself to producing feelings of judgment, and nobody in a group dynamic likes to be judged. If you can provide more information as to why you think something, communicate it effectively, and take responsibility for those feelings, there is a higher probability that the other person will hear what you meant and not feel judged.

To send a clear message use the following skills:

1   Speak for yourself. It identifies you as the source; when you speak for others it produces resistance.

2   Describe what you observe. This links observations to interpretation and gives you a foundation of dialogue.

3   Label your feeling. State what you are experiencing emotionally and actually label it.

4   Express your thoughts. Say what you are thinking, believing, assuming, or expecting.

Example: "When the actor left the stage before the cue was over, to me, it felt as though the music made it seem like a memory. I was thinking that if he leaves later or I shorten my cue, we would remain in the present moment."

I present the statement from my perspective, I describe the actions I observe, I label my response to that behavior, and then I express my opinion.

I did not say, "It feels as though we lose the sense of present time when the actor leaves when he does." The actor may feel as though you are judging them, and the director may feel as though you are judging his or her blocking.

Feedback

Now that we have focused on our own behavior and language, here are few guidelines to giving and receiving feedback that are helpful in collaboration.

Giving and receiving feedback are challenging skills to develop and master, because it makes us vulnerable when we share our feelings and emotions to another person. But if you can improve your feedback skills, you can find a deeper level of sharing, which will show itself positively in an artistic endeavor. This means that it would be in our best interest to create a safe environment for all to share without judgment, to accept one another as people and as artists, and to be responsible for our own behavior.

Ask for feedback when you want it, and offer feedback when asked. If you are offering feedback when not asked, be respectful of how the person may react.

When giving feedback:

- Comment as soon after the behavior as possible, determining if it should be discussed publicly or privately.

- Use "I" statements to ensure accountability.

- Give feedback that is appropriate to the situation.

- Include a request if appropriate.

- Avoid blaming others.

When receiving feedback:

- Acknowledge the feedback.

- Listen and hear what the other person is meaning to say without interruption.

- Be receptive to the other person's need to express their opinion.

- Ask for clarification if needed.

- Avoid rationalizing or defending.

- Decide if and how to use the information effectively.

To accept one another's ideas, listen with an open mind, respecting and considering each suggestion. Ask questions to clarify and to understand, and affirm when another takes a risk or is speaking with honesty. Do not interrupt or have side conversations while others are speaking. Encourage change and growth by identifying another's successes and relating to their failures. And always be patient with the process, being gentle with others' mistakes, as you would want others to be with yours.

To be responsible for yourself, speak from personal experience, honestly and appropriately. Have humility and remain teachable because you will always have something to learn from every situation. Try to not fix or solve another's problem or mistake, or blame others for a problem or mistake of your making. Just offer your response as a means to finding a greater understanding.

The Digital Age—The First Introduction

In the arts, the internet is an excellent resource to learn the style of work and the experience level of each artist with whom you'll be working. But as we all know, on the internet not everything you read is true—so keep an open mind.

By doing a simple internet search, you can ascertain where a person works regularly, at what level of budget they work within, if they work with the same artists repeatedly, if their work pushes boundaries, if they have won awards for their work, and any other details that can inform how you behave when you first meet them.

Having the ability to speak to another artist's success and experience shows curiosity in their work and will help ease the initial conversations when your relationship has yet to develop into a more friendly way of expression.

It's also good to be prepared about someone's process in theatre. If you personally know of someone who has worked with a person on your creative team, ask for his or her opinion. Remember, though, that each theatre experience carries its own dynamic and personality, and one person's opinion of someone else may not be relevant to your experience with them. So when giving someone else feedback about others, be sure to convey that it was situational and from your point of view.

Also remember that if they have done their due diligence, they will have looked you up as well. Know what is on the internet regarding your own work and, if possible, ensure that it represents you the way you like.

Communication in the Digital Age—Email Etiquette

Email etiquette is essential for the twenty-first century communication process. Most of our communication in theatre is in email format. Here are a few guidelines to keep your emails succinct, informative, and efficient.

Who is it to?
Make sure that you are sending the email to the appropriate person and determine if you can selectively reduce the recipients from a reply-all situation. Most of the time not everyone needs to know the specifics. If you are in an environment that relies on reply-all, be especially careful of your word usage and remember who is in the thread. After I've written an email, I like to look again at the recipient list once more before I hit send.

Subject line
Do not state your opinion in a subject line; you do not want the reader to form a judgment before they have read the email. Subject lines are very short and leave too much room for interpretation. Be concise yet not judgmental.

Start with the positive
It is easy and effective to point out the positive of any situation before you comment on the negative. You don't want to put your reader on the defense at the start of the communication.

What is the situation?
Be clear about what the situation is within the beginning of the email. Time is precious for most theatre artists, and you want to get to the point in an efficient manner.

What do you need to convey?
Be comprehensible about why you are presenting the situation and what you are seeking from someone else. Do not over-explain why you need something done or changed; be mindful of the time it will take to read your email. Be assertive by stating the situation, how it affects your work, and what you would like to achieve from this correspondence.

How can they help you?
As specifically as you can, state exactly how this person can help you. Try to not use the word "love," i.e. "I would love it if ..." There are better ways to communicate your meaning through better vocabulary usage, e.g. "It would greatly enhance the production if ..."

Understand how it impacts them
This is really important. It is in your best interest to have an understanding that your request will impact someone else's time and energy. Make it a point to

convey that you understand this and appreciate the extra effort they will give to address your concerns.

Make them feel like a priority

As a freelance artist, every job is a priority. You give 150 percent to everyone, and if you treat each employment as a priority in your life and convey this with whomever you are communicating, you will add to the feeling of trust between you and your team. Answer emails quickly, have all of the information needed to convey your thoughts, and if you do not know the answer to someone's question at the moment of the email, that's okay—be courteous so that they know they were heard and reply to say you don't know yet.

Apologize if necessary

Take responsibility and apologize if you are at fault or a leader of a team that has created an issue. Do not blame anyone at any time, even if it wasn't your fault. In theatre there is no blame, there is only "how do we fix it?"

Take the higher road and don't take anything personally

As much as you can, swallow your pride and remain even-keeled and grounded. There is no reason to add fuel to a fire. Remember that someone else's emotional response may not personally apply to you.

Be assertive, not aggressive in tone

It is hard to determine tone in an email. Choose your vocabulary wisely. If you find that you are receiving negative responses to your emails, create a waiting period of half an hour before sending and reread for tone. Or send it to someone else who is not biased and see if they read any unwanted tone in your message. And, on the flip side, if you have an emotional response to an email sent to you, do not reply immediately. Give yourself time to figure out what provoked the response in you and then respond accordingly and respectfully.

Don't be short

The shorter the length of your email, the more curt and upset you seem to the reader. Even if you are purely stating fact, use expressive vocabulary to create a more conversational approach. The more you create a comfortable exchange of words, the more meaning you will convey. When you know the members of your team well, then you may be able to respond with a sentence and not offend anyone.

Do not use ALL CAPS

We all know that using all-capital letters comes across as yelling and is not appropriate for any business communication.

Punctuation and grammar

Do not use text speak, and use correct punctuation and grammar. When in email format, you want to ensure that your exact meaning is interpreted from your words. The more proficient your language skills in writing, the greater chance your meaning will be understood.

Please, thank you, if you could …

Be gracious with your communication; use words that show respect. "Please" shows that you have an understanding that you are asking something of someone else, "thank you" shows your gratitude towards someone else's time and effort, and "if you could" shows that you know that they are equally busy as you. Words of respect will go far in other people's opinions of how gracious you are as an artist and collaborator.

Greetings and salutations

Use the appropriate greeting and salutation for the situation. Do not be too casual or too stylized. Know the hierarchy in which you work and address people accordingly. Please do not email an artistic director starting with "Hey!" unless you are best friends. Try to avoid exclamation points unless you are really jumping for joy, and "xo" is not an appropriate signoff unless you really want to give them a hug and kiss.

Interpreting Visual Representation

In theatre, it can help greatly if we use a visual thinking strategy when looking at pieces of art as representations of a designer's vision. We all have been around a table when photos are referenced as ideas of style and mood for a production's expression. We want to have a clear understanding of what everyone sees in the visual representation so that we can all apply the same interpretation to our design element.

EXERCISES—VISUAL THINKING

Find pieces of art that have detail and expressive qualities. Everyone is to look at one piece of art and observe what he or she sees. There are three questions that the moderator should ask:

> What do you see?
> What do you see that makes you say that?
> What else to do you see?

The observers respond with specifics to back up their ideas with evidence in the artwork. The first question evokes an open response. The second question makes the observer explain why they responded a certain way that wasn't specific to the visual aspect of the piece. And the third then prompts more response.

What you will see happening is that the visual representation will gain more depth with each response. Also, it will spur agreement or disagreement regarding the response. And it will develop a common language about what you all see collectively.

We want to develop the ability to find meaning in imagery so that we can recreate its emotional impact. Simple identification turns into complex interpretation on metaphoric and philosophical levels, and your response comes from your own associations, questioning, analyzing, speculating, and categorizing.

As sound designers, the visual references are the start for any production. You have to understand the why behind the visual so that you can apply your artistry to the team. As theatre artists, you want everyone to be on the same page when creating the worlds of the production. This exercise helps to attune you to responding with more detail and creates greater communication of a common goal.

Cooperation vs. Collaboration

There are two ways to look at how we work with others. We can collaborate our ideas in a way that makes others feel like they have a stake in what was achieved. And we can cooperate and facilitate what needs to happen in order to create cohesion. There is nothing negative about either of these modes of teamwork. They both exist in theatre. What you want to understand is the difference between them and which way you prefer to work.

EXERCISES—SUPPORTING DIRECTOR'S VISION

You are given text and a sound effect, e.g. a car, birds, train whistle. The person acting as director says that the cue must contain the sound effect as is, with no questions asked.

You create a cue supporting the text and inserting the effect as asked.

After you listen and discuss the cue, you are now asked to create another cue. This time you can ask any question of the director as to how to support the text and the sound effect wanted. Once you have no more questions, you will create another cue where you use the sound effect. But this time you have liberty to use the effect however you want.

You will see that the first way to work is cooperating with what someone else wanted from you. The second way to work is a collaborative discussion to come to consensus before you work. Take note if you respond faster and more efficiently by cooperating or collaborating. Which way did you prefer? What were the differences for you?

People work in many different ways in theatre. And you want to be able to understand how others work as well as yourself. There are times when you will be more collaborative with a director, but you will be more cooperative with your sound team. You will switch between collaboration and cooperation many times even on the same production. It's best if you understand when and where it's appropriate to do either.

Summary

Communication is such a large part of how we collaborate and bring a collective vision of art to fruition. Once we have a better understanding of ourselves, and how we perceive others, we can then apply these communication tools to create a better perception of ourselves in them. The clearer the communication is between a team, the more efficient the collaborative process will be in the end.

Because art is subjective, and we all feel vulnerable with artistic expression, it's important that our communication does not get in the way of achieving our goals. Remember that everyone in the room is also trying to achieve the artistic goals together. And as our passions may make our emotional responses dramatic, it is the goal of serving the production that must be clearly communicated.

CONCLUSION

In this book, we have looked at the essence of how sound is produced. We took the journey into the psyche of how human beings interpret vibrations, perceive them as sound, and then create meaning. We delved further into the metaphysical understanding of how evolution and association aids in emotional response because sound is linked to the limbic system. We looked into spatial awareness and the interpretation of space and place in which we exist aurally. And we have outlined how physiology, psychology, anthropology, and sociology all contribute to the human impression of reaction to sound.

The exercises brought awareness to how we integrate this knowledge into tangible tools that we can use to create our art and discuss its meaning. Through collaboration and communication, artists are able to work with others with respect and understanding. And as you continue in your career, you will develop stronger skills of how to implement your design into a production.

As artists, we want to have a full understanding of our craft. To me, studying sound is an entry into the unknown; it is up to the interpretation of the artist to contribute more meaning to the consideration of sound. Once you begin your exploration, it opens up to such deep significance that it's hard to characterize it by merely putting it into words.

As sound designers, it is up to us to understand the way sound is generated, moves, reacts, and dissipates in any environment. It is the foundation to our understanding of what happens when human beings come into contact with vibration. As an advocate for the field, you will continually have discussions, teach, and explain what you do in order to create a better understanding of how sound designers are artistic collaborators in the world of the theater.

My hope at the conclusion of this book is that I have shed light on the depth and range of thinking we as sound designers explore when we are active participants in a collaborative project. There is a phenomenology to the experience of sound that we draw upon with specific intention to help tell stories.

If the next generation and our fellow collaborators understand the way we think about our field as artists, our communication process can only become more rich and substantive. Awareness and understanding will inevitably create more in-depth discussion, which will produce poignant art.

As artists, we all want to have a life of purpose, and we each have our definition of what that means. For some artists it's legacy, for others it's moment-to-moment fulfillment. Whichever of these is your goal, my hope for you is that you continue to be a lifelong learner in your field of choice.

This book puts into writing the thought process of an artistic sound designer and creates a basis of understanding for those entering the field. This book speaks to the now because we are living in a time where the definition of this field is highly relevant, because we live in a world that is full of technology that has shaped our understanding of sound.

To those who have had this technology all along, look beyond the ease of pushing a button for an effect and see the world of possibility of intention instead. If you have the mindset of human reaction and response through intentional sound, you will develop artistry in this medium.

Everyone believes they understand how music and sound affects them; however, this is solely a personal matter. The goal of interpretation for a sound designer is to understand how sound and music affects *everyone*. How artistry is passed down to the next generation is especially important because of this.

And again, this is just my way of looking at how sound is powerful in theatre.

I thank you for taking the journey into the mind of the artistic sound designer and I urge you to find new and interesting ways to define our field.

GLOSSARY

Abstraction—The quality of dealing with ideas rather than events and freedom from representational qualities in art.

Aesthetic—Concerned with beauty or the appreciation of beauty.

Anachronism—The action of attributing something to a period to which it does not belong.

Anechoic—Free from echo due to a material tending to deaden sound.

Anthropological—Relating to the study of humankind.

Asynchronous—Not existing or occurring at the same time.

Attenuation—The reduction of the amplitude of a signal, electric current, or other oscillation.

Auditory field—The space that represents the limits of ability to hear a particular sound.

Autonomic nervous system—The part of the nervous system responsible for control of the bodily functions not consciously directed, such as breathing, the heartbeat, and digestive processes.

Basso continuo—(In Baroque music) An accompanying part which includes a bass line and harmonies, typically played on a keyboard instrument and with other instruments such as cello or lute.

Biomechanical—Relating to the mechanical laws concerning the movement or structure of living organisms.

Cerebrospinal—Relating to the brain and spine.

Cerebrospinal fluid—Clear watery fluid which fills the space between the arachnoid membrane and the pia mater.

Cochlea—The spiral cavity of the inner ear containing the organ of Corti, which produces nerve impulses in response to sound vibrations.

Commedia dell'arte—An improvised kind of popular comedy in Italian theatres between the sixteenth and eighteenth centuries, based on stock characters. Actors adapted their comic dialogue and action according to a few basic plots (commonly love intrigues) and to topical issues.

Consonance—A combination of notes which are in harmony with each other due to the relationship between their frequencies.

Contrapuntal—(In music) Of or in counterpoint.

Da capo—(In music) Including the repetition of a passage at the beginning.

Denouement—The final part of a play, film, or narrative in which the strands of the plot are drawn together and matters are explained or resolved.

Diegetic—Of or relating to artistic elements that are perceived as existing within the world depicted in a narrative work.

Dissonance—Lack of harmony among musical notes.

Doppler effect—An increase (or decrease) in the frequency of sound, light, or other waves as the source and observer move towards (or away from) each other. The effect causes the sudden change in pitch noticeable in a passing siren, as well as the red shift seen by astronomers.

Echolocation—The location of objects by reflected sound, in particular that used by animals such as dolphins and bats.

Electromechanical—Relating to or denoting a mechanical device, which is electrically operated.

Empathy—The ability to understand and share the feelings of another.

Eukaryote—An organism consisting of a cell or cells in which the genetic material is DNA in the form of chromosomes contained within a distinct nucleus.

Existentialism—A philosophical theory or approach, which emphasizes the existence of the individual person as a free and responsible agent determining their own development through acts of the will.

Figured bass—(In music) A shorthand method of indicating a thorough-bass part in which each bass note is accompanied by figures indicating the intervals to be played in the chord above it in the realization.

Free field—A region in which the effects of bounding surfaces on the behavior of a field are negligible; specifically a sound field in which there is no reflected sound.

Horizon—The limit of a person's knowledge, experience, or interest.

Infrasonic—Relating to or denoting sound waves with a frequency below the lower limit of human audibility.

Kinesthesia—Awareness of the position and movement of the parts of the body by means of sensory organs (proprioceptors) in the muscles and joints.

Limbic system—A complex system of nerves and networks in the brain, involving several areas near the edge of the cortex concerned with instinct and mood. It controls the basic emotions (fear, pleasure, anger) and drives (hunger, sex, dominance, care of offspring).

Mechanosensing—Responsivity to mechanical stimuli, especially at the cellular level or below.

Metaphysics—The branch of philosophy that deals with the first principles of things, including abstract concepts such as being, knowing, identity, time, and space.

Monaural—Having a single melodic line without harmonies or melody in counterpoint.

Organelles—Any of a number of organized or specialized structures within a living cell.

Phenomenology—An approach that concentrates on the study of consciousness and the objects of direct experience.

Physiology—The branch of biology that deals with the normal functions of living organisms and their parts.

Psychobiology—The branch of science that deals with the biological basis of behavior and mental phenomena.

Psychology—The scientific study of the human mind and its functions, especially those affecting behavior in a given context.

Psychophysics—The branch of psychology that deals with the relations between physical stimuli and mental phenomena.

Recitative—Musical declamation of the kind usual in the narrative and dialogue parts of opera and oratorio, sung in the rhythm of ordinary speech with many words on the same note.

Reverberation—Prolongation of a sound; resonance.

Ripieno—The body of instruments accompanying the concertino in Baroque concerto music.

Ritornello—A short instrumental refrain or interlude in a vocal work.

Scenography—Relates to the study and practice of performance design, including all of the elements that contribute to establishing an atmosphere and mood for a theatrical presentation.

Sociological—Concerning the development, structure, and functioning of human society.

Stereophonic—(Sound recording and reproduction) Using two or more channels of transmission and reproduction so that the reproduced sound seems to surround the listener and come from more than one source.

Subarachnoid—Denoting or occurring in the fluid-filled space around the brain between the arachnoid membrane and the pia mater, through which major blood vessels pass.

Sympathetic nervous system—The network of nerve cells and fibers which transmits nerve impulses between parts of the body.

Sympathy—Support in the form of shared feelings or opinions.

Synchronous—Existing or occurring at the same time.

Synesthesia—The production of a sense impression relating to one sense or part of the body by stimulation of another sense or part of the body.

Temporal—Relating to time.

Ternary form—(In music) The form of a movement in which the first subject is repeated after an interposed second subject in a related key.

Tutti—(In music) A passage to be performed with all voices or instruments together.

Valence—Used in psychology, especially in discussing emotions, means the intrinsic attractiveness (positive valence) or averseness (negative valence) of an event, object, or situation.

Zeitgeist—The defining spirit or mood of a particular period of history as shown by the ideas and beliefs of the time.

Zero point—Predetermined central point where the bulk of the action takes place on stage.

BIBLIOGRAPHY

Barton, Bruce. *Collective Creation, Collaboration and Devising*. Toronto: Playwrights Canada, 2008.

Blesser, Barry, and Linda-Ruth Salter. *Spaces Speak, Are You Listening?: Experiencing Aural Architecture*. Cambridge, MA: MIT, 2007.

Booth, Michael R. *Theatre in the Victorian Age*. Cambridge: Cambridge University Press, 1991.

Brotchie, Alastair, and Mel Gooding. "Chain Games." *A Book of Surrealist Games*. Boston, MA: Shambhala Redstone Editions, 1995.

Brown, Ross. *Sound: A Reader in Theatre Practice*. Basingstoke: Palgrave Macmillan, 2010.

Campbell, Tom, C. Philip Beaman, and Dianne C. Berry. "Auditory Memory and the Irrelevant Sound Effect: Further Evidence for Changing-state Disruption." *Memory* 10.3 (2002): 199–214. https://tuhat.helsinki.fi/portal/files/40265634/CamBeaBer2002a.pdf, 2015.

ComputerDJSummit. "The History of Recorded Music." 2007. http://www.computerdjsummit.com/members/documents/musichistory.html, 2016.

Cohen, Robert. *Working Together in Theatre: Collaboration and Leadership*. Basingstoke: Palgrave Macmillan, 2011.

Collison, David. *The Sound of Theatre: A History*. Eastbourne: PLASA, 2008.

Coutinho, Eduardo, and Angelo Cangelosi. "The Use of Spatio-Temporal Connectionist Models in Psychological Studies of Musical Emotions." *Music Perception* 27.1 (2009): 1–15. http://mp.ucpress.edu/content/27/1/1.full.pdf+html, 2015.

Davis, Gary, and Ralph Jones. *The Sound Reinforcement Handbook*. Milwaukee: Hal Leonard, 1989.

Delhommeau, K., S. Dubal, L. Collet, and R. Jouvent. "Auditory Perceptual Learning in Hypothetically Psychosis-Prone Subjects." *Personality and Individual Differences* 35.7 (2003): 1525–36. https://www.sciencedirect.com/science/article/pii/S0191886902003677, 2015.

Dissanayake, Ellen. *Homo Aestheticus: Where Art Comes from and Why*. New York: Free Press, 1992.

Flamme, Gregory A., Mark R. Stephenson, Kristy Deiters, Amanda Tatro, Devon Van Gessel, Kyle Geda, Krista Wyllys, and Kara McGregor. "Typical Noise Exposure in Daily Life." *International Journal of Audiology* 51.Sup1 (2012): S3–S11. https://www.researchgate.net/publication/221765442_Typical_noise_exposure_in_daily_life, 2015.

Gregersen, Erik. "Chapters 1–3." *The Britannica Guide to Sound and Light*. New York: Britannica Educational Pub., 2011.

Hillman, Neil, and Sandra Pauletto. "The Craftsman: The Use of Sound Design to Elicit Emotions." *The Soundtrack* 7.1 (2014): 5–23. https://www.researchgate.net/publication/273480903_The_Craftsman_The_use_of_sound_design_to_elicit_emotions, 2015.

Horowitz, Seth S. *The Universal Sense: How Hearing Shapes the Mind*. New York:
    Bloomsbury, 2012.

Housen, Abigail, and Philip Yenawine. "Visual Thinking Strategies: Understanding the
    Basics." https://vtshome.org/, 2016.

Ihde, Don. *Listening and Voice: Phenomenologies of Sound*. Albany: State U of New
    York, 2007.

Kaye, Deena, and James LeBrecht. *Sound and Music for the Theatre: The Art and
    Technique of Design*. Boston, MA: Focal Press, 2000.

LaBelle, Brandon. *Background Noise: Perspectives on Sound Art*. New York: Continuum
    International, 2006.

Leonard, John A. *Theatre Sound*. New York: Routledge, 2001.

Leonardson, Eric. "Sound and Listening: Beyond the Wall of Broadcast Sound." *Journal
    of Radio & Audio Media* 22.1 (2015): 115–21. http://www.tandfonline.com/doi/abs/1
    0.1080/19376529.2015.1015874, 2015.

Mondor, Todd A., and Launa C. Leboe. "Stimulus and Response Repetition Effects
    in the Detection of Sounds: Evidence of Obligatory Retrieval and Use of a Prior
    Event." *Psychological Research* 72.2 (2006): 183–91. https://link.springer.com/
    article/10.1007/s00426-006-0095-x, 2015.

Moore, Brian C. J. *An Introduction to the Psychology of Hearing*. London: Academic
    Press, 1982.

Nielsen, John. *Effective Communication Skills*. Xlibris, 2008.

Ouzounian, Gascia. "Sound Art and Spatial Practices: Situating Sound Installation Art
    since 1958." Diss., University of California San Diego, 2008. https://escholarship.org/
    uc/item/4d50k2fp, 2015.

Patzia, Michael. "Xenophanes (*c*. 570–*c*. 478 B.C.E.)." *Internet Encyclopedia of
    Philosophy*. N.d. https://www.iep.utm.edu/xenoph, 2016.

Payne, Sarah R., William J. Davies, and Mags D. Adams. "Research into the
    Practical and Policy Applications of Soundscape Concepts and Techniques
    in Urban Areas." London: HMSO, 2007. randd.defra.gov.uk/Document.
    aspx?Document=NO0217_8424_FRP.pdf, 2015.

Peterson, M. Jeanne. *The Medical Profession in Mid-Victorian London*. Berkeley:
    University of California, 1978.

Power, P., W. J. Davies, J. Hurst, and C. Dunn. "Localisation of Elevated Virtual Sources
    in Higher Order Ambisonic Sound Fields." *Proceedings of the Institute of Acoustics*
    Part 4 34 (2012): n.p. https://www.researchgate.net/publication/263925251_
    Localisation_of_elevated_virtual_sources_in_higher_order_Ambisonic_soundfields,
    2015.

Robinson, Bruce. "Victorian Medicine—From Fluke to Theory." BBC, Feb. 17,
    2011. http://www.bbc.co.uk/history/british/victorians/victorian_medicine_01.shtml,
    2016.

Roznowski, Rob, and Kirk Domer. *Collaboration in Theatre: A Practical Guide for
    Designers and Directors*. New York: Palgrave Macmillan, 2009.

Russolo, Luigi. "The Art of Noise (Futurist Manifesto, 1913) Luigi Russolo." *Academia.
    edu*. 2004. http://www.academia.edu/1465274/The_Art_of_Noise_futurist_
    manifesto_1913_Luigi_Russolo, 2015.

Sonnenschein, David. *Sound Design: The Expressive Power of Music, Voice, and Sound
    Effects in Cinema*. Studio City, CA: Michael Wiese Productions, 2001.

Stock, Kathleen. *Philosophers on Music: Experience, Meaning, and Work*. New York:
    Oxford University Press, 2007.

Szalárdy, Orsolya, Alexandra Bendixen, Tamás M. Böhm, Lucy A. Davies, Susan L. Denham, and István Winkler. "The Effects of Rhythm and Melody on Auditory Stream Segregation." *The Journal of the Acoustical Society of America* 135.3 (2014): 1392–405. https://www.ncbi.nlm.nih.gov/pubmed/24606277, 2015.

Till, Rupert. "Sound Archaeology: Terminology, Palaeolithic Cave Art and the Soundscape." *World Archaeology* 46.3 (2014): 292–304.

Truax, Barry. *Acoustic Communication*. Westport, CT: Ablex Pub., 2001.

Zijl, Anemone G. W. Van, Petri Toiviainen, Olivier Lartillot, and Geoff Luck. "The Sound of Emotion." *Music Perception: An Interdisciplinary Journal* 32.1 (2014): 33–50. http://mp.ucpress.edu/content/32/1/33?utm_source=TrendMD&utm_medium=cpc&utm_campaign=Music_Perception%253A_An_Interdisciplinary_Journal_TrendMD_0, 2015.

INDEX

Note: Please note that page references to Figures will be in **bold**; those representing Tables will be in *italics*.